# Family Obligations and Social Change

# Family Life Series

Edited by Martin Richards, Ann Oakley, Christina Hardyment and Jackie Burgoyne

*Published*

Janet Finch, *Family Obligations and Social Change*
Philip Pacey, *Family Art*

*Forthcoming*

David Clark and Douglas Haldane, *Wedlocked?*
Miriam David, *Mum's the Word: Relations between Families and Schools*
Jean La Fontaine, *Child Sexual Abuse*
Lydia Morris, *The Workings of the Household*
Ann Phoenix, *Young Mothers*

# Family Obligations and Social Change

## JANET FINCH

Polity Press

Copyright © Janet Finch 1989

First published 1989 by Polity Press
in association with Basil Blackwell.

Editorial office:
Polity Press, Dales Brewery, Gwydir Street,
Cambridge CB1 2LJ, UK

Marketing and production:
Basil Blackwell Ltd
108 Cowley Road, Oxford OX4 1JF, UK

Basil Blackwell Inc.
3 Cambridge Center
Cambridge, MA 02142, USA

ISBN 0-7456-0323-8
ISBN 0-7456-0324-6 (pbk)

**British Library Cataloguing in Publication Data**

A CIP catalogue record for this book is available
from the British Library.

**Library of Congress Cataloging in Publication Data**

A CIP catalogue record for this book is available
from the Library of Congress.

Typeset in Palatino 10/11pt
by Hope Services (Abingdon) Ltd.

Printed and bound in Great Britain by
Marston Lindsay Ross International,
Oxfordshire

# Contents

# Acknowledgements

I realized long ago the importance of getting other people to read my drafts. It saves me from the more obvious errors of course, and often provides short-cuts into literature of which I am only dimly aware. But most important, it is so often the pencilled comment in the margin, or the perceptive remark when someone is passing back a draft chapter, which gives me the key stimulus to further creative work. I use my colleagues and friends shamelessly for this, and I hope they understand that I will always reciprocate. In this instance, the following people read and commented upon chapters and deserve my warm thanks: Graham Allan, Dulcie Groves, Jennifer Mason, David Morgan, Penny Summerfield. Jennifer and David both maintained a more informal and continuing interest in the book's progress, and I am grateful to each of them for their personal and intellectual support. Ruth Chadwick and Caroline Forder both helped me at an early stage by introducing me to literature in their own fields of expertise. David Held and Martin Richards have retained an active interest in an editorial capacity and have made some very useful comments. The manuscript was typed by Janet Hartley and Sandra Irving, to whom also much thanks.

This book has been written at a time when I have been working also on a research project on Family Obligations. None of the data from that project are included here, and its focus is necessarily much narrower than this book. However, it was work on the background to the project which first stimulated me to consider writing the book, when I realized that the field which I was researching essentially was undefined. The two enterprises inevitably have fed off each other, and in this context I want to mention Jennifer Mason again, who joined me as research officer on the Family Obligations project in 1986 and has proved the most stimulating, supportive and admirable colleague that anyone could wish for. I am aware that she influences my thinking in ways of which I am not always conscious. I hope that she will not recognize too many of her ideas presented here as my own.

The Family Obligations project has been supported by the Economic and Social Research Council (Grant No. GOO 23 2197). I am grateful for their support and especially for enabling me to be released from normal duties during 1986–7. The background reading and the work which I did on the project during that year has been crucial in enabling me to write this book. In turn, working through existing evidence system-atically for this book has helped to shape the research project.

My final acknowledgement is rather special. It is to Jackie Burgoyne, who died in January 1988 at the age of 43. Like most of her friends and colleagues, I still can't quite believe it. It was Jackie who first suggested to me the idea of writing this book, in her capacity as newly appointed series editor for Polity Press. She kept in touch as my ideas developed and the last evening which I spent with her was a splendid sociable and intellectually stimulating occasion, when she commented perceptively and creatively on a detailed outline of this book. But then she was always like that. This is not the place to write generally about her own work and the support which she gave to other people's, but I can certainly place on record that without her this particular book never would have happened.

Janet Finch
University of Lancaster

# Introduction

## The Family

I believe that more unhappiness comes from this source than any other – I mean from the attempt to prolong family connection unduly and to make people hang together artificially who would never naturally do so. The mischief among the lower classes is not so great, but among the middle and upper classes it is killing a large number daily. And the old people do not really like it much better than the young.

This is the bleakest statement of the reality of family life which I have ever seen. Indeed it is just about the bleakest I can imagine. It tells of people locked together in relationships which are stifling, debilitating, even life-threatening. Apparently consenting adults are unable to escape from a situation which has no meaning for them: they are duty bound to continue. The fiction that family relationships are worth holding onto is maintained by old and young alike, all of them unable to reject the bonds of obligation which decree that the family shall be maintained, quite literally, at all costs. The quotation comes from *The Note Books of Samuel Butler* (1919), the late nineteenth-century writer who presented such a sharp and rejecting picture of his own family in the novel *The Way of All Flesh* (Butler, 1903), published thirty years after it had been started and only after most of the people portrayed had already died. Even those of us who have clear-eyed and critical views of family life find difficulty, it would seem, in reconciling this to relationships within our own families.

I first came across this quotation from Butler's notebooks when reading a biography of Ivy Compton-Burnett, the twentieth-century novelist whose works themselves are chronicles of family life in agonizing detail (Spurling, 1974). Her own experience as a child and a young woman is a case example of Butler's quotation. Born in 1884, the eldest child of her father's second marriage, she was brought up in a home where there were considerable tensions between parents, children and stepchildren, yet where distinctively Victorian ideals of family life were meant to prevail. After the death of both her father and her stepmother, Ivy and her brother became trustees for their younger sisters, who were meant to remain in the family home and under parental authority (now transferred to their siblings) until the age of 24. Very soon afterwards her brother was killed in the First World War and Ivy continued to attempt to fulfil the duty which her parents had placed upon her, running a household which was, according to her biographer 'quiet, orderly and cruel', in which her sisters were 'put down and kept under, their proposals overruled' (p. 209). To contemporary eyes, she had been placed in an impossible position. Eventually the sisters staged a successful rebellion, moving out and taking a house together in London without Ivy. A little time after this, Ivy read Butler's notebooks and in her copy the above quotation is scored with six heavy lines in the margin (p. 227). Presumably she had found another writer who could help her to make some sense of her own experience.

All of this has a distinctively Victorian flavour. A definition of the family which is based on authority on the one side, and duty on the other, seemed anachronistic to the Compton-Burnett sisters even in the 1920s – how much more so now. It also has a distinctively middle-class flavour: the suffocating emphasis on maintaining respectability at all costs, the appearance of 'family feeling' being much more important than its reality. Although the Victorian bourgeoisie tried to impose this model on the whole population, they were never totally successful with the 'lower classes', as Butler's comments indicate. Many of us will read of these bleak, unhappy experiences and breathe a sigh of relief family life is no longer like that.

But is that true? I have chosen to make this my starting-point because I believe that these experiences – extreme though they may be – do have some resonances in Britain in the late twentieth century. For example, a number of recent studies of the family care of elderly people show that – for some people at least – duty towards members of one's family feels as if it has an inescapable quality, and failing to acknowledge such duty does still have implications for respectability (Ungerson, 1987; Lewis and Meredith, 1988). There is much more to it than that of course, and I shall discuss these examples in some detail in subsequent chapters. But there are sufficient echoes of Victorian experiences to make it difficult to argue that the profound questions raised by Butler and Compton-Burnett have no contemporary relevance.

Their relevance and importance is greatly enhanced by British politics in the late twentieth century, where the family is very much on the political agenda. Governments in Britain have long been concerned with family life and have made assumptions about it when framing legislation, even though these have seldom been spelled out explicitly (Land, 1978; Morgan, 1985, pp. 57–9). However, since the mid-1970s, it is possible to detect a greater explicit emphasis upon 'supporting the family' amongst all mainstream political parties and this has been tied closely to debates about public expenditure in the fields of welfare, health and social security (Finch and Groves, 1980; West, 1984). In the 1980s, the Conservative government has become increasingly explicit about its desire to encourage families to take care of their members. This is seen as part of its policy to make citizens more self-reliant, and less prone to look to the state for financial and practical support when they are out of work, chronically sick, elderly and infirm and so on. Of the many quotations from politicians which one could use to illustrate this, I have chosen one which was topical at the time of writing. It comes from a speech made by the Prime Minister, Margaret Thatcher, to the general assembly of the Church of Scotland,

The basic ties of the family at the heart of our society are the very nursery of civic virtue. It is on the family that we in the government build our own policies for welfare, education and care. You recall that Timothy was warned by St Paul that everyone who neglects to provide for his own house (meaning his own family) has disowned the faith and is 'worse than an infidel'. (Observer, 22 May 1988)

The reference to the Bible obviously is tailored for the particular audience to which she was speaking, but Margaret Thatcher's remarks encapsulate many of the themes common to other political utterances: an assertion that family ties are the foundation of the whole society and should be accorded a primacy over all others; strong moral disapproval of people who apparently do not acknowledge that they have certain responsibilities towards their relatives; a sense that there is something inherently unnatural about anyone who questions the importance of family life; an implication that 'the family' which is being supported is one in which a man is in the key position of authority; government social and welfare services planned on the assumption that the family is the first port of call in all circumstances where people need assistance of any kind. The continuities with Victorian images of the family are obvious. Indeed the Prime Minister and others have been quite explicit about their desire to encourage us all to return to 'Victorian values', which means, among other things, acknowledging the duty to support our relatives and acting accordingly (West, 1984).

These issues form the topic of this book. My focus is upon assistance and support which is exchanged within kin groups in adult life: Who does what, for whom and in what circumstances? In particular I am concerned to understand how far this is underscored by duty, obligation or responsibility: who believes that they *ought* to do what, for whom, and how does that get translated into practice? I shall be trying to understand these matters particularly in relation to the circumstances of Britain in the later part of the twentieth century. But some comparisons with the past, and with other countries today, are necessary to bring contemporary British experience into perspective and to highlight its distinctive features.

When I speak of 'kin groups' I am referring to adults who are related through blood or marriage, and any others whom people treat as relatives; for example, people who have been adopted, or cohabitees. I have excluded from this discussion responsibilities for young children, since this raises an additional set of issues specific to the care of the young. For a similar reason I have decided also to exclude specific discussion of responsibilities between spouses, although in considering relationships within kin groups as a whole this necessarily forms part of the pattern. But the responsibilities and duties associated with marriage specifically raise another set of issues which, like parent–child relationships, are subject to regulation by law. Both of these have been studied and written about more extensively in recent years than relationships between other kin, which has been something of an unfashionable topic (Wilson and Pahl, 1988). I see it nonetheless as important and worthy of attention at the present time for the reasons which I have outlined.

I define my task in this book as assessing what we know (on the basis of research evidence) about contemporary kin relationships, highlighting the points at which further research seems particularly important, and evaluating what is the appropriate analytical framework for studying the meaning and significance of kinship in the late twentieth century. In so doing, I am moving beyond many earlier studies which (although there are some exceptions) have tended to concentrate upon the *form* of relationships, especially matters which can be quantified (how many kin each person has knowledge of, how frequent is their contact and so on). My focus is more on *content* than on form; on the qualitative aspects of family life which cannot easily be quantified and are concerned with matters of personal identity, social meaning and interpersonal relationships.

At the same time as trying to convey a qualitative feel for the meaning and significance of kin relationships, and especially for what the concepts of duty and obligation mean in this context, I regard it as essential to keep clearly in view the importance of the family as a public as well as a private institution. Recent writing on this topic emphasizes the double-edged character of the family as 'both societal and individual, both institutional and personal, both public and private' (Morgan, 1985, p. 285). I would endorse that position and this is reflected in subsequent chapters. It is the public dimension of family life and its importance in the political arena which also makes it possible, in my view, to go on using the rather vague and ideologically loaded term 'the family' in serious debate. A number of writers have argued that it should be abandoned and Jon Bernades in particular has been responsible for keeping this question in the academic limelight (Bernardes, 1985; 1986; 1988). But the term 'family' is used in the private and the public world and people accord it social meaning. Perhaps it should always be used with quotation marks in serious discussion to denote that one recognizes that it cannot be a simple descriptive word, but has many shifting meanings. I shall continue to use it, however, as a convenient shorthand term and I invite those readers who feel uncomfortable about this to place mental quotation marks around it whenever they see it.

To develop appropriate perspectives upon the private and the public dimensions of kin relationships, I shall use the rest of this introduction first, to introduce some of the analytical issues involved in a discussion of obligations and support within kin groups; second, to explore in an introductory way the role of the state in defining responsibilities within families, as this has occurred in the British context. This enables me to highlight some key themes which will be pursued in later chapters.

## Understanding support between kin: some analytical issues

The starting point for any serious analysis is to define one's terms. I begin here by clarifying the terms in which discussion needs to take place in respect of obligations and support in families. In so doing I define my task more precisely and raise a number of issues which are the subject of more extensive discussion in later chapters.

The first distinction which I want to make is between actual assistance offered to a relative and the reasons why it is offered. When we see an elderly mother still caring for a handicapped child or young man going regularly to do gardening for his grandparents, it is easy to assume that these actions spring from a sense of duty or responsibility. Certainly political statements about family support tend to make that kind of assumption. But is this necessarily so? The mother probably would say that her actions are out of love for the child, and the grandson might be prepared to admit that he had hopes of future financial gain. Both might well see duty mixed in with other motives. My point is the simple one that, in any particular case where support is offered between relatives, we cannot *assume* that its foundations are in a sense of duty or obligation. In any individual case we really need to ask 'What role does duty play *here*?'. Simple though that distinction may be, research on family life often does not distinguish between these two quite so rigorously as I would consider necessary. This will become apparent as I evaluate the available research data in subsequent chapters. Often there is a tendency to assume that evidence of help being given by one relative to another constitutes evidence of family duty. This creates something of a problem when we are trying to separate the two in order to evaluate the role of obligation and duty as the foundations of family support.

So how do we discover the role of duty and responsibility in family life? This is an important methodological question which is beyond my scope to answer fully here, although I have discussed these issues elsewhere (Finch, 1987a; Finch and Mason, forthcoming). However, I shall make some comments about how the available research evidence can be used, and where its limitations are. As I have already indicated, much research on family life does not separate out questions of duty and responsibility and look at them directly. Where studies do attempt this they tend to concentrate upon reflecting 'what people say' about these issues. By asking the right sort of questions, the researchers are able to present their readers with a fairly clear picture, for example, of how someone who has been looking after an elderly person presents her own actions and explains the reasons why she took on this task. Typically the accounts given by people in this situation reflect a mixture of love and duty, affection and obligation (Ungerson, 1987; Lewis and Meredith, 1988).

I would agree that the 'accounts' which people give are an important starting-point for understanding the foundations of any social actions. However, there are problems about taking those accounts at face value. We know from some studies of family life that typically people present accounts of their family in a favourable light, not saying necessarily that everything is perfect, but wishing to present their own family as something which 'works' (Voysey, 1975; Cornwell, 1984). I do not wish to imply that interviewees are deliberately deceiving researchers with these accounts, or indeed that they are unconsciously deceiving themselves, but simply that our experience of everyday life is very complex and when we are asked to 'tell a story' about it, there are many ways in which that story can be told. The whole family therapy industry thrives on helping people to 'see' different stories about their own family relationships.

I have defined my task in this book as developing a framework for analysing and understanding family support and the extent to which it is founded upon duty, obligation or responsibility. That analytical task must take very seriously the way in which people present their own accounts but it cannot rest there: we should not conclude that people are motivated by duty simply because they *say* that they are. We may want to tell a different story, but not necessarily one which implies that our informants have got it wrong. Standing outside their immediate situation, and using the analytical tools provided by social science, we may be able to see the story which our informants have told as part of a broader picture in which their choices are constrained by the economic structure of our society, by gender or ethnic division deeply embedded in social life, or even by the law. These are some of the reasons why the story which I would want to tell might be different from theirs. I define my talk as ranging widely therefore, looking both at the detail of how people relate to each other in face-to-face situations and also at the broader issues of how the social and economic organization of any society has an impact upon the assistance which people give their relatives, and upon the sense of obligation which may or may not underlie it.

I have used the phrase 'sense of obligation' here and I have been using the words duty, obligation and responsibility interchangeably. What do I mean by these terms? To answer that is not simply a matter of giving formal definition, but leads to the heart of some of the questions posed in later chapters. Whilst a dictionary definition of the three words might make some fine distinctions between them, in practice in social life they are used interchangeably and for the most part I shall continue to do that. Where I want to use one in preference to another I shall make that clear.

I have been implying that duty, responsibility and obligation are 'things' which may account for support between kin. But what kind of 'things' are they? Are they feelings or emotions, like anger or happiness? Are they intellectual ideas which any of us are free to accept or reject? Or are they based in a person's assessment of right and wrong, moral evaluations which may run counter to feelings and emotions? In public debate they tend to be treated as a mixture of moral values and 'natural feelings', sometimes implying that they are based on biological impulses. Whether obligations should be seen as emotions, or as moral actions, or neither of these, there is a further set of questions about whether they are characteristically associated with kin relationships, rather than other kinds of relationships, and if so why. In my view, the answers to all these questions cannot be decided in advance to the analysis which follows, since they raise other important questions about the role of emotions and the role of morality in social life, and these in turn can be answered only after careful consideration of relevant evidence and argument. For the moment therefore I shall sidestep these issues and continue to use the rather vague phrase 'sense of obligation'.

Whatever the 'sense of obligation' is in analytical terms it does not develop in a vacuum. As I noted at the beginning of this introduction, for many years governments have attempted to encourage the British population to acknowledge responsibilities towards their relatives. If the sense of obligation does not exist without them, governments need to invent it. In the next section, I shall look at how the 'sense of obligation' has been manipulated in the public domain through the actions of successive governments in Britain.

### The role of the state in defining family obligations

In this section I shall consider in a preliminary way some evidence about how governments have treated family obligations in public policies. This reveals some interesting questions not only about the family, but also about the role of the state and, especially, what is seen as its proper role in defining and reinforcing family responsibilities.

The shape of this relationship as it has developed historically in Britain could be described as reluctant but necessary intervention. It has been a long-running theme in British social policy that families, especially working-class families, regrettably do not always fulfil their natural obligations towards each other, and that therefore the state has to step in to ensure that people do not abandon their responsibilities. Although these views can be traced in much earlier material, the 1832 Royal Commission on the Poor Law articulated the position very clearly and their views were quoted favourably by the Royal Commission which reported in 1909. In Britain the Poor Law was the legislation which, until 1948, gave limited financial assistance from public funds to certain categories of people who were unable to support themselves (see chapters 2 and 4 for further discussion). The views propounded by the Royal Commission ran something like this: support between parents and children is a duty which rests on natural feelings, which are acknowledged in all human societies; England is the only country in Europe where these duties are neglected by some; such deficiences have to be made good by public authorities, who both make alternative provisions and also punish people who do not acknowledge their duties (see Anderson, 1977, for fuller discussion of the Commission reports). The principles involved in the Victorian Poor Law can be seen as a practical expression of this view: public support was given only as a last resort; assistance was at a minimal level; costs of support were reclaimed from relatives if at all possible.

The reasoning which lies behind this long-running consensus betrays some important confusions between duty and natural feelings, between affection and morality. The idea that 'natural feelings' of affection form the basis of family support is of itself undermined by evidence that some people do not give financial or practical support to their relatives. 'Duty' is a prescriptive concept, locked into a particular view of the moral order of the social world, not an empirical description of what happens in practice. Where social policies are designed to encourage a particular version of family responsibilities, they are in fact seeking to create a particular moral order which may or may not accord with what people themselves actually feel is proper. The confusion between 'duty' and 'natural feelings' is useful of course in social policy, because it helps to define those people whose 'natural feelings' lead in another direction as socially unacceptable and therefore legitimate targets for punitive action.

Further, historical writing on these subjects reveals a rather different type of confusion between affection and morality. This is the idea that failure to fulfil one's family responsibilities both saps one's moral fibre and removes the basis for affectionate ties within the family. Helen Bosanquet (1906), for example, writing specifically of men who 'evade' their family responsibilities, says 'it is to this evasion of the responsibility which is the strength of the family that we owe the degenerate family life which is the characteristic of the worst, not necessarily the poorest, parts of our towns' (Bosanquet, 1906, p. 339–40). Charles Booth (1892a), writing of pauperism and the relief of poverty in old age, makes a similar point in a rather different way. In a very curious train of logic, he argues that only certain old people are morally 'fit' to receive the endowment of a pension from public funds, and that their fitness can be tested partly by the way they have lived their own lives, but also by whether the quality of their family relationships has been characterized by 'affectionate duty',

To have lived at all goes for something, to have asked for no relief goes for more, and to have secured through savings, or through friendly feeling, *or through the loving duty of children*, a chimney corner where 5s. a week will be adequate, may be accepted as *proof that the pension is not ill bestowed.* (Booth, 1892a, p. 237, my italics)

Thus the distinctive rationale behind this historical view of family obligations assumes that being morally upright requires that one be affectionate towards one's relatives (especially spouses, parents and children), and also that the actual experience of affection within the family stands proof of one's moral credentials.

How far is this view of reluctant but necessary state intervention to encourage family responsibilities, and the rationale which supports it, still a feature of British social policy? Certainly the political consensus about the desirability of 'supporting the family' in order to enable it properly to 'care for its members' is a rather obvious contemporary version of this. It is a version which clearly makes an assumption about the 'naturalness' of family obligations and the desirability of the state's reinforcing them. However, in comparison with Victorian debates about the same issues, references to matters of morality are somewhat muted for the most part. It is really only in the writings of the radical right on family responsibilities where one finds echoes of the same approach: family units based on ties between spouses and parents and children are the natural order of things; state policies must support and reinforce the 'normal family' rather than deviant versions (such as single-parent households, gay or unmarried couples); family members will support each other as matter of course except where the state has taken these responsibilities away from them (Parker, 1986; Anderson D. and Dawson, 1986; Mount, 1982). Important though these views are in contemporary politics, it would be wrong to assume that they invariably underpin contemporary family policies. The aim of supporting the family commands broad assent in a variety of political traditions, and views upon the relationship between the family and the state cross-cut the conventional left-right spectrum in politics (Morgan, 1985, pp. 57–75).

One way of looking at state policies about family responsibilities is that these policies in effect are concerned with drawing the boundaries between the state and the family and defining the proper role of each. Part of that process entails making a moral and political statement about who can make claims upon whom. An analysis which focuses upon these two processes – drawing the boundaries between the state and the family, and designating upon whom an individual can make claims – can be developed in a number of ways.

First, one can look at where the state family boundary lies and one sees that it is not absolute. It shifts over time, and it also changes between different circumstances, so that we ought properly to speak of boundaries in the plural. Crowther (1982) has shown that in times of economic stringency there is a tendency for the state to redraw the boundaries so that more responsibility is placed upon the family. There is also a very important question about whether people's right to make claims either upon the state or upon their relatives should vary according to both need and resources. Do people who are less well-off have particular rights to make claims upon those who have more resources? Does this principle apply to claims made upon one's family, or upon the state, or to both? As writers upon the political philosophy of welfare have pointed out, it is in this area that we raise 'some of the deepest questions about the nature of human society and moral obligations' (Plant, Lesser and Taylor-Gooby, 1980, p. 52). They are questions which are not resolved clearly in contemporary social policy which, for example, by giving pensions to elderly people acknowledges their right to be financially independent of their families, but implies in other ways that people with need for practical support should make those particular claims upon their families and not upon the state (see chapter 4 for elaboration and discussion).

Second, and leading on from this, it is apparent that drawing the boundaries between family and state responsibility is a process which is politically contentious and where there are a number of competing principles. The dominant view appears to be that for most purposes claims on the family are treated as prior, with claims upon the state only coming into play when these are exhausted (see chapters 2 and 4). Both in welfare policies and in the enforcement of the law, there has always been a considerable reluctance to make provision from state resources for people who 'ought' to be relying on support from their relatives, especially where that support is underpinned by a legal obligation (Smart, 1984, pp. 117–18).

However, running counter to this idea of the state providing only residual support, and having had a considerable impact upon social policy in the twentieth century, is the different principle of citizenship rights. This is the most important political principle which counters a 'strong' view of family obligations, because its emphasis is upon the individual, not the family, as the unit of support. Individual citizens have the right to adequate resources for survival, and the claims which they make to secure these are upon the community as a whole, not upon their own families. The state acts as the mechanism through which such claims are made, by collecting taxes then redistributing resources. The concept of citizenship was embodied most obviously in the changes associated with the establishing of a welfare state in the early part of the twentieth century, and after the Second World War (Anderson, 1977). In so far as many of those policies still operate, the principle of individuals having a right to make claims upon collective resources through the state coexists, in contemporary social policy, with the principle that people in need should first make claims upon their families. The coexistence of those principles is illustrated, for example, in con-temporary policies for the economic support of young people. These concede, to some extent, that individuals have the right to make claims upon collective resources by allowing some level of support from supplementary benefit, but also reduce the amount of money actually available to a point where reliance upon one's family becomes essential to practical survival (see chapter 4 for further discussion).

Another area where the state/family boundary is contested is in relation to gender. It has been the work of feminists since the mid-1970s which has clarified the extent to which 'supporting the family' in effect means that a particular type of household, and set of personal relationships, are being encouraged. In this type of household and kin group, women provide the unpaid labour which secures the reproduction of the population and the care of the sick and elderly. Thus to draw the boundaries between the state and the family in such a way that these activities fall within the sphere of the family rather than the state assumes a particular definition of women's work, and makes specific assumptions about the role of women in our society. As Pascall has pointed out, 'The real meaning of supporting the family is supporting family responsibility, as distinct from state responsibility, for dependents old and young (Pascall, 1986, p. 38). In this respect, feminists have provided a critique of the dominant consensus about supporting the family, although the impact of this upon the direction of policy has been limited (Finch, 1987b).

Third, even the most cursory attempt to understand where and how the boundaries between the state and the family are drawn demonstrates a deep ambivalence about the family and its relationship to the state. This is not surprising, given the competing principles just outlined, and it affects both the points at which boundaries are drawn, and the circumstances in which individuals are seen as properly making claims upon the one rather than the other. It has been centrally the work of Hilary Land (Land, 1978; 1983; Land and Parker, 1979) which has exposed this ambivalence. The mixed messages are: the autonomy of the family must not be interfered with, but as an institution it needs to be protected; the family is the 'natural' unit of support, but the state must ensure that people fulfil their obligations in practice.

The continuities with Victorian social policy are obvious, as also are the pragmatic reasons why any government wishing to restrict public expenditure should seek to strengthen family ties. The ideas which underpin an emphasis on the independence of the family from the state run deep in conservative thought and rest on the belief that the stability of the social order depends upon independent families with a strong, patriarchal head forming the basic unit of society (Nisbet, 1987). Within this tradition, it is easy to see why it is regarded as of utmost importance that the independence of the family should be protected, and that it is proper for the state to secure this end, but paradoxically, excessive interference by the state can undermine the whole enterprise. Ambivalence about the relationship between the state and the family becomes understandable within this context, but of course it produces social policies which sometimes appear quite contradictory in practice. This confusion is exacerbated when the emphasis upon different principles shifts over time, so that policies formulated at a time when there was increased emphasis upon the rights of citizens to make claims on the state (such as the introduction of old age pensions) coexist with policies formed in different political and economic circumstances, when claims upon the family are more prominent (such as policies to remove the practical care of elderly people from the state to the family).

The process of drawing the boundaries between state responsibilities and family responsibilities, and designating where an individual can make claims, is part of the on-going political process and is a contested arena. Therefore, inevitably, there must be circumstances in which the policies formulated at one point in time eventually drift out of line with what some or all of the population see as the proper place for those boundaries to be drawn. Whether this is in fact happening at the present time forms one important theme in later chapters.

### Outline of the book

I have used this introduction to outline some of the most important parameters of the debates which I shall pursue: the distinction between actual assistance given to relatives and the reasons why it is given; different accounts of what is 'natural' in family relationships; the private and public dimensions of family obligations and the ways in which they are closely interlocked; the importance of understanding 'private' relationships in families in the context of the society in which they take place and not in a social vacuum. All these themes are developed further in subsequent chapters.

In chapter 1 my main purpose is to outline, essentially in a descriptive way, what we know about support between adult kin in contemporary Britain, on the basis of existing empirical evidence. This review suggests some analytical issues which are taken up in subsequent chapters. Chapter 2 is an historical review, focused around the question 'Do families support each other less than in the past?'. Chapters 3 and 4 are concerned with the social and economic contexts which may have some impact on the type of support kin give to each other. In chapter 3 I consider economic and demographic structures, while the focus of chapter 4 is upon the law and public policy. In chapters 5 and 6 the emphasis shifts to the personal and interpersonal dimensions of family life, and especially to the question of how any of us arrive at commitments to assist our kin in practice. In chapter 5 I consider the issues of moral and social norms about what constitutes the 'proper thing to do' for one's relatives, and how far these can be said to guide the actions of individuals. The focus of chapter 6 is on the negotiated elements in kin support and obligations, and how people work out commitments to their own kin over a period of time. Chapter 7 draws together the discussion by considering the usefulness of different theoretical frameworks for understanding the distinctive nature of support within families and the sense of obligation which may or may not underpin it. The concluding chapter is brief and returns to some of the larger political questions which I have aired in this introduction.

# 1

# Support between kin:
# who gives what to whom?

## Introduction

We all have experience of family life but it is dangerous to generalize on
the basis of it, especially since contemporary Britain is an ethnically
varied society and one with considerable regional disparities. The
purpose of this chapter is to assess what we know from research
evidence about patterns of support between adult relatives in contemporary Britain. Since this evidence is patchy, the chapter also begins
to identify areas in which future research seems important. The
purpose here essentially is to outline what we know as a prelude to
tackling the themes and patterns which emerge in a more analytical way
in subsequent chapters. Specialists in the field will be familiar with
much of the material reviewed here and may wish to pass over it
quickly. Readers less familiar with these studies may be interested to
weigh their own experience against the research evidence.

The discussion in this chapter is organized around the central
question 'Who does what for whom?'. I have broken this question
down into two component parts, and deal first with the issue of what
types of support pass between relatives, and second with precisely
which relatives offer each other assistance. These questions form the
framework for discussion. As I was reviewing the material to be used
here I had certain issues in my mind which concern the structure and
meaning of the support given, based upon the ideas developed by
anthropologists and sociologists who have studied kinship in Britain
and elsewhere. As these appear as themes threaded through the
discussion it may be useful to identify them here, although I shall
return to them at the end of the chapter.

1 It is obvious that we are bound to find considerable variation in
people's experience of support between kin. Are these variations

personal and idiosyncratic, or does people's experience vary more systematically in relation to their position in the social and economic structure? Do the major social divisions of class, gender and ethnicity really account for the differences? There are also bound to be variations with age, which in terms of family relationships is reflected in a person's position in the structure of generations (for a discussion of age and generation, see Finch, 1986a). Another possibility is regional differences in different areas of the United Kingdom, in both beliefs about and the practice of family support.

2 How reliable is support between kin? There is a sense in which family relationships are regarded as providing structures of support which are uniquely reliable, but at the same time it is obvious that not everyone draws upon such support in practice. Clearly assistance is not given to all kin invariably and whatever the circumstances, but are there certain relationships where it is given almost automatically? In what sense is support from kin reliable, and are there some types of support which are more reliable than others?

3 The polar opposite of automatic support is the idea that people act out of self-interest in family relationships, as in other areas of life. Is there evidence that this happens, and if so when does it happen? At the level of morality, is it regarded as proper to take self-interest into account when deciding whether to offer support to a relative, or to ask for it? Or are you always meant to act in a selfless manner towards your relatives, or at least to give the appearance of doing so? Focusing upon the role of instrumental considerations in family support thus helps us to uncover elements of the morality of duty in family life.

4 The concept of exchange has often been used to describe support in families, and this can be seen as expression of mutual self-interest. How important is the exchange element in structuring kin support? Must there always be a two-way element, or are there circumstances in which a one-way flow of support is regarded as acceptable and even appropriate?

Inevitably the preliminary review presented in this chapter raises more questions than it answers. This is deliberate, in that it helps to identify key questions about support in families which need to be addressed in later chapters.

## What kinds of support do relatives provide for each other?

I shall begin this review by considering the available evidence about different types of support in families, grouping under five main headings: economic support; accommodation; personal care; practical support and child care; emotional and moral support. How important are kin in providing each type of support? On what terms is it given and received?

## Economic support

The most obvious examples of economic support between kin concerns giving and lending money for specified purposes. This can be anything from a loan of £10 to tide your sister over to her next pay cheque, to substantial gifts like giving your grandson the money for the deposit on his first house. Some do not involve the direct exchange of money.

At the outset we need to make a distinction between economic support which passes between one individual and another, and situations where members of a family share resources from a commonly-owned pool, which represents a distinctive type of economic sharing between kin. For example in the farming industry kin ties still form the basis of many businesses (Marsden, 1984; Hutson, 1987). More generally, family businesses still are more significant in the British economy than is often supposed (Scott, 1986) although participation in a family firm does not necessarily imply pooling living expenses. It is also the custom of certain groups who have migrated to Britain to pool resources between kin, either between people living in the same household or sometimes across households (Anwar, 1985, pp. 52–5; Brah, 1986). Whilst these variations are important I shall focus this discussion mainly upon the more common examples, where support is being given by one person to another.

*Money transfers*   What evidence exists about direct transfers of money between relatives, what kind of sums are involved and between whom? A good starting point is Bell's (1968) work on middle-class families in South Wales, which highlighted the importance of financial support in middle-class kin groups and which identified the link between father and son (or son-in-law) as the main channel through which it flowed. Some of this support was on a substantial scale: a large cheque given to enable the parents to 'buy things for the baby'; a capital sum to enable a young architect to buy into a new firm; paying the wages of a home help to assist a family with several young children (pp. 92–4). As Bell points out, because of the composition of his sample, these illustrations all concern flows of money from parents to children at a point in the life course when characteristically resources are stretched, namely in the early years of child-rearing. A much more recent study confirms that similar patterns continue in the 1980s (Wilson, 1987).

This is a useful starting point in that Bell's work highlights two important themes necessary to understand economic support in families: gender and class (in particular, the distribution of income and wealth). The ability to give or lend money to relatives obviously is related to one's own economic resources in some way – although we are unlikely to find that people who have more straightforwardly give more. Equally, gender differences are probably not as straightforward as they first appear. In Bell's work the giving of financial support within middle-class families is 'men's business', and in a sense this is inevitable given that men exercise direct control over economic resources in this setting. However, women can be important as mediators and negotiators of financial assistance to kin, as Stivens (1978) argues on the basis of Australian data.

Data from more recent studies in Britain bear out the observations. Qureshi and Simon's (1987) work, on exchanges of assistance between elderly people and their kin, and Wilson's (1987) findings on grand-parents' support for their grandchildren, both show that women as well as men give economic support to younger generations, but there are some gender differences in the type of support given. Usually women give smaller amounts of money than men, or gifts in kind. Only a minority of women are in a position where they have control over substantial financial resources; however, when they do have such control they give money to their children and grandchildren in the same way that men do. The observed gender differences are a consequence of the different economic position of women and men in society as a whole.

Both of these more recent studies, like Bell's work, indicate that class is a dimension of exchanges of money between kin, in that the purpose of such exchanges in middle-class families is to enable younger generations to establish or maintain a life-style similar to that of their parents. In this sense, sharing economic resources in families helps to reproduce the class structure. On the question of regional differences, these studies of financial exchanges suggest that geographical location is rather unimportant. Similar patterns of exchange emerge from studies undertaken in different parts of Britain: Sheffield, London, South Wales.

Ethnicity represents another important dimension of money transfers, but this is not visible in most specialist studies of family relationships. There is substantial evidence that people who have migrated to Britain quite commonly send sums of money on a regular basis to assist relatives still living in their country of origin. This is reported for people whose origins lie in quite different parts of the world, for example, Poland, Montserrat and Pakistan (Patterson, 1977; Philpott, 1977; Anwar, 1985).

Most of the examples discussed so far imply that transfers of money are gifts rather than loans, although the distinction between these two is not always clear. Hill's (1970) classic American study of transfers between three generations shows that people do distinguish clearly between gifts and loans in principle, but less clearly in practice. It seems that a similar ambiguity is common in Britain in relation to money transfers between kin, although we do lack up-to-date evidence on this point. It is likely that such evidence would show up ethnic and cultural variations; for example, Anwar reports that it is common for migrants from Pakistan to borrow money from kin for major purchases such as a house or a business, but there is a strong obligation to return this loan fully and quickly (Anwar, 1985, p. 72).

*Gifts in kind*   Gifts in kind are no less important than money in family exchanges and there is evidence that these can include both goods and services, including the basic necessities. Baldwin's (1985, p. 142) work on bringing up handicapped children indicates that grandparents often buy necessities such as food and clothing, and this can be vital to the finances of a household where having a handicapped child creates additional expense. Similar findings are reported in McKee's (1987) study of the kin relationships of unemployed people living in Kidderminster. This work offers a good illustration of the range of economic support which is given between kin, and is also important in that it stresses its two-way nature. Even in these circumstances, where one might expect unemployed people to be net receivers, McKee shows that they give as well as receive and the list of what they give looks remarkably similar to the list of items which they receive. The importance of being able to reciprocate gifts in kind is also illustrated by case study data from Pahl's study on household work strategies on the Isle of Sheppey in Kent, in which one man who was long-term unemployed had been helping an uncle to decorate his house, and how the uncle then gave him a large piece of meat. This apparently is the system which works in the family: 'He does favours for them and they do favours back' (Pahl R.E., 1984, p. 340).

For families in less straitened circumstances, one gift in kind which could be of increasing importance is the payment of school fees. In popular discussions of private education, grandparents emerge as people very likely to pay school fees (*Guardian* 27 May 1986) and it certainly has been the case for some time that it is advantageous in taxation terms for them to do so, since grandparents can take out a deed of covenant to cover this payment whereas parents cannot. Evidence that payment of school fees is an established – if a minority – pattern among the English middle classes can be found in the study by Firth, Hubert and Forge (1970, pp. 349–50).

*Inheritance*  For those people who have accumulated assets during their lifetime, leaving money, property and land to relatives after death represents another – and very significant – mechanism through which economic support is given in families. It was the view of Engels (1884) that these inheritance arrangements provided the foundation of the development of capitalism in Britain in the nineteenth century, since they had made it possible to retain property and wealth – and with them all other forms of social privilege and power – within the hands of a small number of families from one generation to the next. In his study of poverty in the United Kingdom, Townsend (1979) argued that the mechanism of inheritance remains an important vehicle for ensuring that the wealthier groups in society maintain their economic position across generations. But what of the majority of people who do not have substantial wealth to bequeath? How significant a part does inheritance play in sustaining or raising standards of living? The available contemporary evidence suggests that very few people accumulate much in capital assets other than the house in which they live (Allan, 1982). The number of people who have this asset to bequeath has been rising.

In 1951 about four million people in Britain owned their own homes; by 1985 this figure had risen to 14 million, with 62 per cent of the total housing stock being owner-occupied (*Social Trends*, 1987, p. 137, table 8.1). Many more people in the future than in the past will benefit from the kind of economic support which people give to their relatives through *post mortem* transfers. Movements in the housing market, especially in the 1980s, have produced wide disparities between the value of property in different parts of Britain. This is one respect in which we can see regional differences opening up in the kind of support which relatives can give to each other, although we know very little about how these matters are handled in families at the present time. Some writers have speculated that we could see the development of new patterns of support such as an increase of private loans within families, or substantial bequests to grandchildren rather than children, since the younger generation are the ones who will find the most difficulty in getting onto the first rung of the housing ladder (Murie and Forrest, 1980; Means, 1987). Clearly these are all matters which would repay up-to-date research, since it seems that we may be witnessing important social changes in patterns of family support at the present time.

I have been making the assumption that people bequeath their assets to their relatives, but is this necessarily so? Under English law this is not straightforwardly a requirement, since one of the cornerstones of the law relating to inheritance is the principle testamentary freedom – the right of each individual to dispose of their assets as they wish. However in the twentieth century this principle has been modified somewhat through both statutory and case law, by introducing the principle that a will should make fair provision for people who have had certain types of relationship with the deceased, mostly but not exclusively kin (Cretney, 1984, ch. 23; Green, 1988).

So the law does acknowledge now that people generate obligations to certain relatives during their lifetime, and that these should be honoured after their death. In addition to spouses the people who make such claims are: former spouses who have not remarried; children; people who were treated as children of the deceased; any other person (relative or not) who was being maintained financially by the deceased at the time of his or her death (Cretney, 1984, pp. 702–7). Such claims in fact are quite rare, running currently at the rate of about 400 a year (Freedman et al., 1988, p. 53). The major reason for this is that a rather small proportion of the population makes a will – only about 20 per cent on the most authoritative figures available (Todd and Jones, 1972; Manners and Rauta, 1979). For the majority who die intestate, separate legal rules apply and these also reflect the idea that certain relatives have the right to claim a share in the resources of the deceased. These rules are fairly complex and depend on the size of the estate. But they demonstrate a fairly clear hierarchy of claims to receive financial benefit from a relative which runs: spouse and/or children; parents; brothers and sisters and their children; grandparents; uncles and aunts. People lower down the hierarchy can only make claims if the deceased did not have relatives who rank above them; and a distinction is made between full and half-blood relatives, the former having prior claims (Cretney, 1984, pp. 698–700). So in the case of all who die intestate, and for most of the rather small number who make a will, the outcome of inheritance will be that relatives are beneficiaries, and the legal procedures which ensure this codify a set of obligations to give support which discriminates between close and more distant kin.

In popular imagery, the reading of a will is the occasion for bitter squabbles to break out over the deceased's preferred distribution of assets, but the limited amount of research data which we have on this issue suggests that overt conflicts are not very common. In the study of middle-class families, Firth, Hubert and Forge were able to find only small numbers of such cases, and then the conflict tended to be expressed as private resentment rather than open hostility (pp. 373–8). However, in a few cases there were serious disputes in families over questions of inheritance, apparently always followed by very cool relationships between the parties, or ceasing contact altogether. In one instance, it was believed in the family that one sister had visited their father during his final illness and had persuaded him to make a new will in her favour, directing his hand as he signed it. Other siblings resented the fact that 'she got the cash and we got a load of old books' (p. 375). In another family, where the inheritance from the father was quite substantial, funds for the brothers and sisters were tied up in a trust which was administered by their mother, and this appeared to result in a series of squabbles about whether each of them was getting their fair share in comparison with the others (p. 376).

Thus disputes between brothers and sisters (who in a formal sense are in the same position in respect of their claims to a parent's estate) is one of the situations where serious conflicts do arise. The other, according to the evidence of Firth and his colleagues, is disputes which involve step-relatives, especially the claims of a second spouse by comparison with the children of a first marriage. The possibilities for disputes of the latter kind of course have increased since this study was done in the 1960s because of rising rates of divorce and remarriage, and we need up-to-date data on how people handle the range of claims of inheritance in families where there is a complex series of step-relationships.

Looking at the effects of inheritance in a broader perspective, it is apparent that the laws and customs associated with it in any society have the effect of shaping kin relationships in ways other than the transmission of economic resources. For example anthropologists have argued that in those societies where women are allowed to inherit as well as men this can determine many other aspects of social relations. Typically it means that steps are taken to ensure that women do not take away a proportion of the kin group's resources when they marry – which can mean variously, that women's sexuality is tightly controlled, that women are given little choice about whom they marry, that there is a preference for choosing marriage partners from within the kin groups (Tillion, 1983; Goddard, 1987).

England traditionally had inheritance laws based on the principle of primogeniture, that is the property should pass to a single heir, usually the eldest son, rather than being divided between all surviving children. This arrangement is particularly suited to a society where wealth is concentrated in the ownership of land, because it ensures that an undivided estate can be passed on to succeeding generations in the family. In their study of the development of the English middle class in the early part of the nineteenth century, based on analysis of wills, Davidoff and Hall have shown that this system did not suit the growing numbers of middle classes who had business or capital to pass on. Increasingly they used the principle of partible inheritance (which had long been characteristic of some other European societies), where the estate was divided between the surviving spouse and children. At this time when women could not hold property after they married, typically daughters were left trust funds which would provide them with an income, while sons received land, property and liquid assets (Davidoff and Hall, 1987, pp. 205–7). These different patterns of inheritance are bound to have an effect upon the relationships between siblings. Under the system of progeniture it will be known from childhood that one sibling will be privileged over all the rest; by contrast partible inheritance requires a much greater degree of co-operation between siblings in adult life, especially if they inherit land or a firm which provides them with a common livelihood. This is an issue to which I shall return later in this chapter, when I consider relationships between siblings specifically.

*Finding work and migration*   It has become the common wisdom that using relatives to help you find work – associated in the past with the early phase of industrialization and more recently with informal methods of recruiting casual labour – is of little significance in the present. This view is challenged by Grieco's (1987) work on the use of social networks, especially kin networks, in job-seeking. Grieco's work is based on a detailed case study in the Northamptonshire steel town of Corby, and smaller studies of women in the fisheries industry in Aberdeen and of people migrating from the East End of London to live and work in the new town of Basildon, on London's outer fringes. Her work shows the continuing importance of kin networks in seeking and finding jobs, even in situations where employers use more formal recruitment strategies. She argues that it often is still in the employers' interest to recruit someone on a relative's recommendation, since this gives employers more control over their workforce. From the point of view of people seeking work, the kin group continues to provide a reliable and up-to-date information network and a means of getting to the head of the queue of potential employees. An example of this can be seen in a story reported by a worker in Corby,

I'd heard they'd started taking people on. I went over to personnel and said, 'What about my son-in-law? His form's been with you for ages. And you're taking other people in front of him. How's that?' So they looked for the form and they couldn't find it. Well it wasn't surprising really; I'd never filled one in. But he got up the front of the line and he got the job. It's the only way. You have to push if you want something, don't you? (Grieco, 1987, p. 86)

Grieco is able to show that in each of the situations she studied in different regions of Britain, proportions of the workforce had kin connections with the firm for which they worked. Women often are as important as men in making and keeping these links, which is one reason why the importance of the kin network in employment frequently has been missed by other researchers, who have looked for people with the same surname. In fact in-laws, and indeed kin as distant as cousins, seem commonly to be included in these employment networks. These conclusions are supported by case study data reported by Wilson and Pahl (1988), based on the detailed study of one kin group on the Isle of Sheppey. In this family both women and men expected to use kin contacts as a way of finding work.

Grieco's major example is Corby which, as a town based upon the steel industry, had an employment history of deliberate recruitment of workers from Scotland. In this situation the kin network operates not only as a means of finding work but also for assisting the process of migration. She argues that if you have been assisted by relatives yourself, this imposes a strong obligation to provide similar support for others, even if that means giving a temporary home to someone whom you do not particularly like (p. 89). So-called chain migration, where one relative gets established and then acts as a bridge for others, is a common feature of many situations both in the past and the present, where people migrate to find work.

The same pattern certainly is found among people who have migrated to Britain from overseas since the end of the Second World War. Chain migration on this pattern is reported for a wide variety of people now living in Britain, including those who originated in Italy, Hong Kong, the Punjab and Pakistan (Palmer, 1977; Watson, 1977; Ballard, 1979; Anwar, 1985). The kind of economic support given from one migrant to the next includes: assistance with the fare; assistance in finding work; a temporary home; personal encouragement and moral support whilst the new migrant is adjusting to Britain.

*The significance of economic support*   Drawing together the different strands of this discussion of economic support, we can ask: Who are the main beneficiaries within a family? Does economic support flow between the generations in both directions, or is the trade one-way?

These questions have been explored more fully by researchers in North America than they have in Britain (Sussman, 1965; Cheal, 1983) but the findings of recent British studies seem broadly to be in line with this work (Qureshi and Simons, 1987; Wilson, 1987). The common pattern seems to be that there is an uneven flow of support across the generations, with a net transfer from older to younger which continues throughout the life cycle, and indeed after death in the form of inheritance. Of course the value of this varies considerably according to the resources available to the older generation. Parents give to their children, and continue to give more than their children ever give them in most cases, although one situation in which this flow often is reversed is where children have migrated to a more affluent country, and expect to send money back to their parents (see for example, Thorogood, 1987).

I began this discussion of economic support between relatives by asking how significant it is in contemporary Britain. The answer is that it is more significant than often it appears, especially if you include examples such as help in finding employment, the importance of which continues to be greater than often is recognized. Although perhaps rather few people rely on their relatives for regular financial support, many people go through times in their lives when such support is important to their capacity to establish or maintain a particular life style. It seems that the central significance of economic support in families lies in its reliability: you always know that you can fall back upon the support of relatives if necessary and that this will be regarded as a legitimate request. In the context of white British culture, all of this applies particularly to middle-class people, who have more substantial resources to share. By the same token it is usually middle-class men who ultimately are in the position to make substantial gifts, although when women can behave in this way, they do. Normally this financial support passes from older to younger generations in families in a one-way flow.

## Accommodation

Sharing accommodation with relatives on a permanent basis is not regarded as a desirable option in contemporary British culture, where the image of the normal household is based firmly upon the nuclear family: typically a married couple and their immature children, with possibly the addition of an elderly parent. This contrasts with many other societies in which sharing a home with relatives has been regarded as the normal option and a permanent arrangement. One example would be traditional arrangements in Turkey, where an adult son would expect to bring his wife into his parents' home to live, and to raise his children there (Stirling, 1965). Whilst scholars debate how far economic changes have been responsible for breaking up these traditional arrangements, there is evidence that the idea persists that this form of joint household is an ideal which people would put into practice if they could (Benedict, 1976). Many similar examples can be found around the world, but in Britain there is substantial historical evidence which suggests that sharing with relatives outside the nuclear family in adult life has never been widely regarded as an ideal to be aimed for (see chapter 2).

Nonetheless the composition of households does change over time, perhaps rather more than much recent research has acknowledged. In reality, the household is a constantly changing social unit as members age and other members come and go (Pahl, J. 1984, p. 201). We need to distinguish, on the one hand between popular imagery and the public ideology of 'the family' and on the other hand what happens in practice, which inevitably is more diverse. Historical evidence suggests that in the past people did share accommodation with their kin, at least on a temporary basis, and they did so essentially for instrumental reasons resulting from social and economic pressures (Anderson, 1971; 1980; Davidoff, 1979; Roberts, 1984). Can we discern contemporary patterns of shared accommodation between kin which might also be the result of such pressures? Are there predictable circumstances in the 1980s where people are likely to live in the home of a relative? How common are these?

One can begin to answer these questions by looking at the proportion of the population who live in households of different types. Evidence from official statistics suggests that the number of households containing two or more elementary families has indeed fallen: from 3 per cent of households in 1961 to 1 per cent in 1981 (*Social Trends, 1987*, p. 41, table 2.1) Clearly this is, and apparently has been for some time, very much a minority arrangement within the British population as a whole. However, for certain groups in that population it is much more common. Small scale studies indicate that households of this type are quite common, for example, for people of Pakistani origin living in Britain (Anwar, 1985) and this is reflected in official statistics by evidence about the overall size of households: in 1985, whilst less than one in ten white households contained more than four people, where people classified themselves as Pakistani, or Bangladeshi, just over 50 per cent of households were of that size (*Social Trends 1987*, p. 45, table 2. 9). The circumstances which have produced such patterns in some ways are similar to those in Britain in the past, namely in the early years after a migration, with the additional dimension that, in the case of migrants say from Pakistan, joint households are a familiar pattern and indeed often are larger than those established in Britain (Saifullah Khan, 1977; Anwar, 1985). In this instance instrumental considerations are reinforced by long-established cultural patterns.

In the majority white British culture, there are phases in people's lives when shared accommodation does feature, especially in young adult life and in old age. I shall look at each of these in turn as a way of helping us to understand when and why people offer help to their relatives in the form of shared accommodation.

*Young adults living with relatives*   The early years of marriage traditionally have been a time when people did live with relatives, before establishing their own household, although this is now less common than it once was. Evidence based upon population censuses and analysed by Holmans (1981) indicates that the number of married couples in shared accommodation fell from three-quarters of a million in 1951 to slightly under a quarter of a million in 1971.

However in practice the change has been less dramatic than it first appears, for two reasons. First, the length of time which couples spend in shared accommodation has fallen from an average of almost three years for people who married before 1955, to around one and a half years for people married in the late 1960s (p. 12). In a study of newly weds' housing, Madge and Brown (1981) calculate that a total of 31 per cent of their sample had shared accommodation at some stage in their early married life, usually with parents. The average length of time in this accommodation was 10 months. Second, the age at which people marry is closely related to their ability to set up an independent household, and for women who married under the age of 20 the numbers sharing accommodation with relatives changed little between the 1950s and the 1970s (Holman, 1981). Thus sharing accommodation with relatives in the early years of marriage still is the experience of a sizeable minority of the population, especially for those who marry young.

Sharing a home with relatives (other than parents) before marriage is another phenomenon which was more common in the past than in the present (Anderson, 1971; 1980) Very little is known about circumstances under which young people now may go to live with a non-parental relative, although Gill Jones (1987) has shown that it still happens for a substantial number, especially those designated as working class on occupational criteria. Basing her analysis on data from a large-scale, representative sample of women and men at the age of 23, she shows that 16 per cent of single working-class men and 22 per cent of single working-class women were living with kin at the time of the survey. The proportions for middle-class people were 6 per cent and 9 per cent respectively; among the middle-class respondents it was much more common to share with friends rather than relatives after leaving the parental home. So for young people from working-class backgrounds in particular, it certainly seems still to be an option to live with kin. However, we know very little in a systematic way about the circumstances under which this is considered a desirable option, or the terms under which young people live in a relative's household.

*Elderly people living with relatives*   Official statistics indicate that living with a relative (other than spouse), in old age is the experience of a rather small minority. Evidence for the year 1985 indicates that whilst 52 per cent of people aged over 65 lived with a spouse and 36 per cent lived alone, only 12 per cent lived with relatives (*Social Trends 1987*, p. 44, table 2.8). However, the experience of living with kin seems to be more common for elderly people of minority ethnic origin. Mays (1983) has calculated that about three times as many elderly people from South Asia live with relatives. Barker's (1984, p. 22) review of the living arrangements of elderly people of Asian and Afro-Caribbean origin indicates that almost three-quarters of Asian elderly people live in large households and as few as 5 per cent live alone, whereas the household composition of elderly people of Afro-Caribbean origin is similar to that in the white population.

Thus, with the important exception of certain ethnic minority groups, living with a relative seems to be a rather uncommon experience for older people. In chapter 2 I shall discuss this in an historical perspective. To anticipate that discussion, the available evidence suggests that elderly people, just like people in the early years of marriage, have always shared a home with relatives for instrumental reasons of a financial kind rather than by personal preference (Wall, 1984). In the case of elderly people these economic considerations seem somewhat more important even than the elderly person's need for physical care. That conclusion is supported by contemporary evidence from Qureshi and Simons's (1987) study in Sheffield, which clearly indicates that it is rare for elderly people to move in with their children in order to be cared for. Where there were examples of co-residence, the joint household had been established some years before the elderly person needed physical care, and a number of these households had been created by the younger generation(s) moving in with the parent, not the other way round.

*Sharing with relatives after divorce*   So far I have concentrated upon two situations in which people may live with relatives, both of which probably would be regarded as a predictable part of the normal life cycle. But are there other circumstances, perhaps less predictable, in which an adult might need to have a home with relatives, at least on a temporary basis? Of particular interest, given that rates of divorce have been rising over the last two decades, is whether relatives commonly provide housing for people who have separated from a married or cohabiting partner.

We know that in general women who have been married (that is, separated divorced or widowed) are more likely to be living with their own parents than those who currently are married (Martin and Roberts, 1984). This suggests that there is a tendency to return to the parental home when a marriage ends, through whatever means, and this is confirmed in the case of separation and divorce by Sullivan's (1986) analysis of data from the period 1976–81. She is able to show that both women and men are much more likely to be living with relatives after a marriage has ended than during it. Data from 1976 for women specifically show that 14 per cent of women whose marriages were intact were living in someone else's household (the most popular choice being the wife's parents), but for divorced and separated women the figure rose to 61 per cent. Data from the Labour Force Survey in 1981 show that high proportions of both women and men who are divorced or separated live in the home of their own parents, although there are some differences related to both gender and social class (as measured by housing tenure). The highest concentrations of divorced people living with parents are to be found among men whose parents live in local authority accommodation. Making the assumption that such men have working-class occupations, Sullivan argues that the housing options for them are very limited after divorce, more limited than for women who, if they have been left as single parents relying upon state benefits for their income, probably will qualify for local authority housing.

The importance of economic considerations is supported by evidence from Burgoyne and Clark's (1984) small-scale study of couples in second marriages. They report that 9 out of 31 divorced women and 11 out of 33 divorced men returned to their parents' home when their first marriage ended. On the whole this was seen as an arrangement that should be temporary if at all possible, even where the relationship with the parents was good and they were supportive of their adult child. In some cases it was necessary to return to the parental home even when parents were not wholly supportive, for lack of viable alternatives, as in the situation described by this respondent,

I got to the stage where I went back to me mum and dad. They said I were wrong for leaving him and that I should go back to him . . . my father didn't agree with it, he's er, very old fashioned, we've never had any divorces or anything in our family . . . (But) I went back to them, well I had nowhere to go . . . my mother and father said I could stay as long as I wanted. (Burgoyne and Clark, 1984, pp. 80–1)

It seems from this evidence that living with relatives when a marriage ends is considered in a rather similar way to living with relatives in other circumstances. It is an option to fall back on if you have to; it is certainly appropriate for relatives, especially parents, to assist in this way, but it is not sought as the most desirable arrangement in the circumstances and therefore it should not last for too long. It also has a strong instrumental element, in the sense that it is most likely to happen when it is economically advantageous.

The theme of instrumentality seems to be as important in understanding support in the form of accommodation, as it is in understanding financial support within families.

### Personal care

By 'personal care' I mean nursing someone who cannot fully look after themselves and/or performing domestic tasks which they are unable to undertake. This may or may not entail living in the same house. Because of the large number of elderly people now in the population it is inevitable that much of the discussion will concern their needs, but they are by no means the only people who need personal care. There are also younger people who have a long term chronic illness or handicap; people who have been psychiatrically ill; people who have a mental handicap. In these cases, some of the 'care' required may not be so much nursing care as a constant or regular presence of another person who will ensure their safety. What part is played by kin in practice in the provision of such care?

*Who provides care for whom?*   What kind of personal care is given to relatives on an unpaid basis? Between which relatives? Are there boundaries to what is considered reasonable for kin to provide?

Evidence about who actually acts as an unpaid carer has to be pieced together from various statistical sources, but the best informed estimates seem to be that very few people are cared for by non-relatives, and that women provide about 75 to 85 per cent of relative care. Single, never-married daughters traditionally have been the group who provided care for their parents in old age. In the present generations of younger women, very few never marry so this particular source of family care has almost dried up, although there is evidence that never-married women still account for a disproportionate number of unpaid carers (Finch and Groves, 1980; Lewis and Meredith, 1988). The only common circumstances in which men provide substantial care is when they are looking after a disabled wife, whereas women care for husbands, parents, handicapped children and sometimes other relatives too (Charlesworth, Wilkin and Durie, 1984; Parker, 1985; Henwood and Wicks, 1985; Finch 1986b).

A consistent feature of unpaid caring, demonstrated by all the available detailed studies, is that once a particular relative has taken on the responsibility for the care of an elderly or handicapped person they get rather limited support, if any, from other relatives or friends. So the care of a highly dependent person by 'the family' in most cases means care by one relative, usually a female relative (Gilhooly, 1982; Nissel and Bonnerjea, 1982; Parker, 1985). This can demand a very high level of commitment, in which caring for a relative completely dominates the carer's own life. In their study of 41 women who had cared for their own mother before she died, Lewis and Meredith comment that to an outside observer 'the majority of respondents led remarkably restricted lives' (Lewis and Meredith, 1988, p. 87). Most spend much of their time feeding and bathing their mother, doing laundry and other household work, and sometimes also holding down a paid job, with only very limited opportunities for a break of any kind. One woman compared it to her experience of being in service in the past: 'It's like being in service. I got one evening off . . . and one afternoon a month' (Lewis and Meredith, 1988, p. 83). Of course taking some responsibility for providing personal care does not always demand quite this level of commitment, but examples of this kind are valuable in specifying just what responsibility towards one's parents *can* mean. Situations such as those described by Lewis and Meredith apparently fall within the range of what is regarded appropriate for a daughter who has a sense of filial duty.

Looking at the evidence available, there seem to be four main principles which determine who offers personal care. This has been characterized by some writers as a hierarchy of obligations (Qureshi and Simons, 1987; Ungerson, 1987).

1   The marriage relationship takes primacy, so that one's spouse becomes the first source of support for married people. This is

confirmed by more detailed research evidence, for example Wenger's (1984) study of elderly people living in rural North Wales, where she found that married and infirm people had distinctive patterns of personal support, where the spouse was the main helper for every task mentioned.

2   Second, it appears that the parent–child relationship is the second port of call, with children being a major source of support for elderly parents and (less commonly in numerical terms) parents being the principal supporters of adult handicapped children. Unlike the personal care between spouses, these patterns of support here are highly gendered, with daughters and mothers being carers much more commonly than sons and fathers (Bayley, 1973; Wilkin, 1979; Glendinning, 1983).

3   People who are members of the same household are also major providers of support. Of course often they also fall into the first two categories mentioned, but it seems that household membership operates separately in relation to giving assistance, so that a particular child who shares a home with their parent is much more likely to be giving personal care than their siblings. The same applies to more distant relatives who may sometimes share a household. Qureshi and Simons (1987) have been able to show this on the basis of data from their Sheffield study of elderly people and their carers.

4   The fourth and very important principle which operates in personal care is gender. There certainly is plenty of evidence that women are much more likely to provide personal care for relatives than are men. Even where there is an apparent choice between a male and female relative, women are much more likely to be carers – daughters and even daughters-in-law rather than sons (Henwood and Wicks, 1985; Parker, 1985; Ungerson, 1987). This is usually taken to reflect a generalized normative expectation that women are the appropriate carers; although empirical evidence about normative expectations is actually fairly sparse (a point which I shall take up in chapter 5).

The operation of these four principles leaves some room for manoeuvre, in the sense that their application may produce more than one possible carer in a given situation. This leaves open the possibility of negotiation between the parties to identify the person who eventually becomes the main carer. The processes by which such negotiations are conducted are considered in some detail in chapter 7.

Gender is an important dimension in personal care. It affects not only who becomes an unpaid carer but also is relevant to two other dimensions of this issue: who receives care, and what kind of support is given. Shanas (1979), in her review of American data on family support for the elderly, notes that women are two or three times more likely than men to say that no one helped them during a period of illness. British evidence demonstrates that women who are ill or handicapped are less likely than men to receive support from formal services or informal sources (Charlesworth, Wilkin and Durie, 1984; Bebbington and

Davies, 1983). Women are presumed to be able to cope domestically in circumstances where men are presumed to be unable to manage: they can cook, clean and care for themselves even if they are physically impaired (Wenger, 1984).

*The foundations of personal care in families*  The picture which emerges from evidence about personal care given to relatives is one of very extensive amounts of support, especially at particular points in the life course. It is possible to do a financial calculation which puts a price on this, by working out the number of hours 'caring' labour contributed by relatives, and the total amount is equivalent to the whole statutory input of health and social services for the equivalent age groups (Family Policy Studies, Centre, 1984; Finch, 1986b).

At the same time, research evidence about how people view this in practice conveys a sense of boundaries: that there are limits to what one can reasonably expect relatives to do, and to what a person would want to rely on relatives for. This is graphically expressed by the phrase 'intimacy at a distance' which was first used by Rosenmayr and Kockeis (1963) and applied to the British context by Townsend (1957), in his study of the family life of old people. The phrase conveys a sense of the desired relationship between elderly people and their relatives, especially their children: they want to be on good terms with them, and to have regular contact with them, but they do not want to rely on them too directly. More recent evidence, whilst not addressing this issue directly, tends to suggest that this desired relationship is still important. Wenger (1984), in discussing her North Wales data, argues that elderly people do turn to their children for support, but they do so reluctantly. Thompson and West in a study of preferences for sheltered housing which included a sample of people of all ages who suffered from rheumatism and arthritis, found among these respondents 'a strong feeling of not wanting to impose on relatives' (Thompson and West, 1984, p. 318), and the older respondents were even less willing than the younger to consider the option of being cared for by kin.

My brief review of personal care given by relatives has stressed the theme of variation, especially by gender. In this respect at least family responsibilities do seem to be very different for women and men, both as givers and receivers. There is obviously also variation by generational position with old age being the most likely – although not the only possible – time when anyone may need personal support from relatives. In these situations we have clear examples of support being one-way, the principle of reciprocal giving necessarily being muted where one party needs substantial care. However, it remains possible that people do see the support which they give to elderly relatives as part of a two-way pattern which stretches over time and across generations, and where they themselves will benefit ultimately from the support of someone in a younger generation. In the case of carers who have their own children this is easier to see than for the classic (and disappearing) case of the single daughter who was presumed to be childless; although in that case the assumption in the past was that the single daughter would be rewarded in material terms through being the major beneficiary of her parents' will, if they had money or property to bequeath. We know rather little about what kind of bargains are struck at the present time although inheritance is always a possible way of ensuring that the balance of support does not tip too much in one direction, even if its use is not spoken about openly.

The theme of instrumentality does not come through so strongly in relation to personal care as it does in other types of support. It is here that we do see examples of apparently selfless giving, where the carer's independent life effectively is suspended for the duration of the caring relationship, which may last many years. In such cases, even if inheritance implicitly is involved, people do not present their own motivations for providing support as part of some bargain in which their own interests are a legitimate concern. Recent studies which have looked at this issue report that people talk in terms of some blend of love and duty, affection and obligation (Ungerson, 1987; Lewis and Meredith, 1988).

Despite this, considerations of self-interest are not entirely absent. Not all carers – still less potential careers – are people acting selflessly out of love or duty. Especially in accounts of how one sibling became the main carer for a parent, there is a sense of people guarding their own position, lest too much should be expected of them. Brothers are more readily excused than sisters, it would seem, although even here Lewis and Meredith report considerable bitterness on the part of carers who felt that their brothers should be playing a more prominent, if minor, role in the care of their parents. As one of their interviewees put it,

I feel it's all wrong that the single one in the family should be the one who does everything. At one stage I told him (the brother) that lots of single daughters dropped dead looking after their mother. He just got in his car and drove off . . . he was a fine sort of brother really. (Lewis and Meredith, 1988, p. 24)

The sense that many potential carers are guarding their own positions in situations where the care of a relative becomes a live issue in a family, is matched by the very clear message that older people in particular are wary of asking too much of their relatives, or of 'having' to rely on them. Paradoxically, since it is in relation to personal care that we see examples of highly committed one-way support, the research evidence suggests that most people do regard it as legitimate for the parties to consider their own interests in this situation, even if it is possible to push that too far. Except unusually, receiving personal care from relatives is not seen by either party as an automatic right.

### Practical support and child care

Small-scale practical support, given either on a regular or occasional basis, is often seen as the essence of kin relationships. Certainly the

British studies of the 1950s and 60s presented and popularized the image of the working-class family which was characterized by extensive and regular sharing of support, especially between women. In societies where the organization of social and economic life is based much more closely on kinship than it is for most people in contemporary Britain, women's involvement in exchanging goods and services with female relatives plays an important role in maintaining the solidarity of the kin group. An example of this can be found in Goddard's (1987) discussion of working-class women in Naples; whose lives are still based very much on this pattern despite economic changes.

What kind of practical support commonly is given to relatives in the British context? It is unavoidable to begin by referring to Young and Willmott's (1957) study of Bethnal Green, and to the much quoted chapter in which they itemize how mothers and daughters and sisters constantly seem to be doing each other's shopping, drying each other's washing and looking after each other's children for the afternoon. In this period, the other influential work on family relationships was Bott's (1957) study, based on an intensive study of 20 married couples. The message here is rather different from the automic and unproblematic sharing of assistance portrayed in the Bethnal Green study. Even in her small sample, Bott was able to document considerable variety. She argues that it is families who see each other frequently where one finds most practical support being given, because frequent contact affords the opportunity for pressure to be put upon individuals to 'keep up their kinship obligations' (Bott, 1957, p. 133). Since women usually are more active than men in keeping contact with relatives, it is not surprising that they are more involved in the giving and receiving of practical support.

There have been no recent studies which have looked at patterns of exchange between kin as their central focus, but relevant data can be gleaned from a number of studies. Of particular interest in this context is Cornwell's study of family relationships in Bethnal Green in the 1980s, in which she explicitly makes comparison with Young and Willmott's earlier work. She shows that there remain some examples of extensive sharing of support between mothers, daughters and sisters, although her interpretation of this is far less romantic than Young and Willmott's. In relation to child care, for example, she documents how assistance given by mothers to daughters typically is more extensive than between sisters. In two instances in her small study, this meant that mothers effectively were caring for a baby instead of their daughter (Cornwell, 1984, pp. 86–90). However, a comparable study which included women of different ethnic origins might show that support between sisters and sisters-in-law was somewhat more significant. As Wilson puts it in her discussion of Asian women living in Britain, these relationships serve to 'cushion a woman against the harshness of her life' (Wilson, 1978, p. 7).

It seems that it is of continuing importance for women to be able to call upon relatives to assist them with child care, and that this still is a key element in women's organization of their daily lives, as it has been in the past (see for example Roberts, 1984). Yeandle's (1984) study of the strategies which women use to combine paid work and domestic work emphasizes that female kin are a common and reliable source of assistance which enables women to combine the two. She found that about two-thirds of the women whom she studied had relied upon female kin at some stage, and that most of the support which they received was child care, coming principally from mothers and mothers-in-law, but also sisters, sisters-in-law, aunts and grandmothers. The findings of Yeandle's small-scale study are broadly supported by data from the Women and Employment survey, which covered the work histories of 6,000 women. Of employed women who needed to make arrangements for a pre-school child, 34 per cent used the child's grandmother and 9 per cent used another relative. Women who worked full time were particularly likely to use the child's grandmother (44 per cent of them did this) (Martin and Roberts, 1984, p. 39, table 4.10).

Help with child care, therefore, is important to enable women to continue in, or return to, paid work. There is also some evidence that it is of particular importance when women (and less frequently men) are left as the custodial parent after a marriage ends. Burgoyne and Clark (1984) report that this was seen as a major reason for returning to live with parents after the break-up of a marriage, and the assistance which grandparents gave with child care in the short term was seen as vital in helping their daughter or son to re-establish themselves economically and to form new relationships.

Regular assistance with child care certainly is important for many women. But for many more the importance of relatives – especially of grandmothers – lies in their availability as people who can be called upon in a crisis, or as people to fall back on when other arrangements break down. In her study of 61 white mothers conducted in London in 1983–4, Wilson (1987) found that none relied upon their children's grandparents to carry the main burden of child care while they themselves went out to work, but most regarded grandmothers as support which they could use on a more casual basis for babysitting, and as help in emergencies. Cunningham-Burley (1985) found a rather similar pattern in a piece of work conducted around the same time in Scotland. The birth of another child seems, predictably, to be a situation in which grandmothers are called upon for assistance. The study of Bell, McKee and Priestly (1983) indicates that maternal grandmothers commonly are the people who care for older children during the period immediately following the birth of a new baby, although sometimes sisters and sisters-in-law also help in this way.

In general, practical support between relatives seems highly gendered, with women much more involved than men. Examples certainly can be found of men giving practical support to relatives on a reciprocal basis, usually involving typically 'male' activities such as gardening and decorating (Pahl, R.E., 1984). But most research studies suggest that sharing practical support is more characteristic of women. It could be that the available studies have concentrated specifically upon women, and that men do give assistance which is less visible. On the other hand, since it is mostly women who are responsible for running households and caring for dependent members of their families, it is not surprising that they are involved in helping each other in these practical ways, which lend themselves to being organized on a reciprocal basis.

As with other types of support, we observe similar patterns in studies undertaken in different regional locations, and at different times over the past 30 years. There is also some evidence to suggest that there is little variation by social class in the amount of practical support given and received. This comes from the study by Goldthorpe, Llewellyn and Payne (1980, pp. 152–6) on patterns of social mobility for men, as measured by a comparison of the occupational status of different generations of the same family. This work was based on a sample survey of over 10,000 men, and a few questions were asked about practical support between kin. Respondents were asked to say whether they had actually received assistance from relatives at the time when their own children were born, and also to indicate whether they would turn to relatives for support in three hypothetical situations, of varying degrees of seriousness: to borrow tools or materials; if the respondent and/or his wife were ill for a couple of days; if illness lasted several weeks. Where men had kin living geographically close, there was no significant difference between classes in the proportions who would turn to kin for support. There was also little difference in the proportions who had actually received help from kin at the time of childbirth.

### Emotional and moral support

The last type of assistance which I shall discuss here is emotional and moral support, by which I mean listening, talking, giving advice, and helping people to put their own lives in perspective. This is support to which the family might seem peculiarly suited, since it is concerned with personal anxieties and fears, the realm of the intimate.

*Routine support and crisis support* Emotional support is given by relatives in a wide range of circumstances, not only in crises. At the more routine end of the scale, studies of the relationship between mothers and daughters, from Young and Willmott onwards, document how daughters turn to their mothers when they are anxious about their children's health, or unsure about some aspect of child rearing (Young and Willmott, 1957), despite the tendency of professional advisers to devalue 'old wives' tales'.

Blaxter and Paterson's more recent study, undertaken in Scotland, suggests that mothers remain an important source of advice to, and support for, young women who are concerned about health matters in relation to their own children – at least for working-class women, with whom their study was concerned. At the same time, some women in the older generation believed that they were a less significant source of advice and support for their daughters than their own mothers had been for them, and all were concerned to ensure that their support did not amount to 'interference' (Blaxter and Paterson, 1982, especially pp. 174–9). A slightly different example of emotional support which is a routine part of women's lives is provided by studies of women who have recently migrated to Britain. For example, a study of women of Pakistani origin living in Bradford shows that the kin group provides a key structure for the guidance and emotional support of women who are newly arrived from Pakistan (Saifullah Khan, 1977).

In calling these examples 'routine', I do not mean to deny their importance to the receiver, nor that they may be very demanding for the giver. But they are of a different order from the kind of personal crisis which people experience as distressing or disabling, such as the break-up of a marriage. How important are kin in giving personal support in these circumstances? The interesting study by Brannen and Collard (1982) on the process of seeking help when marriages are failing, suggests that kin in some ways are less important than earlier studies had suggested. Although kin might be an important source of practical help once the marriage had actually ended, people who were under-going marital difficulties were more likely to turn to someone they considered an 'outsider' for emotional support or guidance. This was particularly true of people who had close knit kin networks, who were unlikely to use individual kin as close confidants, and who often said that there were certain kin – usually parents – whom they would definitely not consult (ibid. pp. 118–25).

*Who gives moral support to whom*   It seems that patterns of emotional support in crisis situations may be somewhat different from those which I have labelled 'routine'. In the more routine situations, there seems to be a common pattern of support between parents and children, especially mothers and daughters, followed by siblings. There is evidence that the latter increases in importance as people get older (Jerrome, 1981). There is also evidence that younger people expect to transfer the source of their main emotional support to their spouse when they marry. In their study of newly-wed couples, Mansfield and Collard found that most expected to be able to apply the contemporary idea that marriage should involve close psychological intimacy to their own circumstances, and many of the women especially were rather disappointed as a result. As one of their interviewees put it referring to her parents,

Now I'm married I've grown a little away from them, but I miss having them to talk to. I don't talk to Alan much as I'd like to because he doesn't respond, doesn't discuss. (Mansfield and Collard, 1988, p. 170)

Data from this study also show that some people do retain relationships which they use for confiding and support, especially with their mothers, and this is regarded as appropriate, especially for women to get support with concerns that essentially are 'women's business'.

The preference for the parent–child relationship as a source of routine moral and emotional support seems to hold good for the white majority, but perhaps less so for people with different ethnic cultural backgrounds. In her study of young unemployed men and women of Asian descent, Brah (1986) indicates that they received that emotional support from various numbers of adult relatives. They felt this was important in helping them to get through the difficulties associated with unemployment.

In relation to support in personal crises, apparently people are more selective in seeking help both from relatives and non-relatives. This conclusion about the selective nature of close confiding is supported by evidence from a variety of sources. Hoyt and Babchuk (1983), in a large study done in the United States, found that people were highly selective in the kin whom they named as confidants and distinguished between people in equivalent genealogical positions, naming one child or sibling as a confidant but not others. In the British context, Wenger (1984) found that married people were most likely to name a spouse as the person in whom they could most easily confide; people who had never been married were most likely to name a brother or sister; widows were most likely to name a child; and in general, the likelihood that a child would be named increased with age. Another very important factor in the selection of a person in whom one confides seems to be the length of the relationship's history. Wenger's data show that 43 per cent of elderly people named as a confidant someone they had known for at least 50 years, and 75 per cent named someone they had known for 30 years. These data suggest that the selection of a relative who gives moral support is related partly to the composition of the kin group and partly to the quality of a particular relationship over a long period of time.

Our understanding of the process of close confiding, and of gaining emotional support from relatives and friends, is greatly enhanced by the linked studies undertaken by Brown and Harris (1978) and O'Connor and Brown (1984). The former is a large scale study of women with depression, and offers an explanation of why certain women develop the clinical symptoms of depression, which focuses on the significance of a close, confiding relationship. Women who had such a relationship with a husband or male partner were much less likely to develop depression than those who did not. The smaller scale study by O'Connor and Brown (1984) takes further the concept of a 'very close relationship' by examining the circumstances under which women develop these, and with whom, in the context of how women manage disruptive life experiences. It is clear from these data that relatives are by no means the only, or even the major, source of support in such circumstances. Less than one third of respondents who had a mother living included her as a person to whom they felt very close, and hardly any had what could be described as a 'true' close relationship with their mother (using criteria developed from the Brown and Harris study). This study further shows that one can distinguish clearly between the kind of 'very close relationship' which will provide emotional support in times of crisis, and closeness in other senses. Women had relationships with relatives which were close in terms of the frequency of contact, but which did not form the basis of a confiding relationship; similarly, they had relationships in which there was quite a high degree of practical inter-dependence which did not function as very close in the confiding sense. This study underlines the highly selective nature of relationships which can be used for emotional support in life circumstances which are personally distressing or disruptive. Certainly such support is not a routine feature of family relationships, even between parents and children.

It will be apparent that much of this discussion has concerned emotional support given to women rather than men, because there is far more empirical evidence about women's close relationships, largely leaving invisible the question of where men derive their emotional support. Some information can be gleaned, although it tends to be more sketchy. For example, Ambrose, Harper and Pemberton's (1983) small study of men after divorce found that just over half their sample relied on parents and/or siblings for support, but they give little detail about the type of support offered and it may well have been practical as much as emotional.

As with other types of support, it is clear that there are considerable variations, especially by gender, in the extent to which emotional support is given within families. For some people it may be of crucial importance, for others the family simply is not a significant source of emotional support.

## Between whom does support flow?

The evidence reviewed here suggests that a good deal of support of various types does pass between members of families. But who are we really talking about? Who counts as 'family' for the purposes of giving and receiving support? Does that vary for different types of support?

In the rest of this chapter I shall slice the data in the opposite direction and look at which kin relationships provide the basis for mutual aid, beginning with parents and children.

### Parents and children

Popular images of parent–child relationships put them in a special category, distinct from other kin relationships, and suggest that this is where we will find the strongest feelings of duty and obligation. Parents, especially mothers, always retain a special bond with the children they have borne; children owe a permanent debt of gratitude to the parents who have reared them. Biology seems to be the foundation of social obligation most obviously in the case of parents and children. Offering support to parents or children is just part of human nature.

How does this popular imagery accord with the reality? There is a sense in which parent–child relationships form the core of kinship in many societies, but the particular shape and form which they take can vary considerably. For example in China, as in many other places, there is a strong expectation that married sons will live with their parents and this continues to be seen as a desirable option, despite the practical difficulties created by restricted housing conditions in the urban environment (Croll, 1978; Wolf, 1985). Both the idea that it is desirable for adult children to live with parents, and the custom that it is most desirable for this arrangement to be with the husband's rather than the wife's parents, contrast with ideas commonly held in Britain about desirable relationships between parents and children in adult life.

What does the evidence tell us about the quality and character between parents and children in Britain? Despite the fact that these relationships are characterized by stronger obligations than any others, we find that in practice there is a wide range of experience of what parents and children actually do for each other. Gender is a key source of variation as is ethnicity, which cross-cuts gender because ideas about men's and women's roles in the family do vary among the ethnically diverse groups of which the British population is now composed (Anthias and Yuval-Davies, 1983). A further source of variation is generational position, with some changes occurring in the type of support which is given and the direction in which it flows over each person's life course.

*Parents to children*  I shall begin by looking at support which flows from parents to children, examples of which can be found in all the categories which I have listed, although personal care in a sense is the least important because most adult children do not need it. But in all the other categories – economic, accommodation, practical and emotional support – the evidence which I reviewed above suggests that parents are regarded the most appropriate relatives to offer support, subject to their capacity to do so. There also seems to be an expectation that children will be favoured over other relatives when assistance is given. That expectation is built into inheritance laws. It is also reflected in an interesting way in data on help with finding employment. Wilson and Pahl (1988) report from their case study data on one kin group, that all expected to help relatives find work if they could but there was an understanding that jobs would go first to 'direct sons' then 'direct daughters', followed by brothers, sisters, nephews, nieces.

The early phase of child-rearing is the time popularly associated with particular reliance upon parental support. The evidence on child care reviewed above suggests that mothers continue to be an important source of support for their daughters, both in practical ways and by giving advice and moral support. However, as I have already noted it seems important that this advice is given in a way which does not compromise the adult child's independence and indeed their status as an adult. This applies also to sons, even in situations where they are receiving significant financial or practical support from parents, as was the case for some of the interviewees in McKee's (1987) study of unemployed men. She found that the recipients fought hard against the idea that they were 'at the receiving end' and went to great lengths to ensure that their parents' support was reciprocated in some way. McKee suggests that it was important to them that they did not return to a pre-adult state of dependence upon their parents.

Whilst there may be a particular need for parental support in the early years of child-rearing there are plenty of examples of significant assistance being given in other circumstances. Unemployment provides us with one such example. Divorce is another, as I indicated above. The desire to ensure that the adult child retains an appropriate degree of independence can be particularly tricky in these circumstances, especially if she or he returns to live in the parents' home and is dependent upon them for accommodation, child care, emotional support and possibly for money as well. Sensitivity to this is reflected in data from Burgoyne and Clark's study of people in second marriages. It is difficult to go back to live with your parents, as one interviewee put it 'after having a home of your own and being a reasonably free agent' (Burgoyne and Clark, 1984, pp. 80–1). Thus the theme of respecting the proper boundaries of independence between parents and children does seem to be present in a variety of situations where parents give support to their adult children.

*Children to parents*   What about support which flows in the opposite direction, from children to parents? The obvious starting point for this discussion is at the other end of the life course, with elderly parents who can no longer live independently. As I have already indicated in the discussion on personal care, there is strong evidence that children, almost always daughters, do provide substantial amounts of personal care in these circumstances. In a small proportion of cases children give their parents financial support (Qureshi, 1986; Qureshi and Simons, 1987).

More generally the evidence of the study of middle-class kinship by Firth, Hubert and Forge indicates that most people acknowledge that parents have a right to make demands upon their adult children, and that most children will do their best to meet those demands (Firth, Hubert and Forge, 1970, pp. 406–7). However, the right to make such demands is not limitless, and in deciding how to respond children may bring in instrumental considerations. For example, as I indicated in discussing personal care, it is regarded as legitimate for children to think about their own interests when deciding whether to support a parent, but this is balanced rather delicately with the morality of obligation and duty, so that children can quite easily get into the position where they are regarded as *too* self-interested.

As with support in the other direction, although it is widely regarded as legitimate for parents to look to their children, it is also possible for them to overstep the boundaries, and the way in which support is requested and delivered is important. Parents who make demands which are regarded as excessive are resented by their children (even if they actually meet some of those demands), as are those who engage in emotional manipulation or divide the sibling group against each other (Firth, Hubert and Forge, 1970, ch. 12). Older people are acutely conscious of the possibility of making too many demands, and commonly try to avoid a situation where they have to rely on their children too much. Again, this becomes apparent in studies of personal care, as I indicated above.

*Foundations of parent–child support*   When we put the two halves of this equation together some important points emerge about the nature of parent–child support in adult life and about the ways in which that support is delivered. The importance of according a proper degree of independence to the adult child is one of these. The idea that elderly people strive for 'intimacy at a distance', as the preferred model for their relationships with their children, is a concrete expression of the norm that adult children's independence and autonomy should be respected and protected. The common phrase 'I don't want to be a burden' encapsulates this. On one level that phrase indicates that it is the old person's own independence which is being guarded, but on another level the idea of wanting to remain independent in old age is a way of according the proper independence to one's children. In both the type of support given and in the way it is delivered, it seems of great importance to sustain a balance between dependence and independence which is regarded as appropriate by all parties.

Another way in which the question of balance arises concerns the direction in which support flows and whether this changes over the course of time. In discussing economic support I indicated that the net flow continues to be from older to younger generations and normally this is not reversed. Does this same pattern apply to other types of assistance? There has been a lively debate in the American literature on this issue, with some researchers arguing that, if one looks at assistance of all types, the model is curvilinear in the sense that the middle generation in three-generation families is net provider of support in both directions (Hill, 1970). Since this means essentially women, Brody (1981) coined the phrase 'women in the middle' to describe those people who have substantial responsibilities to both older and younger generations. More recent evidence (Cheal, 1983) indicates that the flows in fact are linear in other types of support as well as financial, and that in most respects older generations in families are net providers to younger. We lack up-to-date and large-scale British data on this issue but the model of linear flows, in which children are net beneficiaries, does seem to fit the evidence of smaller studies discussed elsewhere in this chapter. One does not get a sense of a strong need for support from parents to children to be reciprocated – certainly not in the short term, and possibly not in the long term either.

The other important dimension of parent–child support is gender, and there are several dimensions to this. First, there is evidence that men, even where they acknowledge that they have responsibilities to parents or children, often exercise those responsibilities through their wives. Sons commonly provide personal care and practical support for their elderly parents through the use of their wives' labour rather than their own (Qureshi and Simons, 1987). Fathers, because ultimately they control financial resources, may be the people who sign cheques or who authorize the payment of money to their children, but it is often women who mediate and negotiate such gifts and loans (Morris, 1983).

Second, there is a sense in which the whole area of kin relationships is women's business more than men's, in that women have a stronger commitment to and interest in keeping the structures of support alive. As Graham (1985) puts it a 'sense of responsibility' permeates women's approach to the whole issue of family relationships. In practical terms, Cornwell's (1984) data show that men play a far less active role in family life than women, and even when they are giving direct and practical support to a relative, their commitments are limited and bounded. This affects the key parent–child relationship in important ways. People who superficially are in the same position in a family – brothers and sisters, mother and fathers – are likely to define their responsibilities very differently and, perhaps more importantly, to be expected by others to define them differently. In Land and Rose's (1985) evocative phrase, altruism is 'compulsory' for women in a way it is not for men.

Finally, there is the question of mother–daughter relationships, which are said to have a special quality and status which has ramifications across the whole of family life. The idea that it is entirely natural for mothers and daughters to be particularly supportive of each other recurs again and again in research studies. An example from Lewis and Meredith's work illustrates the theme common to many other studies. This comment is from a daughter who had been giving substantial care to her mother, and explained the situation thus,

My brothers couldn't wash her and dress her and wash her hair could they? . . . I was the daughter, I would do it, yes. (Lewis and Meredith, 1988, p. 24)

However, support between mothers and daughters is not a universal phenomenon and it varies widely in its scope. Firth, Hubert and Forge (1970) in their study of middle-class families, found that about 15 per cent of parent–child relationships were 'bad' (as perceived by the child and measured by items such as little or no contact, clear dislike from one party to the other) and about one third of those examples of 'bad' relationships concerned mothers and daughters. Even where contact is frequent and based upon mutual affection, that does not mean necessarily that mothers and daughters are significant sources of support for each other, as I indicated in my discussion of emotional support.

Structures of support between mothers and daughters are subject to all the individual variations which I mentioned at the beginning of this discussion, and at a more collective level, ethnic and cultural variation is very important, with some cultural traditions placing a less strong emphasis on this bond than does white Anglo-Saxon culture. For example in the case of people of Asian origin living in Britain, the expectation is much more likely to be that the main supportive bond, especially in respect of financial support, will be between sons and parents. There is evidence that sons make considerable efforts to provide support for their parents even when they are in straitened circumstances themselves. In her study of young Asian men and women who were unemployed, Brah notes that sons with widowed mothers felt under particular pressure to support them financially and practically, and when unemployment made it impossible for them to do so they felt 'an acute sense of failure' as one of her interviewees put it,

I can't live off my mother and my younger brother. I'm supposed to look after them and not the other way round. (Brah, 1986)

Therefore the simple observation that the parent–child bond is where we find family duty and obligation most clearly expressed has to be modified with reference to the gender of the participants, and with reference to a particular cultural context. Also the idea that a strong obligation exists between parents and children, which can be relied upon as a source of support in most circumstances, misses a point of prime significance, namely that such support must be negotiated and provided in a way which does not trespass upon the independence of either party, especially of adult children. Because of this, much of the empirical evidence on parent–child support betrays a sense of wariness and carefulness about offering and accepting such support, which is far removed from the idea that it is the most natural thing in the world for parents and children to support each other.

### Grandparents and grandchildren

Relationships between grandparents and grandchildren have an interesting and distinctive blend of closeness and distance. They focus on the central parent–child bond, but at one generation removed and with a substantial difference in age between the two parties. This blend of closeness and distance is represented in popular imagery of grandparents: they are people who spoil their grandchildren and are indulgent towards their misdemeanours, even if they have brought up their own children rather strictly.

Research evidence supports the view that this relationship is valued highly, especially by the grandparental generation. Firth, Hubert and Forge report that their middle-class respondents almost always named grandchildren as well as children as being part of their close family. However, in the younger generation, most people counted parents but not grandparents (Firth, Hubert and Forge, 1970, pp. 80–91). There is a clear sense therefore in which relationships between grandparents and grandchildren are not symmetrical, with the older generation placing more value upon this relationship than the younger.

In assessing patterns of support between grandparents and grand-children (in either direction) in adult life there is a sense in which we are discussing a rather recent phenomenon, because of the changing age structure of the population and increased life expectancy. In previous generations it was much less likely than it is now that grandparents would have lived to know their grandchildren as adults (see chapters 2 and 3). There also is an empirical problem of understanding how support operates between grandparents and grand-children, in that we must disentangle it from support given to and by the intervening generation. For example, when grandparents look after their young grandchildren for an evening or for a week, are they helping the children or their parents? Or if we find that a grand-daughter is assisting her own mother in caring for an elderly parent, whom is the granddaughter helping? Is she giving assistance to her grandmother, or is she really helping her own mother to bear a heavy burden? In practice one suspects that it would make little sense to the participants in any of these cases to ask who is really being supported: the answer would almost certainly be that both are.

These empirical difficulties tell us something important about the nature of support structures between grandparent and grandchild. They are locked into a broader pattern of support which spans the three generations of parents and children, rather than existing on their own terms. The well-known American research by Hill (1970) has demon-strated the interlocking nature of support structures across the three generations, and has shown that grandchildren do feel responsibility to give assistance to their grandparents in this context, although in practice they actually do less than the intervening generation. Also in relation to the United States, Brody (1981) offers evidence from a three-generation study of women that the youngest generation felt more strongly than the other two about 'grandfilial responsibility', three-quarters of them saying that older people should expect help from their grandchildren, whereas less than a quarter of the oldest generation took this view. Brody speculates that this finding (which runs counter to the evidence which I presented above that grandparents place more value on this relationship than grandchildren) may reflect the idealism of the younger generation and their lack of experience of situations where demands are actually made upon them.

Are these patterns reflected in the British context? There is little up-to-date evidence, but that which exists broadly is consistent with them. The idea that grandchildren, especially granddaughters, are a *possible* choice for the care of elderly people is the key element here, although it has to be seen in the light of the evidence (which I reviewed above) about who actually cares in practice. Grandchildren do not appear on Qureshi and Simons's (1987) hierarchy of preferred carers, indicating that they are very much a minority group subsumed under 'other relatives' and therefore much less likely to be providing personal care than their parents' generation. We lack systematic knowledge of the circumstances under which grandchildren might take on significant responsibility for the support (either personal or financial) for their grandparents in contemporary Britain.

Support from grandparent to grandchild is rather more straightforward, although again rather little evidence exists. Given that the net flow of support is normally from older to younger generations, we should expect support in this direction to be more extensive. Certainly we know that this happens when grandchildren are young, as I suggested in my discussion of child care and also of economic support. Examples can be found of grandparents buying basic necessities such as food and clothing for their grandchildren, as well as more substantial purchases.

So far as assistance to grandchildren in adult life is concerned, the American evidence suggests that grandparents do assist financially and that they define this assistance as a gift, unlike financial support between the other two generations which is more likely to be defined as a loan, or as part of an exchange (Hill, 1970, pp. 69–70). This is consistent with the idea that the older generation in a three-generation family occupies the position of net giver of support, and that this is regarded as proper in a normative sense.

As in the case of parent–child relationships we find here that one-way flows of support can not only be tolerated, but also in a sense are expected, provided the direction of the support is from grandparent to grandchild. However, the form which such support takes means that it is not the kind of support upon which one could rely. If it comes it is a bonus, something which literally is 'in the gift' of the grandparental generation.

Undoubtedly there are differences in people's experiences of support between grandparents and grandchildren, but we have so little up-to-date evidence on this issue that it is difficult to say how far such experiences vary systematically according to gender, ethnicity or social class.

### Brothers and sisters

The relationships between brothers and sisters in any society are governed not only by personal likes and dislikes, but also by wider social and economic arrangements. This is obvious if we consider societies which have systems of partible inheritance, where resources are divided equally between the surviving children on the parents' death. Such arrangements require a high degree of co-operation between siblings in adult life, as is demonstrated by evidence from rural communities – France, for example (Segalen, 1984). These arrangements also may be related to gender, as in the case for example of Tunisia, discussed by Cuisenier (1976), where Islamic law allows both women and men to inherit, but custom presumes that women will not claim their share. When women do try to make such claims, this sets up predictable antagonisms between brothers and sisters. In a case like this, gender divisions interact with inheritance patterns to produce particular forms of relationship between brothers and sisters.

In the British context, does the degree of economic independence accorded to siblings mean that these relationships normally are an insignificant source of all types of support? Evidence from recent empirical research suggests that siblings do provide a source of support in adult life, although this is of less importance between parents and children. Allatt and Yeandle (1986) report findings from their study of young unemployed people that brothers and sisters give each other financial support to help cope with unemployment. McKee (1987) reports that siblings of unemployed men were the second most important category (after parents) to give assistance. The sort of help which siblings gave included loans and gifts of money (these came especially from brothers and sisters who were unmarried), gifts of food and clothing for the children (usually from married sisters) and help in finding employment for the male breadwinner (from brothers). Wilson and Pahl (1988) also report from their case study data that siblings are an important source of assistance when one of them is stretched financially.

More generally, can we identify the circumstances under which siblings are likely to be a significant source of support? First it seems that personal preference and liking is important, certainly to a much greater extent than in relationships between parents and children. Most people feel an obligation to keep in contact with their siblings, but beyond that it is regarded as quite proper for relationships to vary in the level of intimacy and the type of support offered (Firth, Hubert and Forge, 1970; Allan, 1979). La Fontaine, in her review of studies of British kinship suggests that there seems to be 'a preference for particular siblings rather than a general solidarity with brothers and sisters' (La Fontaine, 1985, p. 54).

Second, ethnicity is important in two senses. On the one hand, ethnic minorities currently settled in Britain have been here for a relatively short period of time, and it seems that circumstances of migration and initial settlement are conditions under which support between siblings assumes greater significance than it might otherwise do – a point illustrated by the patterns of chain migration and of joint households which I discussed earlier in this chapter. This argument suggests that support between siblings may become less significant for the ethnic minority British population in the future. On the other hand the cultural expectations which continue to be endorsed in Britain do embody – for some groups at least – a stronger commitment between siblings than is common in white British culture. As Wilson (1978) points out, relationships between sisters and sisters-in-law are very positively valued across the whole of the Indian sub-continent, and patterns based on these relationships seem to be strongly established in the British context.

Third, there are important gender differences, both in the kind of support which passes between siblings (as in McKee's evidence, discussed above) and also more generally in the quality and importance of relationships. Firth, Hubert and Forge (1970) suggest that by and large men have poorer relationships with their siblings than do women, and that relationships between sisters are more likely to be close and supportive. Certainly there is evidence that in the past sisters provided very significant amounts of practical, moral and sometimes financial support for each other (Young and Willmott, 1957; Roberts, 1984). Firth and his colleagues argue that the main reason for this gender difference is that women have much more incentive than men to maintain good relationships through which they can gain support for their domestic and child care responsibilities, whereas men's lives are more dominated by work and careers in which siblings usually cannot help. That is a plausible argument and it points to the importance of economic factors and the prevailing division of labour in shaping sibling relationships. Presumably in circumstances where brothers can help each other to find work, or in some other material way, there *is* an incentive to keep good relationships. That argument certainly would be supported by evidence about migration to Britain, where brothers already settled are an important source of work contacts and economic support for new migrants (Oakley, 1979; Anwar, 1985).

Fourth, it seems that, as with parents and children, we need to be aware that there are likely to be quite wide fluctuations in support passing between siblings over the lifetime of each. Jerrome's (1981) work on older women's friendships indicates that women's relationships with their sisters seem to be intensified in later life, even for people whose relationships had been poor when they were younger. This intensification seemed to be triggered by the loss of other significant relationships, for example the death of a spouse, or retirement from paid work which removed relationships with work-mates and colleagues. Argyle and Henderson (1985), reviewing evidence about contact between siblings, suggest that this follows a U-shape, being high in childhood and teenage years, falling off in the middle of adult life, and then picking up again as the siblings move into old age.

Support between siblings contrasts with support between parents and children in two important ways. First, it seems less reliable, in the sense that whether it is offered depends very much upon personal circumstances and personal liking, at least for the majority white community. Except perhaps in rather trivial matters, there is no real sense that one can expect assistance from someone just because they are your brother or your sister. Second, it much more obviously is two-way support, built upon reciprocal exchange between people who are in equivalent positions in genealogical terms. One would predict that where a particular sibling is not willing or able to give support they are unlikely to receive it, except perhaps if they have given assistance in the past.

*More distant kin*

It is clear from the evidence on British kinship that people do acknowledge a wide range of uncles, aunts, nieces, nephews and cousins as forming part of their kin network in some sense, but whether these people place a significant part in structures of support is quite another matter. In the structure of kinship which is reflected in British research studies – that of the white majority – considerable variation is found in the range of people who 'count' as part of the kin group for different purposes. Simply knowing that two people are linked in a particular genealogical relationship does not necessarily predict that they will acknowledge any responsibilities towards each other, not even whether they have actually kept in contact at a minimal level.

The British data suggest that people commonly think about their total kin universe as divided into two or three categories (represented visually by concentric circles) and these categories do correspond with obligations acknowledged in practice. This is reflected in a number of studies of kinship, but I shall use the terms employed by Firth, Hubert and Forge (1970, ch. 6). First, there is the widest and most exclusive category of 'named' or 'recognized' kin, composed of all the relatives whose existence I am aware of. Second, there are 'effective' kin, the people with whom I keep in contact at a minimal level. The third category is 'intimate' kin, the people with whom contact is close and fairly frequent (for other discussions of these divisions see Schneider, 1968; Allan, 1979).

When we are considering the support which passes between kin we can exclude the outermost circle almost by definition. If kin are recognized but no contact is maintained, then clearly support is not being given. However, it is important to note that such relationships, although dormant for a while, potentially can be reactivated and there is evidence that this does happen (Firth, Hubert and Forge, 1970, p. 155–6). Moving to a different part of the country, for example, or even a chance meeting, may be the trigger to reactivate a relationship with someone in this outermost circle, thus drawing them into the second category. The group which is relevant to the discussion of support is 'effective' kin, which itself is composed of an inner and an outer circle. Precisely who falls into the outer circle of effective kin, or the inner circle of intimate kin, is not entirely predictable in individual cases, although people normally do have a fairly clear notion of two different categories, for whom different terms may be employed. The terms used by the middle-class Londoners studied by Firth and his colleagues were 'family' for the inner circle and 'relatives' for the outer, or sometimes 'immediate family', to distinguish their intimate kin (p. 156).

On the basis of this type of analysis, we can now pose questions about support between more distant kin in slightly different terms. Does support between members of families really only pass between the inner circle of intimate kin? Is there any sense of duty to give support to relatives in the outer circle of effective kin? Do kin who are more distant in genealogical terms necessarily fall in the outer circle? Do they get defined into the inner circle if there is a history of reciprocal support? We do not have adequate and up-to-date evidence which would enable us to answer these questions with certainty, but as elsewhere we can piece together clues from a variety of research studies.

Roberts's evidence suggests that there has been considerable variation historically in how far support structures extend to more distant kin. Her Lancashire data show that families had strong support networks encompassing uncles, aunts, cousins, even great aunts and great uncles; others included none of these (Roberts, 1984, p. 169). That variability is reflected in more recent empirical evidence, especially the study by Firth and his colleagues, which is unusual in giving specific and detailed attention to these relationships. Their evidence suggests that, whilst people do exchange support with more distant kin, it is usually on a fairly small scale and whether one does this is treated as optional not obligatory. Moreover there is a notable tendency to be selective, in that one positively elects to assist a particular aunt, nephew or cousin, with whom one happens to have a good relationship. These good relationships are often the result of contingent factors such as living geographically close, sharing a particular common interest or (in the case of cousins especially) having spent a lot of time together in childhood (Firth, Hubert and Forge, 1970, ch. 12).

The picture which emerges from this study is one where assistance between more distant kin is of relatively minor importance to the total picture (although of course it may be very important in particular cases), and that whether it is likely to be significant is rather idiosyncratic and unpredictable. Whilst in general it does seem that relationships with the 'outer circle' are not particularly important sources of support, one certainly can find predictable – not merely idiosyncratic – exceptions to that rule. One such exception concerns circumstances where a particular person does not have close relatives, where there seems to be an expectation that kin in the outer circle should give more support than they otherwise might, as it were deputizing or substituting for the non-existent children or parents. Examples can be found in the research literature on elderly people, where it is reported that those without children tend to form equivalent ties with whichever kin are available, typically a niece or nephew, although there is some doubt about whether such a person can properly be expected to provide such extensive or reliable support as a 'real' child (Townsend, 1965; Allan, 1983; Wenger, 1984).

Another important exception can be found in Grieco's (1987) data on the use of kin networks to secure employment, where she found that relatives as distant as cousins were as likely to be involved as close kin in arrangements which brought a number of male and female kin into the same workplace or firm. The system works because membership of a particular kin group implies that this person is a good worker and in this instance family reputation extends quite a distance in genealogical terms, well beyond the inner circle of intimate kin, provided a family member gives a recommendation. As one of Grieco's respondents put it,

We're all workers in this family and always have been. We've earned every penny we've ever had. (Grieco, 1987, p. 87)

The idea that the 'good name' of the family is still coveted may be a little surprising in the 1980s, but these data show that there are situations where it is still very important and has direct consequences in material terms.

It would be misleading therefore, effectively to write off the outer circle of kin as significant sources of support in British society. They may not be used routinely, but there certainly are circumstances in which they do provide assistance. Nonetheless the majority British culture does contrast with many others in the relative unimportance of wider kin ties, including arrangements found traditionally elsewhere in Europe. For example, all the work on Mediterranean societies notes a strong preference for marriage between cousins who are the children of two brothers, which contrasts sharply with traditional marriage customs in Britain (and elsewhere in northern Europe), where the marriage between close kin has been prohibited, although the range of kin to whom these prohibitions apply has been whittled down in the past century (Wolfram, 1987). The effect of marriage between cousins is to secure and maintain the boundaries of the kin group and the resources which it controls, by ensuring that no one takes anything out of the kin group when they marry, and that strangers are not introduced (Tillion, 1983).

Using the wider kin group as the basis for organizing social and economic life may not be characteristic of contemporary Britain, but some of the groups who have migrated to this country since the Second World War have brought with them, and retained, a pattern of kin relationships which differs from the white British norm and which in some cases includes a preference for cousin marriage. More generally, there is a wider range of kin whom one is presumed to have some duty to assist. For example, migrants from Pakistan – both women and men – appear to retain a strong sense of obligation to give support to all relatives within their *biraderi* (sometimes spelled *biradari*) which contains a wide range of kin and can represent a network of mutual aid extending across continents (Anwar, 1985). One can certainly see why it makes sense to retain these structures of support in a situation of relatively recent migration into a society which can be extremely hostile. Although the cultural background is different, a similar pattern of using the wider kin network for mutual aid has operated in earlier migrations, for example migration from rural Lancashire into the growing industrial towns in the early nineteenth century (Anderson, 1971), or Irish migration to America and elsewhere (Arensberg and Kimball, 1968). In that sense the present situation of recent migrants to Britain is part of a familiar pattern. Whether structures of support within the wider kin network will continue to make sense when, and if, non-white citizens become accepted as full and established members of British society is an important topic for future research.

## In-laws

Relationships with in-laws form a special category of kin relationships. In his influential discussion of American kinship, Schneider argues that there are two basic principles built into the kinship system: blood and marriage. Blood relatives in some sense are bound together by genetic material, but relations by marriage are bound together by law and a code of conduct which accompanies this (Schneider, 1968). Broadening this analysis, we might note that there is considerable variation in different cultures about how the two principles of blood and marriage relate to each other, and therefore in the code of conduct upon which in-law relationships are based. The different cultural traditions represented in the British Isles are no exception.

What importance do in-law relationships have, especially in relation to structures of support, in the dominant white British culture? Wolfram (1987) suggests that a distinctive feature of British kinship is the concept of the unity of husband and wife, and thus a strong sense that spouses 'own' each other's kin. Research evidence suggests, however, that for the most part a mother-in-law is not treated as equivalent to a mother, nor a sister-in-law to a sister, and so on. Also there is some evidence that in-law relationships entail different types of exchange: mothers *do* things for their married daughters whereas mothers-in-law *give* items to them (Argyle and Henderson, 1985, p. 223).

Relationships with in-laws, especially with parents-in-law, conventionally are regarded as problematic and therefore it is not surprising to find that patterns of support seem to be affected by the quality of the relationship. Firth, Hubert and Forge report that some people get on with their mothers-in-law better than their own mothers, but for the most part these relationships are regarded as likely to be tricky: people treat them as an 'occupational risk' of marriage and regard themselves as 'lucky' if they work out satisfactorily (1970, pp. 414–15). Anxiety about in-law relationships, and evidence that some considerable adjustment can be necessary, is found also in Mansfield and Collard's (1988) study of the early years of marriage. It was not uncommon for interviewees to report that at least one set of parents had been unhappy initially about their plans to marry and this was often connected in some way with disappointment or disapproval over the choice of spouse.

As with the other relationships considered here, there are clear gender differences, certainly in relation to support which passes between in-laws. Cornwell reports that the men in her study have very little to do with their own families and even less with their wife's kin. She cites one example of a man who spent several years living in his parents-in-law's house but still had little to do with them afterwards; another where a man had helped to nurse his father-in-law through an illness, but when that was over had as little contact with him as he had before (Cornwell, 1984, p. 89). Women, by contrast, not only support their own kin but their husband's as well in some cases. In the evidence presented by Qureshi and Simons (1987) and also by Ungerson (1987) on who cares for elderly people, daughters-in-law ranked above sons as people likely to be providing such care.

Beyond the relationship between parents-in-law and children-in-law, there is little evidence of support, except in cases where for individual and idiosyncratic reasons people happen to form a good relationship, say with a sister-in-law. Such situations seem to be experienced as appropriate and a bonus, but by no means expected. Indeed, as Wolfram points out, such relationships are of so little importance within British kinship that there are no recognized kinship terms for many of these relationships gained through marriage (Wolfram, 1987, p. 4).

The pattern is very different in some of the minority cultures represented in the British Isles. The sharpest contrast is with migrants who have brought with them the expectation that sons will bring their wives into the homes of their parents, where in some sense the wives will be under the authority of their mothers-in-law. As I have indicated, shared households of this type are more common among groups whose ethnic origins are in the Indian sub-continent, than for white British people or for migrants from the Caribbean, although such households are often smaller than their equivalents in India, Pakistan or Bangladesh.

Such arrangements are also often associated with the custom of keeping men's and women's worlds sharply segregated, although as Saifullah Khan (1976) points out in her discussion of purdah in Bradford, the luxury of remaining truly separate could only ever be afforded by the comparatively wealthy. What such arrangements traditionally have provided is a large group of women, related to each other as in-laws and living in the same household, who operate their own quite complex social organization in which each gains significant support. In the more restricted circumstances in Britain, where such households are smaller and contacts between women in different households in some respects more difficult, women lose something of this support network although they may gain a greater degree of independence in their interactions with men. It remains to be seen whether these arrangements will continue to make sense in the future. Indeed Saifullah Khan was able to report even from her data collected in the mid-1970s that some recent migrants, especially those best equipped to survive in Britain economically without the support of kin, already were considerably relaxing arrangements based on the purdah system.

Looking at in-law relationships generally, it is apparent that one of their distinctive features in any culture is that they are conducted both through, and in a sense for the sake of, a third party. There would be literally no relationship between a man and his son-in-law were it not for his daughter, and so on. This means that support which in-laws receive from each other is ambiguous in a way which does not apply to other relationships. Is the support which is given to the son-in-law 'really' being given to the daughter by proxy? In many cases the answers to that question would be difficult to unravel, and if challenged most people probably would say that they were doing both. But there are some instances documented in the literature where people are quite clear that support given to in-laws is really being given to the blood relative. In Grieco's study of the use of kin networks to gain employment for example, one of her female respondents, a worker in a tobacco factory in Basildon, told her,

If he weren't my son-in-law I wouldn't lift a finger to help him. If she ever left him I'd cut him completely adrift. I'm helping her really. He thinks I'm helping him but I'm not. I wouldn't give him the time of day if I could help it. (Grieco, 1987, p. 28)

This raises interesting questions about what actually does happen to such relationships when the third party is no longer there, that is, when the marriage is broken through death or divorce. Does the relationship continue as before? Does it cease altogether? Does something between those two extremes happen? Is it different for marriages which end in death and those which end in divorce? These are interesting questions of increasing importance as the divorce rate continues to rise, but we have little empirical evidence to go on. In a sense these are situations where 'the rules' are currently being written through individual and collective experiences.

Some clues can be found in existing literature. Schneider's discussion of American kinship argues that the removal of the third party makes the continuation of the relationship voluntary: the divorced or widowed spouse of a blood relative will still be treated as a relative only if there is a continuing relationship in the qualitative sense 1968, pp. 92–4). Existing British evidence on widowhood seems to support that conclusion, reporting a tendency for many widows gradually to lose contact with their husband's relatives, although some do stay close (Marris, 1958). Whether divorce operates in the same way as widowhood in this regard is really a matter of speculation at the present time. In relation to white British culture in particular, various factors combine to create a sense of unreliability in in-law support: the ambiguity about whether the in-laws are 'really' part of your kin group; the possibility that the linking third party will be removed at some stage; the expectation that in-law relationships are likely to be tricky at an interpersonal level.

## Conclusion

In this conclusion I shall not attempt to summarize the richness of the patterns which I have identified in the available data, concerning who does what for whom. However, I shall return to the four themes which I identified at the beginning, and which have been threaded through the discussion. A reconsideration of these moves us onto a more analytical plane, and points the way forward to discussion in subsequent chapters.

*Variations in the experience of kin support*   The issue here is whether variations in people's experience of support within families can be attributed to personal and idiosyncratic factors, or whether those variations are related systematically to the position of the parties in economic and social structures. The evidence suggests that variations are systematic to an extent, but that this does not account completely for the considerable differences in family support which one can observe in practice.

In the preceding review, social class emerges as the least important of the major social divisions in structuring our experience of kin support. This could well be a consequence of a lack of up-to-date evidence offering systematic comparisons between classes. We need such data and it needs to be sensitive to regional variations. But on the basis of evidence available now, it seems reasonable to conclude that class is not of the first importance in structuring our experiences of family life. An exception to this general conclusion concerns economic support where class is important because, even using the rather crude categories of middle class and working class, we can see that these do represent different levels of access to financial and other economic resources. Economic support of all kinds seems to be much more significant of middle-class kin groups, who on the whole have more to share and use that capacity in a distinctive way to enable family members, especially the younger generations, to maintain a suitable style and standard of living.

Researchers working in the 1950s perhaps could be forgiven for not recognizing the importance of ethnicity in family relations, since Britain was a more monolithic society in ethnic terms than it became subsequently. We can see now that ethnicity is an important source of variation in individual experience and no studies of family life can afford to ignore it. Indeed it is an important priority to generate new data which make ethnicity visible, because on the basis of existing evidence it is difficult to distinguish whether the different patterns of support which we can see in minority ethnic kin groups are likely to persist as patterns of settlement stabilize.

Without doubt variation by gender is a key element in patterns of support between kin. In the data there is some support for the notion that certain matters such as child care and support for elderly people are regarded as women's business in families, while men's business is money; but it would be too crude to assume that this simple division of responsibilities could explain all the gender differences which occur in kin support. In practice women and men are involved in different ways in giving and receiving support, but much of this is explained not by a cultural definition of what counts as women's business or men's business, but by three other factors.

First, women and men have different access to resources which could be shared, especially financial resources. We saw that there is some evidence that, where women do have command over financial resources in a way normally associated with men, they share in financial support in families in a way rather similar to men. Second, women and men have different responsibilities accorded to them in the domestic division of labour. Men do not share support with child care simply because so few of them are responsible for the care of children, and so on. Third, because women's and men's lives are organized very differently in our society as a whole, women seem to be more available to provide any assistance which involves input of time and domestic labour. A sister with a part-time job looks more available to care for a parent than a brother who works full-time. Since paid work still is much more likely to be distributed this way than the reverse, there is a built-in tendency for caring responsibilities to fall on women, even without cultural expectations that women are particularly suited to these tasks. So both as givers and receivers of support, men and women normally are in very different positions and it is not surprising to find therefore that gender permeates all aspects of support structures.

Age and generational position are important in families almost by definition. The evidence suggests that they operate in a particular way, namely that there are predictable patterns in flows of support between older and younger generations, in which support flows in both directions, but on balance the older generation are the givers and the younger the receivers. Contrary to some popular images, normally this does not seem to be reversed in a significant way during the last years of life of the older generation, except perhaps where a person receives substantial personal care, but is not in a position to repay it through bequests after their death.

Regional variations have proved the most difficult to uncover. The problem is partly conceptual, partly empirical. Where research studies have been carried out in different parts of the country it is difficult to disentangle anything which might be attributed to regional variations specifically, from other systematic variations by gender, class, ethnicity or variations over time (that is where changes in patterns of family relationships have occurred between the 1960s and the 1980s). Short of a series of studies which is designed directly to compare regional patterns, holding other variables constant, we cannot be certain that *any* observed variations can be attributed to, say, people's views about family responsibilities being different in the north-east of England from the prevailing norms in the south-west.

Without studies of that kind, which we certainly do not have, it is proper to remain agnostic on the question of whether regional variations are of any significance. However, it is noticeable in a number of studies reviewed here that rather similar patterns are reported from studies undertaken in different locations. To pick out just a few examples: grandparents treat their grandchildren in the same way whether they live in Aberdeen or London; middle-class people use money to support their close relatives in similar ways whether they live in Swansea, Sheffield or London; people use their kin network to help them find employment whether they live in Glasgow, Basildon or Corby. In so far as we have evidence about regional comparisons, it points to continuities rather than differences. On the other hand, there are some regional variations in economic terms which may have increasing impact on the resources available to be shared in families, especially the rising value of property in the south of England and the better job opportunities there.

*Reliability*   I posed a series of questions about whether support from relatives can be seen as reliable, and what reliability actually means in this context. It seems that there are very few situations in which support from relatives is totally reliable in the sense that it would be given automatically, and without further thought, when a need is identified. There may well be some examples of families which operate like that but it is not the general pattern, even in relationships between parents and children which come closest to it.

The real significance of reliability is something rather different: it is the reliability of knowing that there is something to fall back on, with family support acting as a safety net if really needed. The analogy of the safety net seems to me to be a good one, not least because it is an image commonly employed in everyday life. A safety net is something which you hope that you will never have to use, and you endeavour to arrange matters so that you do not need it, but if necessary it will catch you. One gets this sense of the safety net in relation to various different types of assistance: money, child care, accommodation, even personal care, where it runs counter to the notion that the most natural first line of support for elderly and dependent people is their families. The research evidence suggests that support from one's family should be the last resort and not the first, and that even then it must be handled carefully to ensure that each party retains a proper independence of the other. That need to draw the boundaries of independence applies particularly to parents and adult children, between whom this safety net operates most predictably.

*Instrumentality*   My focus on instrumentality has been concerned with the issue of whether people are allowed to act out of self-interest in family relationships. The answer seems to be that this is regarded as quite proper if the advantage is mutual – possibly less so if it is not. Indeed there is a sense in which it is positively desirable to act out of self-interest in offering support to a relative, since if the donor also benefits, there is less chance that one party will become over-dependent upon the other. That consideration of one's own advantage can be entirely proper is particularly clear in relation to sharing accommodation, where it seems that it is the foundation of most such arrangements. Particularly important is the evidence that, where elderly people are sharing with younger relatives, these arrangements often were entered into in the first instance for the benefit of the younger as much as the older generation.

In arguing that the instrumental response is quite proper in some circumstances I do not mean to imply that it always can operate. There are certainly some situations in which it would be seen as entirely inappropriate, for example in relationships between grandchildren and their grandparents, where support is normally given from the older to the younger generation, but in the form of a gift. This is given out of generosity and grandchildren do not necessarily have the right to expect it. Indeed, wherever assistance is defined as a gift (rather than, for example, part of a broader pattern of exchange), it is likely to be regarded as inappropriate that the potential beneficiary should behave in an instrumental way towards the potential donor.

*Reciprocity* The concept of reciprocity has been central to academic studies of kinship, especially in anthropology. I shall deal with it more fully in chapter 5. In reviewing the material in this chapter, I have simply posed the question about whether, and in what circumstances, support within kin groups can be one-way, or whether there is always some pressure to reciprocate.

Flows of assistance between generations provide us with an important example where, in practice, support is often one way, and where apparently this is regarded as quite proper. Parents give to their children and their grandchildren and they continue to give. Whilst certainly they may receive something in return, there does not seem to be a pressure to balance out the gifts. One-way flows are tolerated here, perhaps expected.

Apart from these generational patterns of support between parents and children, there does seem to be pressure for assistance to be reciprocated. In relationships between siblings or between other kin, the two-way principle seems to be the foundation of support structures. Indeed, it is an important way in which the principle of maintaining each person's independence can be protected.

These four themes do seem to highlight some important features of support within families: how it operates and its meaning to people who participate. The general picture which emerges is one in which, whilst a considerable amount of assistance does pass between relatives, the procedures for asking for, offering and accepting it are quite tricky to handle in practice. There are very few cases in which it is automatic for one relative to offer support and unproblematic for the other to accept it. In that sense, helping one's relatives, even one's parents or children, is by no means the most natural thing in the world. There are no unambiguous rules about how this should be done, and there is considerable room for manoeuvre on both sides.

Because of all this, there is a sense in which all assistance between relatives must be the subject of negotiations about when it is to be given, by whom, for how long, and on what terms. This conclusion highlights the importance of seeing support between kin in the context of the interpersonal relationships of the parties to these negotiations. I do not expect my father to lend me money simply because he is *a* father. He is *my* father, and our relationship has a past, a present and an anticipated future, all of which will affect the terms upon which we can consider a transfer of money without compromising our own personal identities, or the relationship between us.

Despite the limitations of the available data, the picture which emerges from this review is complex and interesting. People do give support to their kin but they do so in a way which is patchy, possibly idiosyncratic, and which certainly cannot be predicted simply from knowing how they are related to each other. This chapter has been devoted principally to describing what happens; the rest of the book is concerned with understanding this rather complex picture.

# 2

# Do families support each other more or less than in the past?

## Introduction

How have patterns of support between members of the same kin group changed in Britain over time, and especially over the past two centuries? Are the rather variable and unpredictable patterns of kin support, which I identified in chapter 1, of recent origin? Have people lost a clearer 'sense of obligation' to assist their kin which existed in the past? The expansion of the study of family history in recent years, and the coming together of historical and sociological concerns in this field in particular, makes it possible at least to attempt answers to these questions in a way that would not have been possible even ten years ago, for lack of appropriate sources of evidence. At the same time, the limitations of the data are very apparent, and mean that the answers to these questions must be partial and to some extent speculative, rather than detailed and authoritative.

The most obvious limitation is that much of the available data concern relationships within households, rather than relationships between kin in different households. Further, the data can be used to reveal a good deal about the composition of households – who lived with whom – but far less about the character and quality of relationships which people had with each other (Laslett, 1972a, p. 1; Anderson, 1980, pp. 36–7). Where data do exist on support between kin across households, this tends in effect to be limited to documenting the networks through which support flowed and the kind of support which was given, and can give very little direct evidence about the underlying structure of social relations which supported these exchanges. We often simply do not know in what ways people in the past were drawing on ideas about obligations, rights or duties when they provided assistance for their kin (Medick and Sabean, 1984, pp. 20–1). In addition to the specific limitations, there is the general caution which should be exercised in using historical data to document social change. As Morgan (1985, pp. 169–70) points out in his review of studies in family history, history never just tells us a single story – there are many possible stories, depending upon what questions we ask. There is also the tendency when comparing the past with the present to draw too sharp a distinction between 'then and now', a tendency often linked to a view of the present as either vastly superior or inferior to the past.

This last point is particularly pertinent to the issue of how responsibilities between kin have changed, because the idea persists that in the past there was a time when 'the family' had a stronger sense of responsibility towards looking after its young, old and sick members. This notion has a strong hold on popular consciousness, political debate, and even some writing in social science (for further discussion, see Finch, 1987b). By contrast, the present day is seen as a time when people's sense of duty and responsibility is much weaker, so that they are less prepared to acknowledge obligation or to take responsibility for kin. For some commentators on the political right such as Marsland (1986, p. 87), the apparent weakening of family responsibility has been encouraged by the growth of state services which provide alternative sources of support.

When, if ever, did this golden age exist? Assumptions vary: some people take the more recent past as their benchmark, others look to a more distant Utopia. In contemporary political debate it is 'Victorian values' which are presented as the high point of family responsibilities, implying that Utopia existed somewhere around the middle to end of the nineteenth century (West, 1984). In academic writings it is probably more common to look to an earlier period as the time when family solidarity was of prime importance. In this perspective, it was industrialization and urbanization which triggered those processes and which led ultimately to a weakening of family ties, and especially ties with kin outside the so-called 'conjugal family' composed of a couple and their immature children (Morgan, 1975, ch. 2; Harris, 1983, chs. 6–8). A completely contrasting interpretation of history is represented by MacFarlane's (1978) work on the origins of English individualism, where he argues that the structure of kinship which prioritizes the nuclear family and de-emphasizes other kin has been characteristic of England at least since the thirteenth century.

The scope of the discussion in this chapter will be broad and will cover the past two centuries, sketchy though that necessarily will be. To structure the discussion, I shall focus on the idea of a golden age of family responsibilities in the past as the starting-point for understanding how these have changed over time. That idea raises three interlinked questions, answers to which should enlarge our understanding of social change as it has affected family relationships. These are:

1 Has social and economic change over the past two centuries led to a reduction in the actual support which kin give to each other?

2 Has social and economic change weakened people's sense of obligation or responsibility to provide support?

3 Has change had the effect not necessarily of reducing the amount of support, or of weakening the sense of obligation, but simply of changing its character?

These three questions clearly overlap, but can be treated as conceptually separate, and it is helpful to disentangle them in this way at least initially. I shall come back to them at the end of this chapter, having reviewed the empirical evidence.

## The changing shape of kin groups

Patterns of support between kin cannot be understood without first making some reference to the ways in which the structure of the population, and patterns of family formation associated with it, have themselves changed over time. These factors have affected profoundly the composition of families – quite literally, what relatives people actually have – and hence they form the essential building blocks from which family support is constructed. Since there have been very significant changes in population structure and family composition over the last two centuries, any discussion of how family relationships have changed must always acknowledge that we are not comparing like with like – an observation which of course itself calls into question the over-simplified view of a gradual deterioration of family ties from pre-industrial society to the present day. In chapter 3 I shall discuss more fully the question of how far these demographic structures do affect the nature of family obligations, at any given point in historical time, considering in particular how far demographic factors in the late twentieth century have given a particular shape to kin groups. In this chapter, I shall set the context, by highlighting some of the key features which affected kin relationships in earlier generations.

The relationship between fertility rates and mortality rates has created a population structure which has varied substantially during the period in question. In the mid-eighteenth century the expected age of death for a woman was 35; by the 1970s it had risen to 80. In the mid-nineteenth century more people were being born by comparison with pre-industrial Britain, but also more people were dying relatively young. This created a relatively youthful population with large numbers of young people (some of whom of course would die before full adulthood) and relatively few people over the age of 50. This means that in individual families it must have been rather unusual to have grandparents surviving much beyond the infancy of their grandchildren, and thus relationships across three generations would have been comparatively rare. There have also been changes in the length of a 'generation' and the overlap between generations in families as a result of changing patterns of marriage and family formation. The average age at which people marry remained more or less stable for the preceding two centuries until the end of the Second World War, when it began to fall, but there were notable changes in the pattern of childbearing, especially between 1870 and 1930. Women started to have fewer children in total, and to concentrate childbearing in early adulthood, rather than spreading it throughout their fertile years. Thus increasingly in the twentieth century children have been born when both their parents and grandparents were younger, further reinforcing the likelihood that the generations will overlap in adult life (see Anderson, 1985, for an elaboration of these patterns).

Another effect of high fertility plus high mortality in the nineteenth century was a much wider age spread between siblings than we have been familiar with in the twentieth century, with the older siblings (if they survived) being on the verge of adulthood while their younger brothers and sisters were still being born. One consequence of this, as Hareven (1978, p. 62) has pointed out, is that the experience of parent–child relationships was very different for siblings at different positions in birth order. For example, older children were much more likely than younger ones to overlap with their parents in adult life, whereas for younger children there was a good chance that, by the time they were grown up, their parents would be dead. Again, the concentration of childbearing into a short period, which began in the late nineteenth century, now makes this much rarer.

The consequences of these same changes can also be seen at the other end of the life course, in old age. Most obviously, both women and men can expect to have a recognizable period of 'old age' when they have ceased paid work, the creation of a standard age of retirement from work being a twentieth century phenomenon. In terms of family responsibilities, the various changes I have identified have combined to produce a phase of life in later adulthood when people are free from direct responsibility for rearing children. Such a period was largely unknown to earlier generations, and the implications of this change are especially important in women's lives (Titmuss, 1958; Anderson, 1980).

Finally, there have been changes over time in the rates of divorce and marriage, although the significance of these for patterns of kin relations may be not so obvious as it first appears. In the nineteenth century, divorce was more or less impossible except for the very wealthy, initially only through a private Act of Parliament. Even after 1857, when divorce came easier, the numbers involved were not large, averaging about 600 per year up to the start of the First World War. Thereafter the number of divorces started to grow rapidly and following legislation in 1971 which made divorce easier there was a further expansion. There is some evidence that the rate of increase has slowed down in the 1980s, but there still were more than 160,000 divorces in 1985. Remarriage after divorce is also a much more common experience than in the past. In 1940 only 2 per cent of marriages involved a divorced partner; by 1985 this had risen to 33 per cent. However, the proportion of marriages involving widows or widowers has decreased steadily over the past 150 years (for an elaboration of all these trends, see Haskey, 1987a).

Patterns of disruption and reconstitution of kin groups do seem very different now by comparison with the past. However, it is easy to overstate the significance of this change. The ending of a marriage before old age and the creation of step-families through remarriage is by no means a recent phenomenon, but in the past these events occurred more commonly through the early death of one partner than through divorce. Single-parent families headed by widows were fairly common, for example, in Anderson's study of mid-nineteenth-century Preston, and this was a circumstance in which people might well look to their relatives for support (Anderson, 1971, pp. 144–7). The historical evidence does not really support the view that kin groups were much more stable in the past than in the present. As Gittins has put it, 'The commonsense notion that all families in the past were much more solidaristic and stable institutions cannot be borne out – death saw to that' (Gittins, 1985, p. 9). This is not to deny that the ending of a marriage through death, and through divorce, are in many ways very different experiences, nor that they may be handled differently in families, but the point here is that the idea that kin groups used to be much more stable over time than they are today has to be modified by historical evidence. In summary, the evidence shows that the shape of kin groups is subject to very significant variation over the course of time. The importance of this for understanding structures of kin support are important. It means that necessarily there have been variations in people's need for support from their kin, and in the capacity of kin to provide it. Most importantly, there have been fluctuations over time in the actual existence of kin who might provide such support for each other.

## What kind of assistance did kin give each other in the past?

A thorough and systematic evaluation of the kinds of support which have passed between kin over the past two centuries is a separate project in its own right. I do not claim to be comprehensive in what follows, rather my aim has been to assess some of the main features of kin support in the past which have particular relevance to the central theme of this book – how important are duty, obligation and responsibility in motivating the support which people give to their relatives? I have chosen to focus on three types of support which help us to address this question: sharing a household, money and practical support.

### Sharing a household

Proceeding with due caution therefore, we can ask: what do we know about patterns of support between kin over the past two centuries? I shall begin with household composition, the issue around which much work on the history of the family has been centred. We know that it is fairly uncommon for adult relatives to share households today: only 12 per cent of households contain three or more adults and not all of these will involve relatives sharing (*Social Trends*, 1988, p. 36, table 2.2).

The predominant interest of much of the historical work, especially the early work, on household composition, was to examine one of the key elements in the idea of a golden age of family support – that in the past it was common for members of the extended family actually to live together, and that a major effect of industrialization was to shrink the household, typically to the nuclear family unit. The earlier work of historical demographers of households was concentrated on examining the simple measure of household size, and they were able to establish by a variety of evidence that the average size remained remarkably consistent between the seventeenth century and the twentieth. In fact, the average household size remained between four and five throughout this period and only fell to three during the twentieth century (Laslett, 1972b; Wall, 1972). Although the methods used in these studies have been criticized (Berkner, 1975) they have been very influential. Certainly the simple notion that industrialization altered radically the size of the household cannot be correct, since the relatively small change which has actually occurred is of quite recent origin. The large extended family household in any case seems only to have existed for a small minority, if at all.

Although the overall size of households may not have altered dramatically, this still leaves open the question of whether household composition has changed. Did different people share households with each other in the past? Was it more common for at least one or two adult relatives to be added to a household in addition to a nuclear family unit? That question is more difficult, because of the level of detailed evidence which is required to answer it with certainty.

Wall's (1986) evidence suggests that there have been fluctuations over time in patterns of who actually shares households, but that these have not been in a single direction. Between the mid-seventeenth and the mid-twentieth centuries there have been three discernible periods, each characterized by different patterns of sharing. The picture is complicated by the existence at certain points in the past of a relatively large number of households which contained servants; but people classified as servants could also be kin, for example older children of a family whose parents could not support them economically. They went to live with relatives, but also worked for them (Gittins, 1985, pp. 15–16). Wall's (1986) evidence shows that the really notable change between the mid-nineteenth and mid-twentieth centuries was in the smaller number of people living in other people's homes as servants or lodgers. The number of kin living together rose during the early industrial period (up to the middle of the nineteenth century) and remained fairly constant thereafter. So far as elderly people in particular are concerned, there has been relatively little change in patterns of co-residence with relatives until the later part of the twentieth century; although there have been some fluctuations, the overall pattern shows more continuities than changes. For example, most elderly people who are married have always lived only with their spouse, and small but fairly constant proportions have always lived in residential institutions of one kind or another (Wall, 1984).

If we look at the reasons why kin shared homes with each other in the past, three themes emerge which help us further to understand why there have been fluctuations in co-residence. These are: demographic change, affecting the need to seek accommodation with relatives; the economic circumstances of all parties; changing ideologies of family and household.

Demographic change has affected most obviously the position of elderly people. From about the middle of the twentieth century onwards, the number of elderly people in the population has been rising, and it will continue to rise until the end of the century. This means that there are more people who might need support in old age, including sharing a home with relatives. But at the same time the number of available children with whom they might reside is much reduced by comparison, say, with the mid-nineteenth century, because of the reduction in the birth rate. Indeed as many as one-third of all elderly people have no surviving children (Parker, 1985). Thus we now have many more older people and many fewer children with whom they might live, and it is not surprising therefore that the last half-century has been characterized by a reduction in the proportion of single elderly people living with relatives.

Demographic changes of a rather different kind have had the effect of substantially reducing the categories of people who once lived with kin. If we look at the evidence of Roberts's study of Lancashire households between 1890 and 1940, we see that the various categories of kin who co-resided included: unmarried daughters living with parents; unmarried brothers and sisters living with a married sibling; orphaned children; children whose parents were still alive, but who had gone to live with relatives because of parental poverty or lack of space in the parental household (Roberts, 1984, pp. 72–7). In each of these cases, demographic change, coupled with a rise in living standards, has largely removed the need for these categories of people to live with relatives. For example, almost everyone now marries at least once and the category of never-married people has virtually disappeared. Increased life expectancy means that it is now a rare occurrence for children to be orphaned. In chapter 3 I shall look more closely at the impact of these demographic patterns on the need for support from relatives. My point here is simply that they do go some way to explaining why patterns of co-residence fluctuate over time.

The economic circumstances of both parties seem to offer another important explanation of why it is more common for people to share a home with relatives at some points of historical time than at others.

Michael Anderson's work has been particularly important in establishing the significance of considering the material gains for either or both parties, if we wish to understand why people lived with relatives in the past. In his review of the historical data now available on household composition in the past, Anderson (1980) emphasizes in particular the distinction between the rural and urban economies. If one takes simply the early industrial period, up to about 1820, it is possible to show that almost one third of rural households contained servants, typically young people in their early teens who left home to spend about 10 to 15 years in service before marrying. However, in urban areas this was less common and there seems to have been more opportunity for young people to stay in the parental home for longer, because of the greater availability of work in the locality (Anderson, 1980, pp. 25–6).

Drawing on his own earlier study of Preston in the mid-nineteenth century, Anderson (1972) also has used arguments about economic advantage to examine the question of why the average household size seemed to be larger in the developing cotton towns than elsewhere. Indeed, it is possible to show that there was a marked increase in the number of married children living with parents during the nineteenth century and into the twentieth century in cotton towns – quite the reverse of what one would expect if it is true that industrialization broke up the extended family. Anderson argues strongly that such patterns can be explained only by looking at the material advantages and disadvantages of people living together. He applies it to the particular case of young people living with their parents after marriage, by arguing that in the expanding industrial towns there was every opportunity for young people to be wage earners and therefore to be net contributors to the parental household, at a time when wages were at a very low level. In the same period, kin links were an important mechanism for recruiting labour, and so living in the parental household would have given young people increased chances of finding work, as well as providing them with accommodation which they might not have been able to afford on their own.

However, material circumstances on their own do not account fully for changes in co-residence. Ideological change apparently is a further element in explaining why it is more common to find people living with relatives in particular historical periods than in others. Over the past century, there have been ideological pressures – expressed, among other ways, through public policies – to define what constitutes a 'proper' family, and to encourage people to live in these units. As Davidoff puts it,

it was during the Victorian and Edwardian periods that 'the shape of the private household was being officially defined' (Davidoff, 1979, p. 78). The desired family form was a household consisting of a married couple and their children, where the man is the breadwinner and the woman a domestic worker. These definitions were consolidated further through public policies put into operation during and after the Second World War. (Summerfield, 1984, ch. 3)

These ideological definitions of a normal or proper household therefore are of relatively recent origin. Because they are also incorporated into, they are bound to shape, people's aspirations and their actions to some extent (see chapter 4 for a discussion of the impact of public policies on family responsibilities). They have meant, for example, that housing policies have endorsed the view that each nuclear family should have its own household, and thus increasingly it has become possible for people to take that option. As I indicated in chapter 1, it is now less common for young married couples to begin married life in the home of a relative, except on a very temporary basis.

In summary, the pattern of change in household composition certainly does not involve a simple shrinkage from large to small units. Nor does it entail a straightforward shrinking to the nuclear family unit as a consequence of industrialization. It is the case that typical households in the later part of the twentieth century are much less likely than they were in earlier times to contain anyone other than the conjugal family. The pattern of movement, however, is not wholly in one direction. It seems that people take kin, and indeed non-kin, into their households in situations where this is mutually advantageous, but the balance of those advantages fluctuates over time, and varies between different localities in the same historical period. It is also very significantly related to the structure of the population and the composition of families, which affect both the supply of and the demand for shared households.

It is very difficult to say what part was played in these processes by notions of duty to assist kin, but the significance of the principle of mutual advantage, in understanding fluctuations in household composition, rather challenges the idea that people took relatives into their own home solely out of a sense of obligation towards them.

### Financial support

The evidence about other types of kin support in the past – whether within or across households – is much more fragmented than evidence about household composition. Financial support is perhaps the most accessible to documentation, although even this is not always clear, especially for the great majority of the population who did not codify their financial support for kin through wills and settlements, simply because they lived from hand to mouth.

For the classes who did have enough to bequeath, we have valuable evidence about the patterns of inheritance preferred in the early nineteenth century from a variety of sources, especially a study by Davidoff and Hall (1987) of 622 wills made in two different areas of England during the period 1780–1850. As I indicated in chapter 1, whilst the system of primogeniture had been used traditionally by the aristocracy as a way of passing on an estate intact, the expanding entrepreneurial business class of the early industrial period tended to favour partible inheritance. This meant that a man's estate was increasingly likely to be divided between his wife (if she survived him) and his children, although not necessarily in equal measure. One example given by Davidoff and Hall is of Samuel Galton, a wealthy Birmingham banker who had also bought land. When he died, he divided his liquid assets and his land between his sons, having first provided for each of his daughters through setting up trust funds which would provide them with a good income. This example apparently was fairly typical of the wealthy sectors of the middle class (p. 208).

It appears that in the earlier part of the nineteenth century a change took place in the kind of family responsibilities which are implied by inheritance practices. Whereas previously those who had wealth to bequeath typically provided very handsomely for the eldest son, and at a much reduced level for the rest of their children, a practice became common which implied that children had roughly equal claims on a parent's resources, with some distinction made on grounds of gender so that women and men inherited different kinds of property. This idea that parents have equal responsibilities towards their children has remained the dominant one in the twentieth century, as is evidenced by the contemporary research data on inheritance which I discussed in chapter 1.

Financial support between relatives has one feature which is not shared by other types of support, namely that it has been regulated by the law. This applies most obviously to inheritance, but also the law has been used to regulate financial support in families in a different way, namely through the Poor Law which has applied to many more people than ever have been affected by inheritance. The vestiges of this remain in the legal requirement that spouses should support each other financially. But until the Poor Law was abolished finally in 1948, the principle of financial support between kin applied more broadly. In particular there was a requirement under English law for children to support their parents financially. Sons carried this legal responsibility throughout their lives; daughters relinquished it when they married. The nineteenth-century origins of these provisions are closely tied into a desire to hold down state expenditure and to ensure that the wealthier classes did not have to dig too deep into their pockets to support people who could not work for wages. In that sense, the Poor Law was a mechanism whereby one class imposed a particular view of family responsibility upon another.

However, we must beware of interpretations which are deceptively simple. The role of the law in constraining and shaping responsibilities in families is an important topic in its own right and I discuss it in chapter 4, using the Victorian Poor Law as a key example. I mention it here in order to signal that the existence of legal rules and sanctions makes it more difficult to uncover from historical evidence why people in the past gave financial assistance to their relatives, if they did, and in particular, to decide how far such assistance was based upon feelings of obligation or duty. How do we know whether people gave money to their parents because they felt a sense of duty to support them financially or because they feared prosecution? Does it even make sense to pose the question in this form? Problems of interpreting the historical material are compounded by the fact that contemporary evidence from the nineteenth and early twentieth centuries tends to treat examples of working-class people who did not support their parents as evidence of individuals lacking 'filial affection' (Anderson, 1977). But of course, people may feel very affectionate towards their parents but be unable to give them money, or indeed, be able to give them money but feel that this is not the proper thing to do. These issues are difficult enough to disentangle in contemporary research, and there are major problems in gaining access to data which would really enable those distinctions to be made in an historical context.

The evidence which is available does enable us, however, to draw some conclusions. The most important of these is that there seems to be no evidence that people assumed automatic responsibility for their relatives – including parents – who were old, sick, or in some other circumstance where they were unable to work to maintain themselves. The evidence suggests that even in the pre-industrial period there was no automatic assumption of financial responsibility for elderly parents. This emerges clearly from Clark's (1982) discussion of social security in medieval England, where the emphasis is upon the comparative unimportance of financial support from kin, although this certainly existed. Clark demonstrates that older people tried, where possible, to set up contractually based arrangements (some of them enforceable through the courts) to secure their livelihood and care in old age, through a system whereby they surrendered some of their rights to their land to a specified individual, in return for agreed services – 'individually arranged pension benefits' (ibid. p. 308). The fact that the transfer of property rights was only partial and conditional gave them the guarantee of security in old age, and the people involved in such transactions were not necessarily children or even relatives. The services promised were to provide a room, fuel, clothing, to wash clothing, or to visit if sick.

The theme of mutual advantage rather than a sense of duty in financial relationships between kin again emerges from this example; or to put it another way, it suggests that historically in Britain financial relationships between adult kin have been regarded typically as two-way exchange rather than one-way support. One can find examples from the more recent past to support that view. For example, Ellen Ross's (1983) discussion of the lifestyle of the working poor in the East End of London, in the period leading up to the First World War, contains evidence about financial relationships between young working adults and their parents, based partly on the surveys of Charles Booth (1892b). She suggests that the 'board' money which young people paid for living in the parental household was seen as an exchange, especially for daughters: they handed over their wages to their mothers and in exchange their mothers equipped them to enable them to go into service.

The resistance to the idea of one-way financial support can also be deduced from evidence about the circumstances under which people tried to evade legally defined financial responsibilities to kin. I shall discuss these in detail in chapter 4. But at this point it is worth mentioning briefly that there are plenty of examples of people 'losing touch' with their elderly parents as a way of avoiding maintenance payments, during the period in the late nineteenth and early twentieth centuries, when certain Boards of Guardians were trying rigidly to enforce financial liabilities. A rather similar pattern can be seen in the very different circumstances of the inter-war economic depression, when the Household Means Test meant effectively that young working adults living in the same household as their unemployed parents were expected to support them financially. Many young people with the encouragement of their parents, left home at this time to avoid these responsibilities.

Both these examples raise issues other than the question of whether support is one-way, but they do indicate that there certainly have been historical circumstances in which people have felt that the requirement to provide financial support to parents, in circumstances where they were apparently unable to reciprocate, went well beyond their normal expectations of support between kin. Financial need, even on the part of a close relative, has apparently never been seen as a situation which required an automatic response. Even when people *could* give money to relatives, it has never been obvious that they *should* do so, whatever other circumstances obtain.

We also learn from the historical evidence that gender has been an important source of variation in people's experience of financial support within families. In the past women's capacity to give assistance was even more constrained than it is now, by their lack of control over financial resources. This was actually recognized in the Poor Law which limited women's liability to support their parents to unmarried women, thus reinforcing the idea that a married women's economic position is complete dependence upon her husband.

### Practical support

Practical support provides the third example which I shall use in this discussion of patterns of support in the past. Child care is one obvious example, but there are also the many day-to-day tasks which enable households to be maintained and to function at a reasonable level of efficiency. Hareven, in her discussion of early industrial society in America (1978), suggests that this type of exchange was more common than sharing households, but that it could only operate on a reciprocal basis. Between close kin it was possible for the exchanges to be one-way over a longer term, one person a net 'giver' at a particular point in time because of a reasonable confidence that he or she could be a net 'receiver' at a later stage. But between more distant kin, routine day-to-day assistance had to entail exchange of a two-way kind in the short term because 'the need for reciprocity [was] dictated by the insecurities of urban life' (p. 65). Because of their place in maintaining and servicing a household and its members, it is of course likely that most of these exchanges entailing practical support were between women.

Another interesting feature of exchanges of this type is that, under certain conditions, money could be used to fulfil one part of the bargin, i.e. if practical services were being offered in only one direction, or if those services went beyond that which could be contained in normal, on-going reciprocal exchange. For example, Ross (1983, p. 12) cites evidence of young working adults paying their younger siblings to perform services such as cleaning their shoes. Roberts (1984, p. 180) found examples of women paying their mothers and mothers-in-law to look after their children while they went out to work. She comments that people seemed to feel that child care was an appropriate service for kin to perform for each other, but also that they should not be exploited. In common with other types of support which I have considered here it seems that practical help, even when on a fairly small scale, has never been given to relatives automatically and without some assessment being made of the wider social context. Reciprocal exchange of services seems to be a particularly important feature of this type of support in the past, as it is indeed in the present.

## Givers and receivers of support

The idea that patterns of support in the past were linked to mutual advantage emerges in relation to all three of the types of support which I have considered: sharing households, financial support, and practical day-to-day services. The picture is incomplete, however, if one thinks solely in terms of undifferentiated 'kin', without asking between *whom* these services flowed. We need to look, therefore, at how the patterns of support varied between those two major divisions in kin groups: gender and generation.

### Women and men

First, variations by gender. In the past, did different types of support, or varying amounts of support, flow between women and men and have those gendered patterns changed over time? This obviously is a very difficult question to answer, given the lack of detailed evidence about precisely those kinds of day-to-day support where gendered patterns are likely to be most apparent. Financial support, however, is relatively easy to document where it concerns those wealthy enough to have money, property and other possessions to dispose of in wills, or indeed in their lifetimes. As I have already indicated the evidence here suggests that although English inheritance law traditionally privileged the eldest son, from the early nineteenth century onwards the equal claims of all children began to be acknowledged, although daughters and sons received different types of bequest (Davidoff and Hall, 1987).

The English Poor Law also allocated differential responsibilities to women and men, in respect of giving support to relatives.

Looking at examples of day-to-day practical assistance, it is apparent that women have been involved in exchanging this with other women much more commonly than men have been involved in exchanges with women, or with other men. One possible explanation lies in the division of labour between women and men. Because women have been allocated the tasks associated with running a household and rearing children as their particular responsibility, one could argue that they need practical day-to-day support in a way which men do not. It is likely that they will seek this support from other women rather than from men, even their husbands, because the tasks involved have been defined as women's work. Thus in the past women had a particular interest in maintaining a pattern of exchanges with female kin, in which they both gave and received day-to-day support. I made a similar argument in chapter 1 about practical support in contemporary society.

That is an hypothesis about the foundations of practical support between kin in the past which could be tested systematically against historical data, although it would be a major task and certainly is beyond my scope here. However, it is relatively easy to find illustrative examples which suggest that, in the past, the sharing of day-to-day assistance between kin was rooted in the responsibilities allocated to women in their domestic lives. Elizabeth Roberts, in her study of working-class women in three Lancashire towns from 1890 to 1940 (Roberts, 1984, pp. 169–81), demonstrates the importance of women helping other women in extended family networks, through minding children, caring for the elderly, providing clothing, and sometimes taking a relative's child into their own home. Men also provided some support for their relatives, usually minor property repairs or help with an allotment, but the volume of this was much less. Jamieson (1986) in her study of working-class mothers and daughters in urban Scotland in roughly the same period, found that young adult women living in the parental home would take on domestic work to assist their mothers routinely and extensively, in a way not replicated by their male counterparts. Again, in Ellen Ross's study of the East End of London before the First World War, the theme of women assisting other women comes across strongly. With both kin and neighbours, women shared 'extensively and unsentimentally' on the basis of reciprocal exchange (Ross, 1983, p. 6), including such items as food, clothing, domestic items, such as washtubs, and small amounts of money, such as a penny for the gas. There was indeed, she argues, a tendency for women to bypass support from men and to rely on other women as being more dependable sources of support, a tendency found in other cultures of the very poor (p. 6). In such circumstances as these, the major example of men assisting their kin seems to be the use of kin networks to secure employment (Anderson, 1971, pp. 111–23; Roberts, 1984, p. 180).

If the above argument is correct one might expect to find that, in other situations where the division of labour is less fixed, there would be more diverse patterns of kin support across gender lines. Whether this is the case in contemporary societies is an issue to which I shall return in later chapters. However, even where a less rigid gender division of labour prevails, it seems to be the case that women commonly act as the 'kin keepers', that is to say, the people who keep up regular contacts with members of the wider kin group. In so far as women have these contacts rather than men – even if sometimes they are, as it were, on behalf of men – it is likely that they are in a position to mobilize support in a way that men are not. That would lead to a situation where more assistance passes between women than between men even in situations where their 'needs' are more similar than in the examples I quoted above. Only in the case of money, over which men may retain control even when the domestic division of labour is less rigid, might one expect them to be more actively involved in exchanges of support with kin. Again, this is an hypothesis which would repay systematic investigation in respect of historical examples with contrasting forms of division of labour.

## Older and younger generations

The second major principle along which kin relations are divided is that of generation. I noted in chapter 1 that the contemporary evidence suggests predictable patterns of the flow of support between generations. Has this changed over time?

This question cannot be considered separately from the issue of how 'needs' for different kinds of support vary between generations and, for an individual, across a lifetime, and how both of these vary historically. A useful way of considering this is to use the concept of the dependency ratio, that is the ratio of people who are out of the labour market in relation to those who are in it. This, it can be argued, is socially constructed and varies over time. I shall discuss the implications of the dependency ratio for the construction of family obligations in more detail in chapter 3. The point on which I want to concentrate here is that during the last two centuries changes in the law and in employment policies progressively have excluded both the youngest and the oldest generations from the labour market, and therefore from the means to support themselves through earning wages. The impact of that has been different for older and younger generations and has affected the position of each generation in relation to financial support from relatives, and also assistance with accommodation. In the twentieth century increasingly it has become possible for older people who have withdrawn from the labour market to support themselves from resources provided by the state rather than rely on their families; the same has not been true of the youngest generation. I shall consider briefly how these historical changes have affected patterns of support between family members.

*Young people* So far as children and young people are concerned, it is well recognized in historical work on the nineteenth century that the growth of state intervention to control the employment of children, and to establish and expand compulsory education, had the effect of altering the balance of obligations between parents and children. The effect was to make it difficult for children to contribute to their own support, let alone the support of other people, thus removing the reciprocal nature of support between the young and their parents' generation, and establishing childhood and youth as a period of one-way dependence of the young on their parents (Pinchbeck and Hewitt, 1973; Anderson, 1980; Gittins, 1986). By the end of the nineteenth century, children under school-leaving age effectively could not be contributing a wage to the household economy and had become very clearly a net drain on resources. The effects of the economic burden which children imposed were felt first in the middle classes, for a variety of reasons, and led to significant family limitation in the late nineteenth century, as Banks's (1954) classic study shows. Of course there was still some opportunity for children to earn money while they were at school, and where those opportunities were taken there is evidence that parents considered this as part of the household income and expected it to be handed over (Jamieson, 1986). There were also a whole range of ways in which children could contribute to the household economy through domestic labour and child care, both within their own households, and as part of the pattern of exchange between kin and neighbours. Ross (1983) cites evidence of mothers 'loaning' the services of daughters in particular. They were used to perform tasks such as child care or running errands as part of the system of exchange in which their mothers were involved.

There certainly were opportunities, therefore, for children and young people to contribute both directly and indirectly to the household economy even before they entered the labour market, and on balance the evidence suggests that girls were likely to be more substantial contributors than boys, especially in the provision and exchange of domestic services, although boys may have had more opportunities to earn money. However, all of this has to be set in the context that whilst still at school children were dependent for their own basic economic support upon the parental generation. By the later part of the nineteenth century the pattern of inter-generational exchanges which had characterized pre-industrial and early industrial society clearly had shrunk to a pattern of very limited contributions by children to the household economy, except for those children who were allowed to work as 'half timers' until this possibility was also removed in 1918 (Hurt, 1979). After leaving school the situation of course is different, although the position of young wage earners in the household may well have depended upon the employment opportunities available for them in the local economy. Anderson (1971, pp. 125–7) argues that the good wages which young people could earn in the cotton towns in the mid-nineteenth century altered the balance between parents and children and put them on more equal terms when they shared a household, and also made it more possible for them to leave the parental home – although boys did this more often than girls. Anderson's comparison is with the rural economy of the period, where young people were more dependent upon the family for access to their livelihood. His argument has relevance for any set of historical circumstances, including the present day, in that it suggests that relationships between young adults and their parents, including patterns of reciprocal exchange between them, are closely related to the capacity of young people to earn a wage.

The major point which I want to take from this discussion of young people's situation is that their need to be supported economically by their parents, and more generally their position in structures of reciprocal support within families, to a large extent depend upon factors outside the control of individual families: laws relating to schooling and employment, and the operation of the labour market. Since these factors can and do change, the position of the younger generation in structures of family support must be seen as specific to particular points in historical time. The major changes in their economic position which began in the late nineteenth century and have lasted until the present, essentially are responsible for creating the dependence of younger people which now appears such a natural part of human life.

*Older people*　I have indicated already that the exclusion of older people from the labour market over the same period has had a somewhat different impact upon their position in reciprocal support within families. However, we can see that their position also is constructed largely by factors which are outside the control of individuals.

Evidence from the middle of the nineteenth century, in Anderson's study of Preston, indicates that older people were involved in structures of family support very much on a reciprocal basis. His work demonstrates that an older person was much more likely to be taken into the household of a relative if they were able to contribute something in return, for example doing domestic work, or looking after children while their mother went out to a job. Of course it is more likely that women rather than men would be in a position to offer such assistance (Anderson, 1971, pp. 139–44). At the beginning of the twentieth century, Poor Law administrators were still noting that older women seemed more able than older men to survive without any apparent source of income, because of the domestic services which they could perform (Roebuck and Slaughter, 1979).

Against the background that people expected support for an elderly person to be reciprocated in some fairly immediate way, the pressure to exclude older people from the labour market was accompanied by a pressure to give them some independent means of support which would prevent their having to rely on their children or other relatives. This was reinforced further by demographic changes which, by the early years of the twentieth century, already meant that an increasing number of people survived into old age without any children at all. Even if they had been willing to rely on relatives, they could not do so (Anderson, 1977).

The idea that older people should leave the labour force at some point gained ground in the earlier part of the twentieth century with the popularity of ideas about scientific management, which implied that older people were bound to be inefficient workers. Older people were not necessarily unwilling to be excluded, as the existence of 'retirement movements' in various industrialized countries demonstrates (Guillemaud, 1983). The issue of retirement had never been on the agenda previously, quite simply because people died much younger in earlier generations. However, there was considerable pressure for the terms of retirement to be such that older people could maintain economic independence. Although some could do this through using their savings or drawing on insurances, many could not, with women much less likely than men to be able to support themselves by these means (Roebuck and Slaughter, 1979). The issue was resolved eventually in the introduction of old age pensions, in a limited form, for the first time in 1908. Only people over 70 were eligible, and initially there was an income test and also a test of good character. People who had been convicted of criminal offences, including drunkenness, or people who had habitually failed to work, were not to be supported from state resources. It was, as Thane puts it, 'a pension for the very poor, the very respectable and the very old' (Thane, 1982, p. 83).

Nonetheless the principle of retirement pension was accepted from this point onwards, and it enabled older people to maintain their position as active partners in structures of kin support, at least in financial terms. Unlike younger people, who have become more dependent upon the 'middle' generation over the last century, the position of older people has moved, if anywhere, in the direction of greater independence. However, the situation of older and younger generations is similar in a different sense, in that in both cases the position of individuals within those structures is determined very largely by factors outside their control – very obviously so at the time when the issue of old age pensions was first on the agenda.

Thus there *have* been changes over time in patterns of support between generations, but these are not necessarily a result of individuals' changing beliefs and values about family responsibilities. Indeed, factors such as changes in employment law, in regulations about compulsory schooling, and the introduction of state benefits have very obviously shaped such changes.

## Processes and principles of kin support in families

Certain themes emerge from this discussion of patterns of kin support in the past which give some clues to the type of social processes that underlie the giving and receiving of support in families, and the principles upon which it is based. I shall draw out three of these themes, each of which serves to raise further questions about understanding family obligations in contemporary societies.

## Reciprocity in family exchanges

The first of these concerns the reciprocal nature of kin exchanges. In relation to all the major types of support I have considered – the sharing of households, the giving or lending of money, the provision of practical support – the principle that support is most likely to be given if the advantage is mutual, or if there is a clear expectation that assistance will be given in return, is a prominent feature. The idea that people operate 'strategies' in which they assess a range of options, and act to maximize their opportunities, has become an increasingly important insight in historical work on the family, and one which accords an active role to human beings in constructing their own lives, rather than seeing individuals at the mercy of large scale social forces (Morgan, 1985, p. 175). It also has been the subject of considerable historical debate.

The common ground between historians is that reciprocal exchange on the basis of mutual advantage is the essence of support between kin, making the family a group whose relationships are rooted in material considerations and not simply one which is bound together by moral imperatives and ties of affection. Historians with very different sets of concerns agree upon this (for example, Anderson, 1971; Humphries, 1977; Roberts, 1984). Indeed, it would be difficult to imagine a situation in which mutual advantage was not a factor conducive to the development of structures of support. The real issue, and one where there clearly is disagreement among historians, is how far support will be given between kin when the element of mutuality is absent. In the past did people really deny support to relatives who were in no position to reciprocate, or at least who seemed unlikely to be able to do so? Were such calculations always based on short-term considerations? Or was it possible for one individual to be in the position of a net 'receiver' for some considerable time because of an expectation that they would be able to reciprocate at some stage in the future? Did such calculations vary in different kin relationships, especially between kin who were closer or more distant in genealogical terms? These are the key questions to be asked about reciprocity within families, both historical and contemporary.

The contrast between the two major opposing historical interpretations is brought out well by comparing two studies of urban Lancashire: Anderson's (1971) study of Preston in the mid-nineteenth century based on documentary data, and the study of Roberts (1984) of Preston, Barrow and Lancaster in the period 1890–1940, based on oral history. This is a significant comparison, because of the key place which Anderson's work occupies in developing an interpretation of kin relations in the past which emphasizes the importance of calculations about the capacity of another person to reciprocate. This work has also been significant in shaping the thinking of contemporary sociologists of the family (Harris, 1983, pp. 127–30).

Anderson does not deny that kin probably continued to be the main and the most reliable source of aid for migrants into the expanding towns, as they had been in the rural communities (mostly in Lancashire and Ireland) from which the migrants came. However, there was an important contrast between rural and urban settings. In rural communities, pressures to conform to a fixed structure of normative obligations were strong, since most people's livelihood depended upon remaining within the family unit. However, in the new urban environments it was possible for the young and fit to earn good wages and therefore to be independent of their families. The effect, for them at least, was that these normative bonds were loosened. At the same time, kin ties remained a structured link which offered the potential for mutual support, and this was probably more reliable than ties between non-kin and more acceptable than those bureaucratic forms of public support available in the period. In a rapidly changing society, with many people living on the margins of subsistence, such support was limited in cost and likely to bring benefits to the giver in return. Thus in this setting, 'family and kinship relations tended to have strong short-term instrumental overtones of a calculative kind' (Anderson, 1971, p. 171). In a later elaboration of his perspective, Anderson argues more generally that kin relations must always be understood in terms of the kind of calculations people make, and this should provide the starting-point for any analysis: 'if we are to understand variations and patterns of kinship relationships, the only worthwhile approach is to consciously and explicitly investigate the manifold advantages and disadvantages that any actor can obtain from maintaining one relational pattern rather than another' (Anderson, 1972, p. 226).

The contrast with Elizabeth Roberts's position is stark. She documents the extensive structures of support across households as well as within them, and finds little evidence of a calculative orientation towards kin. Indeed she argues that support given to kin was often at considerable cost to the giver in terms of time, energy and even money. People in her study, she argues, supported their kin out of a mixture of duty and genuine affection, plus feelings of pride, especially a desire to keep a member of one's own family out of the workhouse (Roberts, 1984, pp. 170–2).

How are we to reconcile or decide between these competing and very different accounts of the basis of support between kin in the past? One possible interpretation is that, since they are talking about different historical periods, the nature of family relationships in Lancashire had actually changed between the middle of the nineteenth century and the early part of the twentieth (Lewis, 1984, p. 54). That interpretation of an extent is consistent with Anderson's arguments, if one assumes that working-class life in Lancashire towns was more stable in the later period and somewhat less harsh, removing the absolute necessity for short-term instrumental calculation, while at the same time making predictions about the likelihood of reciprocal support in the future more reliable. Another possible source of the difference in the two sets of data concerns gender. Since Roberts's book focuses on women, she necessarily highlights patterns of exchange which are specific to women, and it is quite possible that both duty and affection were (and are) more prominent in exchanges between women than when men are involved.

A further possible way of reconciling the two accounts is to say that both express important elements in kin relations, but each has to be modified with reference to the other. The argument for taking this position is partly methodological. Because the authors were using different types of data, it is quite possible that they have seen different dimensions of an essentially complex process. Indeed, Roberts herself makes the point that, for example, Anderson's reliance upon census data made it difficult for him to see the extent of exchanges across households. It would certainly not have given him access to the kind of personalized data about effective relationships which her oral history interviews unearthed. At the same time, one must exercise a certain note of methodological caution about this kind of interview in which people in a sense present public accounts of private relationships. In such a situation, the features of those relationships which reflect less well upon the interviewee may not emerge easily – an important point demonstrated very effectively by Cornwell's (1984) research on contemporary family relationships. Anderson and Roberts can perhaps be seen as offering us different facets of essentially a similar situation, where feelings of affection and concepts of duty are taken into calculations about mutual advantage based on material considerations. The result is patterns of support whose basis is probably far more complex than it appears to an outsider and which also perhaps includes the expectation that love and affection themselves will be reciprocated (Summerfield, 1986).

The work of historians on kin relations in the past raises some very important questions about the nature of reciprocity and how it operates in particular economic circumstances, which have direct applications to the present and the future. The core of this is to understand the delicate balance between feelings of affection, moral imperatives of duty, and calculations about personal advantage and disadvantage, and to understand how the particular sets of economic circumstances in which women and men are placed shape the character of that balance at any point in time.

*Maximizing resources*

The second underlying process of kin support which is highlighted by the examination of historical evidence is the process of maximizing and making the best use of resources within the kin group. The emphasis here is rather less upon the calculation of personal advantage, and rather more on the kin group as a co-operative unit, taking collective decisions which are to the advantage of all. In fact much of the actual evidence that these processes have operated in the past concerns

households, rather than wider kin groups which operate across households (Chaytor, 1980). This is as much a consequence of data on
households being more easily available as necessarily a reflection of real
differences between household and non-household kin.

Historical studies of strategies for maximizing resources are concerned
with the household (and sometimes the kin group) as essentially an
economic unit within which resources are shared. Such strategies
therefore vary considerably according to the economic conditions under
which family members operate. In the early industrial period, where
there was an expansion of domestic industrial production, one can see
very clearly that co-operative strategies were developed to ensure that
the domestic industry was viable. These strategies included the
formation of complex households, containing several nuclear family
units, as a response to the severe economic pressures which prevailed at
that time (Anderson, 1980, pp. 77–8). This of course is a situation in
which the direct labour of family members was needed, and could be
incorporated into a strategy for collective survival. Once work for wages
became the norm, different kinds of strategies necessarily took shape,
although individual waged work did not remove the importance of the
collective unit. Wall (1986) argues that some historians have drawn too
sharp a distinction between the 'family economy' and the 'family wage
economy' and that, in circumstances which offered possibilities for
both, family production coexisted with waged work. One example can
be found in Osterud's (1986) study of the hosiery industry in Leicester,
where some domestic production continued long after factories were
established. Of course it was convenient for factory-owners to build an
element of flexibility into their businesses by using women as out-
workers when they needed to. But also one can see families in these
situations creating maximum flexibility by using some members for
household-based production and some for different types of waged
work in what Wall calls the adaptive family economy: 'their economic
activities were diversified against the prospect of bad times and to
make the most of the good' (1986, p. 294).

The picture which emerges from this kind of work highlights
collective action and collective advantage, but often says little about
whether all the individuals involved in this enterprise benefited from it
in equal measure. Indeed the whole concept of maximizing household
resources tends to imply that all do benefit, although it can be very
difficult to know the precise distribution of resources in such households. However, such historical studies as do address this question
indicate that all members do not benefit equally. Again, gender and
generation are the key principles dividing household members, with
children and especially women receiving a smaller share of household
resources than adult men (Rathbone, 1924; Oren, 1973).

Thus the co-operation of kin either within or across households to
maximize resources contains an element of mutual support, but is
structured by gender. The obligation to pool and share resources with
one's kin would be felt differently by women and men. This is

highlighted in Gittins's (1986) study of a Devon town in the years 1850–1930, where she argues that relationships with kin were more important than marriage for the women in terms of the structures of support within which they were engaged. Further, women felt a responsibility to remain locked into that system of kin support in a way not replicated for men, who were more at liberty to 'get better jobs, migrate, emigrate and abrogate all responsibility for parents and siblings' (ibid. p. 264). Women, on the other hand, were more confined by a sense of responsibility to kin,

the most salient and persistent attitude to work and families was the overriding sense of responsibility they felt to parents, brothers and children. This responsibility might or might not involve wage labour, marriage and unpaid domestic work, although there was *always* some of it whatever situation they lived and worked in. (Gittins, 1986, p. 262, italics original)

In fact Gittins sees women as individuals who use such structures to maximize their own resources as well as feeling responsibility to support others, and she argues that women are involved in an informal economy to a far greater extent than are men. In that sense women have a greater range of strategies for maximizing support at their disposal, although of course their capacity as wage earners in the formal economy has usually been far more limited than men's. Typically women have been engaged in exchanges of goods and services based on kinship, but these have also helped to create women's kin relations in particular forms and based upon essentially economic relationships: the care of each other's children; lending and borrowing money and other items; lending and borrowing children's labour. Gittins's work is useful not only because of the way in which she highlights gender, but also because her empirical data broaden out from the household and show that women at least have, under certain circumstances in the past, been involved in the use of kin relations to maximize resources across households. The corollary is that they have accepted a range of obligations to provide support for non-household kin.

## Patterns of support over time

The third theme which emerges from historical studies is also concerned with maximizing resources and acknowledging obligations, but introduces an important additional perspective, namely time. It is obvious that historical perspectives oblige one to give due weight to the passage of time and to see ideas about duty or obligation, and patterns of support associated with them, as features of family relationships which are adapted to suit the prevailing economic and social conditions. That is an extremely important insight into the nature of family obligations, and is significant for understanding the nature of contemporary obligations (see chapters 3 and 6 for further discussion).

Introducing the perspective of time also requires us to consider an individual's 'lifetime', and how the lives of specific individuals are woven together over the lifespan of each. We can then see that any person's inclination to acknowledge obligations and responsibilities to specific relatives is subject to change over time in ways which are patterned and predictable, at least in part. This perspective gives us important analytical tools for understanding the nature of contemporary obligations to kin, as I have argued elsewhere (Finch, 1987c). The particular focus which I find valuable is the concept of the 'life course', which is different from the more orthodox conception of the 'life cycle' and 'family life cycle', in that it allows for more variation and does not assume that family relationships go through a series of modifications which are totally predictable in advance. By developing perspective, historians of the family have influenced considerably the work of other social scientists in recent years (Morgan, 1985, pp. 177–9).

A key figure in the development of concepts of the life course has been Tamara Hareven. She argues that a central task of the historian is to understand the interweaving of three elements: historical time, family time and individual time. By 'individual time' she means individual life transitions and how they are shaped into an individual timetable (for example, into marriage, childbearing, or retirement). 'Family time', refers to the ways in which the individual timetables of members of a family group are woven together, to keep the family unit as a viable concern, or to maximize resources. The central empirical question which arises out of this perspective is: How far, in a given set of historical circumstances, do individuals feel constrained to bring their own timetables into line with family time by, for example, postponing certain transitions until the time is more auspicious for the family group as a whole? Hareven's view is that economic circumstances have eased in the twentieth century, for most people, so that the alignment of individual time and family time has increasingly become a voluntary matter, whereas the stark economic conditions of the nineteenth century made this an absolute necessity (Hareven, 1978). I would argue that this remains an issue open to empirical exploration even under contemporary conditions (Finch, 1987c).

This concept of individual timetables enables us to get away from the focus on the family or household as an undifferentiated unit, and to understand something of the complex patterns which evolve when individuals' lives are woven together over the period of their lifetimes. In this perspective, individuals are both part of the group and separate from it. Further, decisions about the needs of kin, and whether one has a duty to put them before one's own interests, cease to be static sets of responsibilities and become matters for judgement at a particular point in time, with such judgements being related both to the economic circumstances then prevailing, and to the situation of all the other members of the family group.

The focus on timetabling also adds a different dimension to the concept of reciprocity in family responsibilities, in showing how the nature of the calculations which individuals must make itself changes over time. Indeed, the three themes which become visible through historical material – reciprocity, maximizing resources, and timetabling – all clearly are interwoven in practice.

## Conclusion: what has changed?

I introduced this historical discussion by posing three questions about whether there has been a reduction in people's actual support for their kin, or in their sense of obligation to kin, or simply change in both. We can return to these questions now, and draw together the strands of the preceding argument.

The main point which emerges from considering the historical evidence is that there certainly has been change in the amount and type of support offered, but that this cannot be seen simply as a decline from a high to a low point. The idea that there was a golden age of family obligations in the past was born out of a desire to ensure that increasing numbers of elderly people (and other dependent groups) in the population did not become too heavy a burden financially upon the wealthier classes; hence the anxieties about whether working-class people had an adequate sense of 'filial affection', which can be documented from at least the nineteenth century. But in reality the amount and type of support which kin give each other varies with the particular historical circumstances within which family relationships are played out, so that looking at patterns of support at different points in time means that one is not comparing like with like in quite significant ways: there is variation both in people's need for support and in the capacity of relatives to provide it.

These points can be illustrated in a variety of ways. Simply looking at demographic patterns is one. The 'need' for large numbers of very old people to be cared for, because they are unable fully to look after themselves is a phenomenon of the later part of the twentieth century, when the age structure of the population has shifted to give high proportions of older people, at the same time as advances in medical care have enabled many more people to survive into very old age, despite infirmities. By contrast the nineteenth century was characterized by a youthful population structure and much shorter life expectancy. Although it is true that more people would have contracted serious illnesses of a type which have now been eradicated – especially tuberculosis, which struck large numbers of people (women more frequently than men) throughout the nineteenth century – very few people would have survived into a long and infirm old age (Johansson, 1977). The issue of whether female relatives – or anyone else – would provide unpaid care for relatives simply would never have arisen for most people.

It is meaningless therefore to ask whether people are less willing to look after their elderly relatives than in the past, when this particular dimension of family obligation was simply not put to the test for most people in previous generations. Even if we make the comparison with the earlier part of the twentieth century when people were beginning to live longer, the economic conditions of family life were so different as to make a decision to take an old person into one's home, if they could not maintain themselves, a very different decision from its equivalent today. For the middle classes, able to live a comfortable life with servants to take care of domestic matters and to minister to the needs of dependent members of the household, giving a home to an elderly relative would not have meant the automatic provision of unpaid care by female relatives. For working-class women, especially the many who lived still in conditions of severe poverty where their own wages were essential to the household, a decision to share a household with an elderly person simply could not mean full-time unpaid caring. Even a writer such as Elizabeth Roberts, who has a very strong view of women's sense of responsibility towards their relatives during this period, acknowledges that old people living with relatives but unable to contribute any longer to the household economy might well be 'neglected' or 'pushed into a corner' through force of circumstances: 'Although the duty to care for relatives was a paramount one, rarely ignored, it is also true to say that the quality of care varied from the dreadful to the superb' (Roberts, 1984, p. 179).

The variation in people's need for support, and in the capacity of relatives to provide it, is not simply a matter of demography or the force of economic circumstances. The history of the past two centuries in Britain demonstrates very clearly that both 'need' and 'capacity' are socially constructed. In particular, the acts of governments in shaping forms of social, political and economic life through legislation and social policies, determines them significantly. This point will be considered in more detail in chapter 4. Equally people's need for support from relatives specifically has to be related to whatever alternative provisions exist at any given time. Offering a home to an elderly parent – or more particularly, *not* offering a home – can be a very different kind of decision, according to whether or not there are acceptable alternatives readily available. The British approach to social policy as developed in the nineteenth century both understood this distinction and exploited it by making the workhouse the only alternative to family care and then deliberately creating conditions in workhouses which were both undesirable in terms of physical conditions and also reinforced a sense of shame, so that any relative who could be considered available would feel obliged to offer support. This idea that relatives will acknowledge their responsibilities more effectively if alternatives are kept to the minimum has retained a strong hold on British social policy – a point to which I shall return.

When we look at circumstances in the past, and see the patterns of support between kin which prevailed at any given point, we are looking at situations very different from our own in important and relevant ways. Those differences seem very largely to account for the variations in actual patterns of support which have occurred over time. But what of an underlying 'sense of obligation'? It could be argued that variations in economic and social circumstances are very largely responsible for shaping the visible patterns of support, but that these only occur because of an underlying sense of duty and responsibility towards relatives; this operates independently of external circumstances. Could it be that this underlying sense of obligation has weakened over time? Has there, for example, been a restriction in the circumstances in which it applies, or in the range of kin to whom it applies? In principle, it would be quite possible to argue that this sense of obligation had weakened, even if the actual volume of support between kin remained at a substantial level, because more people are now in a situation where they need support, and because the economic circumstances of the majority of the population (by comparison with a century earlier) are much easier. Therefore some support can be given at relatively little cost to oneself, and without really testing feelings of duty to their limits.

These questions are extremely difficult to answer from empirical data historically, but their importance means inevitably that I shall return to them in later chapters. They relate closely to some key debates about the nature of historical explanation of family relationships and family change, as between the 'household economics' and the 'sentiments' schools of historical explanation (Anderson, 1980). Both schools of thought contain writers of diverse views, but to oversimplify, the former broadly can be characterized as writers who focus on the economic behaviour of members of households and families as the key to understanding family relationships and how they change. The latter place rather more emphasis on the social values and cultural meanings associated with family life, and look at change over time in the sentiments, attachments and emotions associated with different family relationships – usually between spouses and between parents and immature children, although in principle the same kind of analysis can be applied to the wider kin group. For example, the work of Stone (1977) is concerned with documenting the dominant pattern of change associated with family relationships since the sixteenth century. He sees a movement away from a situation where there were extensive kin ties but a lack of really close relationships in the conjugal family, through the emergence of a family based on the patriarchal authority of the father, to a dominant form of family life which began to take shape around the middle of the seventeenth century, and was characterized by close emotional bonds between parents and children and a strong sense of privacy in the nuclear family household. Similar analyses which place values and sentiments at the centre of family change are offered by Shorter (1975), Flandrin (1979) and also by Aries (1972), who is concerned mainly with the changing nature of childhood.

This complex debate cannot be dealt with in detail here. But the general issues which it poses do have importance for understanding contemporary family life and responsibilities. Writers in this tradition emphasize that there has been an historical change in the cultural and social meaning of the term 'family' over time, so that it has come to mean essentially the unit based on marriage and parenthood, with a secondary role only accorded to other kin relationships. Whilst the quality of empirical evidence on which their arguments rest is doubted by many commentators (Morgan, 1985, p. 165), the perspectives which they offer can be translated into important questions of contemporary relevance. Do people now think of their 'family' solely or principally as a conjugal unit, according other kin a very limited place? Are there a destructive set of values associated with family life in late twentieth-century Britain? Do such values provide a central motivating force in behaviour between kin? Do they operate independently of the economic and material circumstances in which individuals are placed?

Another slightly different angle on these issues is to consider the distinction between instrumentality and expressiveness which has been made use of by sociologists, and is usefully applied to a discussion of kin relations by Morgan (1975, pp. 78–85). Much of the historical evidence presented in this chapter suggests that under the harsh conditions of poverty which prevailed for most people in the early industrial period, family relationships necessarily were highly instrumental, with support being offered only if there was some hope of mutual benefit precisely because anything else would have been an unaffordable luxury. It is only as economic circumstances have eased, for most people at least, that the expressive aspects of relationships have become more prominent, although whether family relationships can ever be regarded as 'purely' expressive is very questionable (ibid. p. 78). The particular blend of instrumentality and expressiveness for given individuals is a matter for empirical investigation.

Thus a focus on the emotional dimensions of relationships – whether on feelings of affection or feelings of duty – tends to suggest that if there has been any discernible change in a single direction over time, it has been an increase rather than a decrease in the significance of the feelings which people have for their relatives. That tentative conclusion probably is as far as one can go on the basis of empirical evidence. So far as the actual patterns of support are concerned, one can say more confidently that these have not simply declined from a high point, but have undergone various changes and fluctuations, according to the circumstances under which people lived. All of this makes sense in relation to the historical context of England in particular where, on MacFarlane's (1978) evidence, social and economic structures have been based upon a strong sense of individualism, and not upon traditional ties of kinship, for at least 600 years.

People in late twentieth-century Britain do not necessarily do less for their relatives than they have done for the past two centuries, nor do they necessarily have a weaker sense of obligation, but they do have to work out the nature of their relationships and the patterns of support associated with them, in circumstances which are very different from the past. These differences, which mean that in comparing the present and the past we are not comparing like with like, are paralleled by changes in the composition of the population as a whole. In addition to all the differences which I have itemized in terms of age structure, family formation and lengths of generations, we should note also that the British population in the past was less racially and ethnically diverse, being almost exclusively white.

The idea of the golden age in which family responsibilities were stronger than they are today is clearly a myth, without foundation in historical evidence. Industrialization and urbanization did not destroy either domestic relations or kin relations but clearly they did – as Harris has put it – transform their character (Harris, 1983, p. 130). However, this was not a once-for-all change. The character of family relationships has been changing and continues to change to suit the particular circumstances in which individuals find themselves – often very subtly but sometimes quite visibly.

That conclusion in a way seems rather obvious and a matter of common sense. So why does the myth of the golden age persist? A full discussion of that issue is beyond the scope of this book, but I would agree with those commentators who argue that its persistence tells us a great deal more about the present than the past. Laslett (1972a), for example, argues that the desire to believe that extended family households, and the relationships associated with them, were the norm in Britain in the past is a matter of 'family ideology' rather than 'family experience'. He places the blame squarely at the door of social scientists, whose theories have directed them to look for this pattern in pre-industrial and non-industrial societies. I would agree that social scientists have probably helped to sustain the myth but not that we have created it: the power of social science is not that significant. We need to look rather to the social conditions of our own time and the recent past to understand why such a myth seems plausible and important. As Raymond Williams puts it, speaking not specifically about the family but more generally about myths of a rural past which was happier and more stable, such myths stem from the contradictions of the present which are difficult to contain. They are idealizations which serve to 'cover and to evade the actual and bitter contradictions of the time' (Williams, 1973, p. 45).

To understand the myth of the golden age in the past, we therefore need to understand family relationships and family responsibilities in the present and the circumstances in which they have to be worked out: the topic with which the rest of this book is concerned.

# 3

# Contexts: economy and demography

## Introduction

Feelings of duty and responsibility in families would be treated by many people as a very personal matter. Whether I choose to lend money to my sister, or to nurse my mother when she is ill, is an issue between me and them and no one else. My motives for doing this (or for choosing not to do it) are no one else's business. These are matters reserved for the private and intimate relationships of family life, where I can make my own choices for my own reasons.

That view of responsibilities and assistance within families is very much at odds with the arguments which I have developed in the first two chapters of this book. In chapter 2 I argued that the support that people give to their relatives is governed to a considerable extent by the prevailing social, economic and demographic conditions at any particular point in time. We cannot understand support in families simply as a matter of individual preferences and choices. It is a product of wider social processes, at least in part. Also in chapter 1, in my review of contemporary evidence about support and responsibilities in families, I suggested that variations in the assistance which people give to each other are not wholly individual and idiosyncratic, but are patterned by the position of individuals in wider social structures – their class position, their gender, their ethnic identity. The arguments which I have been developing also run counter to the idea that support for kin is a natural part of human existence, based on psychological bonding or genetic ties.

I shall now go on to look more explicitly at the place we should accord to social, economic and political support and also norms of obligation and duty in families. In this chapter I consider economic and demographic structures; the next chapter concentrates on the law and social policy. Together these form the context within which people's responsibilities to their relatives have to be worked out. The emphasis here is upon contemporary Britain, although some historical examples will be used, to help bring into focus more recent experience. The kind of questions posed in this chapter are: How far is the amount of support given and received in families determined by factors outside the control of the individual? Does it depend on factors such as how many sisters and brothers you have, whether your parents happen to survive into late old age, or whether there is money in the family? Even if these external factors set limiting conditions upon possible structures of support, how much room for manoeuvre do individuals have within those limits?

These questions bring us to the heart of debates which have been central to sociologists' attempts to understand the nature of social life, namely the relationship between the structures of a society on the one hand, and the possibilities for independent human action on the other. In recent social theory the formulation by Giddens (1979) of this problem as the relationship between 'structure' and 'agency' has been particularly influential. Whilst it is not part of my purpose to engage with these debates in a general way, Giddens's work offers some tools of analysis which are useful in the present discussion.

Giddens takes the view – as have many others – that any adequate social theory must give proper weight to both social structure and human agency, and must tell us how the two relate to each other. He argues that human action creates and recreates social structures, but at the same time social structures make it possible for human beings to interact with one another – they facilitate action as well as constrain it. He sees social structure as part of human action, rather than separate from it, since no actions make sense without reference to the social context in which they occur,

[in one sense] every process of action is the production of something new, a fresh act; but at the same time all action exists in continuity with the past, which supplies the means of its initiation. Structure is not to be conceptualized as a barrier to action, but as essentially involved in its production. (Giddens, 1979, p. 70)

Thus Giddens's view of social structure is that it provides resources which people can use when they are interacting with others in daily life. In that process social structure also is reinforced and reconstituted. We need to see human beings acting purposefully in their use of such resources, although the outcome of their actions may have consequences which they did not intend. In the context of this theory, Giddens rejects the view that patterns of action are straightforwardly imposed on people, including those theories which tell us that people internalize the norms of the wider society and then produce appropriate action. He argues that, if we wish to understand human motivation, we need also to see this as part of purposeful action. People need to, and are able to, explain what they have done and why they have done it and this itself forms part of the action. We all do this by drawing upon our understanding of how the social world works, by using the same shared knowledge of our society which we use to formulate our conduct (pp. 56–8).

Giddens's work raises complex but important issues to which I shall need to return at various points in subsequent chapters. His formulation of these ideas is at an abstract level of social theory, but can be used and applied in the context of family responsibilities. As we consider the importance of economic and demographic structures in shaping support within families, Giddens's work offers an important corrective to a common tendency in social science to view external structures as constraining human beings, by emphasizing that they can also facilitate people's attempts to construct their own lives and relationships. Essentially he directs us to look at the role of social structure in shaping family responsibilities as an example – to paraphrase Marx – of the way people make their own lives, but in circumstances which are not of their own choosing.

I shall organize this discussion by looking at three different types of factors, which have emerged in earlier chapters as potentially important in understanding family obligations. These are: socio-economic factors; demographic factors; patterns of family formation. Although I consider them separately, it is important to remember that they are also inter-linked, a point which should become apparent in the course of discussion.

## Socio-economic factors

### *The economic climate*

If we take a very broad focus, we can see that the shape and significance of kin relationships are affected in some way by the economic organization of any society. It has been argued that in most societies which have undergone capitalist development, one effect has been the 'domestication' of kin relationships. If the kin group previously was a centre of economic production, control over this is lost, although it remains the centre for organization and control of the domestic sphere, and especially for reproduction (Stivens, 1981). That particular analysis of economic change and its effects on kin relationships probably does not fit the case of Britain, as I suggested in the previous chapter, and as some historians would argue strongly (MacFarlane, 1978). But the debate about these issues points us to look at the questions of how far the economic organization of any society, or the general economic climate of prosperity or decline sets the context for the development of specific forms of family support. To continue the analysis developed in the last chapter, this is likely to affect both people's need to be assisted by their relatives, and the capacity of relatives to provide such support. Such effects of course are not uniform; economic circumstances vary in different localities (as perhaps with regional economic differences in contemporary Britain), because people with different skills are affected differently by economic decline, or because of the inequalities built into the labour market. In the latter case there is clear evidence that people from ethnic minority groups have suffered disproportionately in the recent economic recession (Brown, 1984). The effects of the economic climate upon people's lives are also modified by other social and political forces, especially whether there are alternative sources of support provided through public resources. This latter issue will be taken up in the next chapter.

Is it possible to draw any general conclusions from the available evidence about how economic circumstances affect assistance between relatives? When is this likely to be extensive and when more limited? Do people give more to their relatives when times are hard or do they give less? It would be difficult to generate sufficient systematic evidence on a range of comparable circumstances to answer this question authoritatively, but a case can be constructed that mutual aid between kin particularly flourishes in harsh economic circumstances (Morgan 1975, p. 83). Historical examples discussed in the last chapter could illustrate this case: Anderson's (1971) study of the working classes in mid-nineteenth century Preston, for example, or Ross's (1983) research on support between women in the East End of London at the turn of the century. Comparative examples also suggest that this is a fairly widespread phenomenon. Carol Stack's (1975) account of a study of a poor black community in the United States, in the 1970s, documents how residents of The Flats had developed distinctive patterns of reciprocal exchange based upon 'swapping' of resources between kin, and sometimes between friends. The whole system worked by creating sets of people who became obligated to each other over time, in co-operating groups whose identity was thus collectively defined. A similar picture of mutual aid and sharing, especially extensive sharing between female kin, of course also emerged from the sociological studies which were conducted in Bethnal Green and elsewhere in the 1950s (Young and Willmott, 1959), in circumstances where the increase in prosperity characteristic of the immediate post-war period had not yet begun to have its effect.

The evidence that harsh economic conditions are likely to foster strong mutual aid between kin can lead to an over-romanticized view of the joys of life for the urban poor, and to a regret that increased prosperity destroys the essence of reciprocity and responsibility in family life. Such an interpretation is not justified by the evidence, for a variety of reasons. First, there is strong historical evidence, which I considered in the previous chapter, to suggest that the kind of sharing and support which is generated by harsh economic conditions is necessarily bounded and limited, and very dependent on the capacity of the receiver to reciprocate. Whilst it may be a mistake to over-emphasize the calculating nature of such exchanges, it is equally wrong to conclude that poverty and economic uncertainty breed a climate of family relations where there is unbounded warmth and generosity (Tilly, 1984).

Second, there is a moral and political point to be drawn out of this debate, which is put most effectively by Philip Abrams in his discussion of the social and economic basis of informal neighbourhood care for elderly people and others (Bulmer, 1986). Abrams's particular concern was to elucidate the conditions under which different forms of neighbouring can flourish. His argument essentially is that 'traditional neighbouring', based centrally upon kin networks, does flourish most effectively in harsh economic climates, but that no one ought properly to be in favour of re-creating those conditions as the price of recreating neighbourhood support.

Third, and in some ways connected with Abrams's point, it is easy to take an over-romanticized view of family support under harsh economic conditions if one fails to ask whether people actually experience such support as desirable and preferable to any alternatives. It is all very well for political commentators to regret – as many have done – that structures of family support among the working classes have been replaced by state services, but is that how the working classes see it?

Probably not. There is certainly some evidence that necessity rather than desirability is the motivating force in such circumstances: as Hareven puts it in relation to early industrial society 'the need for reciprocity [was] dictated by the insecurities of urban life' (Hareven, 1978, p. 65). Stack's study echoes the same theme even more strongly: the urban poor involved in mutual aid through the swapping of resources routinely complained about the sacrifices which they made for their kin, and those who had experienced such exchanges over a long period expressed feelings of 'both generosity and martyrdom' (Stack, 1975, p. 38).

There is no inherent connection between giving support to a relative and believing that this is the way in which that relative ought to be supported. Indeed, it is precisely in a harsh economic climate, and when there are few alternative sources of support that people are likely to support their kin out of necessity rather than spontaneity. I shall take this argument further in the next chapter, where I consider some evidence which suggests strongly that when the pressure is taken off a little by the provision of some state support, people are actually more willing, not less willing, to give their relatives some assistance.

Another different line of reasoning which supports this argument is to look at what happens in the case of people who are wealthy. If the argument about harsh economic circumstances were correct, one would expect to find that wealthy people had very weak kin networks and relied very little upon their relatives. In fact such evidence as exists about the relationships of wealthy people (and research on this topic is very scarce) suggests the reverse. The establishment and continuation of a family – the word dynasty might be more appropriate – has always been a preoccupation of the aristocratic classes in western Europe (Powis, 1984). The development of capitalist businesses in the eighteenth and nineteenth centuries depended fundamentally upon kin ties to generate capital and to form business networks. Some social groups – notably Quakers and Unitarians – drew almost exclusively on kin ties to build up their business links, and there was a widespread practice of consolidating this through finding marriage partners for one's children from among business associates. As I noted in chapter 1, inheritance provided the mechanism through which the fruits of this could be transmitted to younger generations in the same family (Scott, 1982).

Although family firms represent a less significant sector of the economy now than in the past, Scott (1986; pp. 75–9) has shown that almost one third of the 'top' firms in Britain remain in active family control, and many more have a strong influence at board level from one kin network. The ties of kinship remain a key factor in sustaining the privilege of families who own businesses or property, supported by a conscious strategy of 'perpetuating the family name and increasing the family property' (Scott, 1982, p. 158).

So in general terms, I think it is reasonable to draw the conclusion that there is no necessary link between harsh economic circumstances and strong support networks in kin groups. If anything, there is a case to be made that it is people in privileged circumstances who are more likely to have strong family ties. I turn now from general discussion to some specific examples of economic circumstances which might be expected to affect support networks in kin groups.

## Unemployment

In the particular economic circumstances of the late-twentieth century, the issue of how far high levels of unemployment affect support between relatives is likely to be of particular interest. In fact there is only a limited amount of evidence about the contemporary effects of unemployment upon family relationships, and most of this concentrates upon the conjugal family, rather than wider kin relationships. The major concern of these studies is with the effects of male unemployment, and even less is known about the effects of female unemployment on family relationships. From this evidence some possible trends can be gleaned, but these can be no more than hypotheses which require further empirical investigation.

To begin with an issue where the evidence is firmest: a clear consequence of unemployment is that both individual and household income is reduced, in comparison with household circumstances when the same people are in paid work. Despite popular beliefs about people being better off on the dole, the authoritative DHSS cohort study of 2,300 men who became unemployed in the autumn of 1978 shows that only 6 per cent were better off on benefits than when in work. All the rest had their income reduced, and for about half of them the replacement income was less than half of their previous net earnings (Moylan, Davies and Millar, 1984, ch. 6). Moreover, there is no evidence that the deficit in the male income is commonly made up by wives' earnings. The same study confirms that wives of unemployed men are *more* likely to be out of the labour market than wives of men in paid work, and this tendency increases the longer a man is unemployed (see also Cooke, 1987).

It is clear that unemployment increases the 'need' for support, particularly financial support. But do other members of the kin group step in and supply that need? Is unemployment the contemporary equivalent of the harsh economic circumstances which foster structures of support between kin? In chapter 1 I gave some examples of unemployed people receiving gifts from their relatives: food, children's clothing, sometimes money. However, if we ask whether unemployment generally can be said to elicit support from relatives, the evidence on this is inconclusive. Certainly there are some empirical examples which illustrate that this does happen. The study by Lydia Morris of the households of 40 redundant steel workers in South Wales, in the early 1980s, shows that kin had stepped in with extra support in 12 out of the 40 households. In all these cases, the help came from parents, with the wife's mother being the most common source of support. The form in which the aid came reflected and reinforced traditional gender responsibilities within the household. In most cases the aid came to the wives, in the form of contributions to the housekeeping through gifts of food, or clothes or money for the children. In the two cases where the men were recipients, the assistance was given as small sums of money from the man's own father, for use in his personal spending (Morris, 1983).

Although this evidence suggests that unemployment *can* lead to an increase in kin support, even in the Morris study this was a minority experience. So it is important to ask why kin support apparently is *not* increased in a majority of cases. That is an issue on which currently there is very little evidence although various possible explanations spring to mind: the relatives of unemployed people themselves do not have the capacity to provide support; in contemporary society the conjugal household is regarded as an independent financial unit, and therefore support from kin would be inappropriate; financial support from relatives further undermines a man's status as the breadwinner, which is already severely dented by unemployment. This last explanation certainly would be supported in general terms by the available evidence: both in Morris's own study and in McKee and Bell's study (1986) of unemployed men in Kidderminster, the importance of men's retaining the breadwinner status in principle emerges as a strong message.

An explanation of a rather different kind for lack of support from relatives when people are unemployed is that the system of state benefits positively discourages this. If unemployed people are receiving supplementary benefit (which many do), then they are subject to the regulation which 'counts' any gifts from relatives (or any other source) in their assessment for benefit. Only occasional gifts below £100 can be discounted and then only if the gift is for certain purposes. Receiving any amount of money in excess of four pounds per week from relatives on a regular basis has the effect of reducing the money which an unemployed person receives from the state resources – assuming of course that they obey the law and declare this (Lynes 1985; Lakhani, 1988). It may seem paradoxical that governments concerned to reinforce family responsibilities actually create disincentives to family support in this way, but it is understandable as part of the view of unemployment which wishes to discourage it as a permanent way of life and treats unemployed people as if they should always be waiting to be re-engaged as wage labourers (Pahl, R.E., 1984).

There are some ethnic variations in the way in which unemployment is handled in families, and the arguments just developed almost certainly do not apply in the same way to some situations where non-white people are unemployed. Brah (1986) studied young unemployed Asian women and men who were living in a household with other relatives, and she shows that they benefited from the fact that household income is pooled. To that extent, support from relatives is more automatic than for the majority white community. However, there was a strong countervailing pressure, experienced by men in particular, deriving from the cultural expectation that they should be providers of financial support for parents and other relatives. Unemployment reduced their capacity to fulfil this expectation and put them under severe personal pressure, as I indicated in chapter 1. Although financial assistance might be available more readily to Asian men, to rely on relatives in this way is apparently even more damaging to their social identity than is the case for white unemployed men.

Moving away from financial support explicitly, there is another important issue which is more difficult to document, but which in fact may be one of the reasons why financial support is not forthcoming in many cases. There are some hints in the data that the experience of unemployment may have the effect of generally weakening kin ties rather than strengthening them. The apparent reason for this is that being unemployed reduces the capacity of both men and women to participate in the on-going patterns of activities on which such ties are based. At the sharp end, being unemployed reduces people's capacity to provide support in return for support received. Whilst one-way flows can be tolerated over short periods of time, and between close kin for longer periods (see chapter 1), the longer a person's income remains at a reduced level, the fewer become their options for entering into reciprocal relationships of support. This applies not only to financial support. R.E. Pahl's (1984) study of both employed and unemployed households demonstrates that where people are not in work they do not actually have the resources to engage in 'self provisioning' in the way that households can when one, and especially two, members have incomes from work. They are unable, for example, to purchase the equipment and materials needed to decorate or repair their own homes. By the same token, they do not have the resources to provide these services for others. This means that unemployed men are less, not more, able to engage in structures of mutual aid, although in Pahl's view this affects women less than men, since the kind of informal support networks which they are involved in require time rather than tools.

More generally, there is evidence that unemployment tends to trigger something of a withdrawal from the previous pattern of social contacts for both men and women, although for different reasons. Men's social contacts are sustained through activities which entail spending money so that, although some unemployed men certainly appear to retain a disproportionate amount of the reduced household resources for this purpose, their capacity to remain full members of such networks clearly is reduced (Morris, 1983). Women's social networks do not require financial resources in the same way, partly because most women do not have 'personal money' to the same extent even as unemployed men. Especially if women themselves are not in paid work, there is evidence that their networks are based more on visiting other women's homes. However, opportunities for this also are reduced when men are unemployed, because women do not have their homes so fully at their own disposal in these circumstances (McKee and Bell, 1985).

The general picture which emerges from this limited and patchy evidence is that unemployment under contemporary conditions is more likely to lead to the restriction of family ties and withdrawal from structures of mutual support, rather than their strengthening. More systematic research on that issue clearly is needed.

## Mobility: geographical and social

One common effect of economic change is that people move away from their relatives, both in the literal and the metaphorical sense. What effect does either geographical or social mobility have upon support between kin, or on the sense of responsibility associated with it?

*Geographical mobility*　At a commonsense level, geographical distance is bound to affect the kind of support which is possible between kin. If you live 200 miles away from your father you cannot pop round to see him every day, as you could if you lived just round the corner. Well-known studies of the 1950s and 60s documented how re-housing and slum clearance policies, which sent people off to superior dwellings on distant estates, had the effect of breaking up structures of family support (Willmott and Young, 1960). More generally the evidence of a number of studies of kin support suggests that geographical distance affects kin relationships, in that it determines both the frequency of contact and the degree of choice which individuals have about the nature of their interaction with relatives (Morgan, 1975, p. 83).

However, it would be a mistake to assume that there is a simple linear relationship between geographical distance and the level of support between kin. That becomes particularly unsatisfactory if one inserts into the equation the idea of duty or responsibility. Geographical distance clearly has some effect on the opportunities for mutual aid, but it does not necessarily weaken support in any straightforward way. The key to understanding this is to consider the social meaning of distance. What counts as 'near enough' or 'too far away' for a particular obligation to be honoured is some mixture of practical constraints and a sense of how compelling is that particular responsibility. In principle, geographical distance may simply lead to finding different ways of fulfilling a particular obligation (like moving your father to live with you, or near you), rather than to abandoning it (see Ungerson 1987, pp. 43–59, for some examples).

Various studies provide evidence which supports this argument. Colin Bell's (1968) work on middle-class families, which was undertaken as reaction against the concentration upon working-class families in previous studies, was concerned with this issue. He found that middle-class families, although more geographically dispersed than their counterparts in traditional working-class communities, nonetheless used their greater financial resources to retain contact over longer distances, and gave both practical and financial support to each other at key points rather than on a day-to-day basis. Cars and telephones made this possible for middle-class people. The spread of those commodities more widely through the population 20 years later probably has reduced the class difference, but by the same token it means that more people have the capacity to keep regular contact with geographically distant kin.

A rather different example of support being retained over very long distances can be found in Wallman's study of eight London households, where the key emotional support for one of her respondents continued to be provided by the woman's mother who lived in the West Indies, and whom she had not seen for 20 years (Wallman, 1983, pp. 96–7). Practical and financial support also can flow between kin over very long distances, and indeed commonly does so in circumstances of long distance migration. In chapter 1, I reviewed evidence which indicates that people who have migrated to Britain in the past 30 years quite commonly send money to relatives in south-east Asia and the Caribbean, expect to keep in contact through letters and visits, and give practical assistance when others wish to migrate.

The example of migration over long distances shows very clearly the fallacy in the argument that kin support is necessarily reduced in proportion to the distance between relatives. Indeed in some circumstances this kind of migration can, if anything, strengthen structures of support, as we see in the historical example of migrants into the expanding British industrial towns in the nineteenth century, where links between kin provided a key mechanism for facilitating the movement of labour. Geographical mobility represents one factor in the structural context within which family obligations need to be worked out, but we cannot necessarily predict what its effects will be. For example, in Britain during the 1980s it has been relatively easy to find work in the south-east of England, by comparison with some other regions where the unemployment rate has been high. There has been some attempt by the government to encourage people to move to find work. Where that has been successful will it lead to a weakening of family ties, thus undermining another aim of government policy, namely to strengthen the family as a mutual support system? Since the existing evidence suggests that geographical mobility does not weaken family ties necessarily, if we want to know whether it has done so in this instance, that must be a matter for empirical investigation.

*Social mobility*   Do the same kind of arguments apply to social mobility, that is, to families where some members have moved into a different social class, leaving others in the same class position? Studies of social mobility tend to define class in orthodox terms, tying a person's class position to their occupation – or in the case of women, to their husband's occupation – although some attempts have been made in recent years to get away from the crude middle/working-class distinction and to re-define where the boundaries between classes lie (Goldthorpe, Llewellyn and Payne, 1980).

So far as family relationships are concerned, what we are really talking about is a family whose occupational profile looks something like this: father was a steel-worker, now retired; mother still works as a part-time shop assistant; one son followed his father into the steel industry but is now unemployed; the other son has qualified as a solicitor; the daughter is a nurse, married to a doctor. In conventional social class terms, the second son and the daughter have been upwardly socially mobile, leaving behind one brother and their parents. Downward social mobility can also occur. Consider, for example, the case of a family with this occupational profile: father was a bank manager, now retired; mother has worked full-time in the home throughout her married life; their son is a qualified accountant; one daughter is a dentist; another daughter qualified as a teacher but when she married she bought a corner shop with her husband; the business was unsuccessful and both are now unemployed. In this case the second daughter has dropped into a lower occupational class, and a disadvantaged economic position, by comparison with her parents and both her siblings. In both these cases we have some members of the family whose class position is anomalous in relation to the others. What difference, if any, does this make to support given and received, and to feelings of duty and obligation in such families? Do the children who have been upwardly socially mobile end up giving more support to their relatives because they are in an advantageous financial position, or do they tend to cut themselves off? Does the downwardly mobile daughter receive extra help from her parents and her siblings, from her parents only, or is she rather an embarrassment to them all?

The most authoritative evidence on occupational social mobility comes from the Oxford mobility study, which looked at changing patterns of mobility for men over the period since the Second World War in Britain (Goldthorpe, Llewellyn and Payne, 1980). In this period there have been considerable opportunities for upward social mobility, because of the expansion of occupations which are designated conventionally as middle class. As the authors of this study note, there has been a longstanding assumption in the literature (especially American literature) on social class that upward social mobility is bound to weaken kin ties. This has persisted despite the fact that the empirical evidence on this point has always been ambiguous at the very least (p. 148). Their own study provides evidence to suggest that upward social mobility does not weaken kin ties, especially the tendency to give and receive practical support, although apparently it does have some impact on whether men are likely to spend their leisure time with relatives. For men who have been upwardly mobile into class I (composed of higher professional and administrative occupations), at first sight the data do seem to show a tendency to lose contact with kin, more than for men from comparable families whose class position has been stable across the generations. However, when one takes into account the factor of geographical mobility this apparent difference disappears. Men in these occupations do have to be geographically mobile and this appears to lead to some loss of kin contact according to the data presented by Goldthorpe and his colleagues, but when the comparison is confined to people who have kin living geographically close, it appears that upward social mobility has not caused a lessening of contacts. A similar pattern appears in respect of relying on kin for practical support. Indeed, men who have been upwardly mobile if anything were more inclined than those 'born into' class I to say that they would rely on relatives for various kinds of practical support, and that they had had the experience of doing so in reality (pp. 160–3).

The findings of this study are interesting and important, being based on a representative of over 10,000 men. They have to be treated with some caution however, because one cannot assume that equivalent patterns necessarily would be found in a parallel study of women. The Oxford mobility study also made no attempt to address ethnic variations. Additionally the questions asked about kin contacts and support were fairly limited. Nonetheless we can say that it gives us some strong clues about the likely impact of occupational social mobility upon structures of kin support, especially that it is a less significant factor than many people have imagined. However, data of this kind, taken from a large-scale survey, can tell us little beyond surface appearances. To return to the examples I used at the beginning of this discussion, we could predict that the upwardly mobile children in the first example, and the downwardly mobile daughter in the second, would retain contacts with their parents and their siblings especially if they all lived in the same district, but would the quality of those contacts change in ways that are too subtle to be picked up in a survey questionnaire?

We can see that there are good reasons why they should change if we consider the evidence which I reviewed in chapter 1 about support between siblings and between parents and children. In the case of siblings, there is a very strong message that these should operate on a reciprocal basis; neither party should be in the position of net giver or receiver. For parents and children the situation is slightly different: there is an expectation that parents will give to their children and that they will not expect equivalent gifts or services in return, but it is also clear that people make great efforts to ensure that the balance is not tipped too far and that adult children do not become too dependent upon their parents. Upward or downward social mobility potentially makes it more difficult to achieve these desired balances, since it means that the command over resources of 'the parties' is not equivalent: the person who has ended up in a higher social class probably is in a position to give more, especially money, than the relative whose class position is lower. The examples which I gave earlier in this chapter, and in chapter 1, of unemployed people and their family relationships, illustrate that people do find it difficult to produce the desired balance in kin support in these situations, although they try hard to accomplish it. Whether this applies to people who have been mobile in either direction, but nonetheless are in employment, is less clear. There is also an issue of how all this changes over the life course, which again is difficult to uncover in a survey. For example, we know that family relationships become increasingly important for many people as they grow older, especially relationships with siblings (Jerrome, 1981). Once people are approaching old age, and have retired from their former occupations, do the effects of occupational mobility become easier to handle? To examine all this properly would require an empirical study which compares different types of situations in which people have been socially mobile, but does so in a way which allows the more subtle consequences to be revealed.

## Demographic factors

### Age structure and the dependency ratio

As I noted in chapter 2, the most significant set of changes in the British population in the second half of the twentieth century has concerned the age structure. I shall spell out here the nature of these changes and their effects upon family support and ideas about family responsibilities.

As is well known, the most dramatic change through which we are currently passing is the progressive ageing of the population: that is, an increasingly high proportion of the population falls in the older age groups. Simply, during the twentieth century the proportion of people over 65 has trebled from 5 to 15 per cent; or in absolute terms, from half a million to over three million. For the younger elderly group (between retirement age and 74) this increase is now evening out, but the size of the very elderly population will continue to grow until the end of this century, especially the population of people over 85. Thus more people are surviving into late old age. As a consequence, although medical care and improved standards of living generally mean that most people can expect to remain healthy and active for longer than in previous generations, we have an increasing number who will reach a point somewhere over the age of 80 when they cannot fully care for themselves (Henwood and Wicks, 1985, p. 359). Again by comparison with earlier generations, in old age people will not have large numbers of children and grandchildren; indeed, at the present time as many as one-third of elderly people have no surviving children at all (Rimmer and Wicks, 1983).

A slightly different way of looking at this and associated changes is to use the concept of the dependency ratio. This is a way of summarizing the proportion of people of working age in the population, by comparison with those above and below it (children under school age, and people over retirement age). There has been a dramatic 'worsening' of this ratio during the present century; that is, proportionately fewer people of working age, and more outside it. From about 50 per cent in the 1930s, the proportion outside working age rose to 72 per cent in 1971, although by 1981 it had fallen a little to 67 per cent. It is unlikely to rise again during this century, although there will be a shift of the balance within the population outside working age, because of the continuing increase in the numbers of elderly people (Craig, 1983; Rimmer and Wicks, 1983; Parker, 1985). The reasons for this of course are the growth in the numbers of people surviving into old age and very old age, plus fluctuations in the birth rate. Although average family size has not risen over the period as a whole, there have been increases in the numbers of children being born at particular points, notably the post-war 'bulge'. Although numerically they do not form a significant group, in the context of the present discussion it is also worth noting that more children born with severe handicaps are now surviving infancy because of advances in medicine. Exact numbers are not known, nor is it clear whether this rate of survival will continue to increase (Parker, 1985, pp. 11–13).

Do these shifts in the dependency ratio have any discernible effect upon individual families, in terms of the need for support or the capacity to provide it? As far as the younger dependent population is concerned, one could interpret the increased tendency to compress childbearing into a short period (the details of which I discussed above), as arising from a need to have both parents in the labour market for as long as possible. In a society which allocates full responsibility to parents for looking after their children, both practically and financially, we can see this as one of the ways in which the population of working age exercise their responsibility for young dependents, who are now a net drain on parental resources very much more than they were in the past (see chapter 2).

However, the most obvious consequences of the worsening of the dependency ratio concerns the care of growing numbers of elderly people which – if it falls upon relatives – will have to be carried by a much smaller number of people in younger generations than would have been the case in the past. As I noted in chapter 2, earlier generations simply were not faced with a situation of this magnitude, because the majority of people did not survive into old age. Thus I would agree with Graham Allan that the idea that people in the past cared for their relatives more readily than they do now is historically naive, because such views 'fail to appreciate the degree to which care for the elderly is, in a real sense, a new problem' (Allan, 1985, p. 126).

Elsewhere in this book I discuss evidence which helps us to understand how older people and their relatives (if they have any) are coping with this 'new problem' in terms of family support. In chapter 1 I noted that there is evidence of female relatives in particular providing a substantial amount of personal and practical care for elderly people who cannot care for themselves, often stressing that they do so out of duty and obligation as well as affection. At the same time, it is clear that there is considerable resistance on the part of elderly people themselves to the feeling that they may become 'too dependent' upon their children and other relatives. In that context, demographic changes have had a very significant impact upon family support and family obligations. From the perspective of financial support, I suggested in chapter 1 that in many cases older people are net givers of support rather than receivers, although clearly that varies in different sectors of the population. People's occupational and class position during their working lives gives them differential access to pensions in old age, and it is worth noting that women are more likely than men to experience poverty when they are elderly (Groves, 1987; Walker, 1987). Some older people in ethnic minority groups have been brought into Britain as dependents of younger relatives, and have no independent source of income even from public funds. The extent to which relatives feel responsible for the financial or practical support of older people is related not only to demographic structures, but also to public policies which may supply the means for older people to remain more or less independent, or may actively encourage family support. This is an issue to which I return in chapter 4.

Changes in the dependency ratio have expanded the need for younger generations to provide care to older people, but have also affected their capacity to do so. I have already noted that large numbers of elderly people do not have surviving children. If they do have children, there will be fewer of them to share the burden of care than would have been the case in the past. Another important issue is the increasing tendency for women to remain in the labour market, or to be drawn back into it after childbearing more quickly than was the case in the past. Since usually women are the people allocated the practical tasks of caring for an elderly relative, at first sight it looks as if the capacity of the younger generations to provide care is reduced at a time when the need for them to do so is increasing. However, it is by no means clear that when women are in paid work they thereby become unavailable to provide personal care for a relative. The authoritative study of women's employment patterns by Martin and Roberts contains evidence that there is little direct relationship between employment and caring for a dependent relative: the proportion of women who undertook such a responsibility was similar among the working and non-working population. This is not to say, however, that there is *no* relationship between the two. In fact in the same study it was found that women working part-time were more likely also to be caring for a dependent relative than women working full-time (Martin and Roberts, 1984, p. 113; Parker, 1985). The interplay between decisions about paid work and care of a dependent relative is likely to be complex and to be affected by other factors, such as the range of available alternatives for care. I shall return in later chapters to the nature of such decisions, but in fact little is known systematically about how they are negotiated.

Changes in the age structure of the population, and the associated issue of the dependency ratio, do therefore form part of the context within which individuals have to work out their family relationships, but their impact cannot be charted directly. In the late twentieth century in Britain, they have created a demographic context which is distinctive by comparison with the past.

*The gender ratio*

Another significant feature of the population structure of Britain in the later part of the twentieth century concerns the gender ratio: we now have roughly equal numbers of men and women in the adult population. Although in one sense an equal gender balance is the 'normal' state of affairs in any population, since roughly equal numbers of male and female children are born, in the context of recent British history it is relatively unusual. From the middle of the nineteenth century, the proportion of men in the population fell steadily, reaching a low point around 1920. Thereafter it began to rise again and by 1986 it had almost evened out: 950 men for every 1,000 women (Britton and Edison, 1986). The implications of these fluctuations for family obligations can be understood relatively easily.

The most obvious implication of the gender ratio concerns the proportion of the population who have the opportunity of marrying. In a society which is monogamous by law, there have to be enough people of both sexes to 'go round' if most of the population is to be married at any point in time. Of course it is possible for most people to be married at some point during their lifetimes even in a population which is unbalanced in terms of gender, if there is also a certain amount of divorce and remarriage, so that the gender in shorter supply spread themselves around, so to speak. In fact what has happened in Britain is that the evening out of the gender ratio, possibly assisted by increasing rates of second marriages, has led to a situation where very high proportions of the population do marry. In the most recent birth cohorts for whom evidence is available, 93 per cent of men and 96 per cent of women have married at least once by the time they reach the age of 50 (Haskey, 1987a). There is a tendency for women who remain unmarried to be in the highest social classes, measured on occupational criteria, but the reverse is true for men (Haskey, 1983).

The major effect of these changes so far as possibilities for family support are concerned is to have vastly reduced the supply of single daughters who, in past generations and with a surplus of women over men, traditionally provided the source of labour which cared for elderly relatives – especially, but not exclusively, parents. Although there are debates among historians about how widely spread this phenomenon was in different sectors of the population, the classic pattern was for single women to be 'kept at home' to care for their parents although they could expect their devotion to family duty to be recognized and rewarded through inheritance, at least in the middle classes. Even when women have not lived permanently in the parental home, there has been an expectation that single women will bear the burden of parental care in old age, either taking a parent to live in their own home or managing care without co-residence if they live sufficiently close to each other. Lewis and Meredith's (1988) study of daughters who had cared for their mothers demonstrates that single women were expected to do this in the relatively recent past (specific examples from this study are quoted elsewhere in this book, see especially chapters 1, 5 and 6).

At present, the number of single (that is, never married) women in the population is very much smaller than in the past and it may diminish further in the future. Even where women do remain unmarried we cannot expect necessarily that they will behave as single women did in the past. Many will have successful and high status careers which they would have to give up in order to become unpaid carers for elderly parents; conversely, very few indeed will have remained in the parental home and dependent upon parental resources, so that the implicit bargain which entailed eventual gains for a single daughter in the past would no longer apply.

A further consequence of the fact that almost everyone does marry at some time in their lives – less obvious perhaps than the reduced supply of single carers, but at least as important in relation to family obligations – is that the majority of the population does have a family of procreation, that is a section of their kin group based upon their own marriage and any children associated with it. The proportions of women who have children have been rising steadily for cohorts born during the twentieth century, reaching a peak for women born in 1945, of whom 90 per cent will have at least one child. There is evidence that the numbers are falling slightly for younger cohorts, so that women born after 1955 are more likely to remain childless. Even then, it is estimated that 82 per cent will have a child (*Social Trends*, 1988, p. 47–8). This contrasts sharply with the situation which prevailed in the whole of western Europe between the seventeenth century and the twentieth century, where larger numbers of people never married and were, in terms of kinship, rooted permanently and exclusively in their family of origin. Although in fact it is this latter situation which was 'unique in human history' (Anderson, 1980, p. 18), if we are comparing our present society with British society in the last few centuries, we do have a situation which has changed significantly, especially since the end of the Second World War.

This new phenomenon where most people do form a family of procreation (and some form more than one) is significant for family obligations because, as I indicated in chapter 1, there are cultural rules which accord precedence to the family of procreation over the family of origin. Among the white majority these operate in most circumstances; for men whose ethnic origins are Asian there are circumstances when responsibilities to parents have a particularly strong claim. Broadly speaking, if a person is experiencing a conflict of duty and loyalty between their parents and their spouse or children, the proper thing to do, in the context of white British society, would be to favour the spouse and children. Of course choices are usually not so simple in practice, but the point is that we now have only very small numbers of people in British society who can never experience such conflicts and whose sole allegiance in kinship terms is to their family of origin. The demographic context of kin relations in contemporary Britain means that practically everyone must be faced at some time in their lives with a situation where the demands of the family of origin and the family of procreation have to be balanced against each other.

## Patterns of family formation

Finally in this chapter, I shall consider another group of demographic factors which are concerned with changing patterns of marriage, divorce and remarriage. I have already noted that most people do now marry at least once. Now I shall consider the circumstances under which they do this and the consequences thereafter. In particular I shall be concerned with the ages at which marriage, divorce and remarriage occur and the length of time between them; the number, timing and spacing of children; the processes of forming independent households. These interlinked factors have a direct bearing upon the shape and size of the family group, and significant implications for structures of family support. Much of the discussion here focuses inevitably upon the practices of the white majority, consideration of ethnic variations being hampered by the fact that major data sets such as the census give no information about ethnicity.

### Marriage, childbearing and generational overlap

A number of interlinked changes during the twentieth century have combined to produce kin groups which have a distinctively different shape, particularly in generational terms, from those which prevailed in earlier generations. The main factors here are: age at marriage; number, timing and spacing of children; improved mortality rates generally and increased life expectancy in particular. I shall say a little about each of these in turn, and then consider their combined implications for structures of family support.

*Contemporary patterns are distinctive*  It is well known that the age at which people marry (at least for the first time) has fallen, although this fall is perhaps not so dramatic as is sometimes supposed. As I noted in chapter 2, there has been little change in the median age at marriage between the eighteenth and the twentieth centuries (Anderson, 1985). However, there have been significant fluctuations during that period. From the beginning of the twentieth century in particular, there has been a tendency for people to marry younger, culminating in the cohorts born in the 1940s who had the youngest average age at marriage since statistical records began. In these cohorts, the median age at marriage was 21.5 years, and 90 per cent were married by the age of 30. Cohorts born since then have shown a somewhat more variable pattern, and the projected median marriage age for the cohort born in 1961, for example, is 23 years (Kiernan and Eldridge, 1987). There are some differences related to social class, as measured conventionally by occupation: people in social classes IV and V tend to marry a little younger than those in I and II (Haskey, 1983). Projections into the future obviously are difficult to accomplish with any accuracy, but Kiernan and Eldridge have put forward a plausible case, based on the analysis of the marriage patterns of different sub-groups within the population, that if anything the median age at marriage is likely to rise further and certainly will not drop again in the foreseeable future.

The fall in the median age at marriage has been accompanied by another trend, namely a narrower spread round the median. Whereas in earlier generations people married at very varied ages, in the second half of the twentieth century the great majority of the population has married for the first time within a very narrow age band. By the 1970s we had reached a situation in Britain where people married between the ages of 17 and 25 (Anderson, 1985). Thus not only do more people marry than in earlier generations, but there is much more uniformity in the timing of this event, although age at marriage shows some variation by social class, as defined in occupational terms. In a study of people marrying in 1979, Haskey (1983) has shown that both men and women from social classes IV and V (semi-skilled and unskilled occupations) tend to marry at the youngest ages, and people in social classes I and II tend to marry when a little older.

This compression of the age at marriage into a narrow, and quite youthful age band, coupled with the strong likelihood that most people will marry, means that there is very much a norm of 'the right age to marry', in a sense that there was not in earlier generations when patterns were much more diverse. This is one element in the increasing predictability of patterns of family formation which Anderson (1985) sees as a central and distinctive feature of twentieth century family life.

A parallel area where experience has also become more homogeneous and more predictable concerns the number of children born per couple, and the timing of their birth. The most dramatic drop in the number of children born per couple came between about 1870 and 1930. During this period, average completed family size fell from five or six to just over two. At the same time, there was an increasing tendency to compress childbearing in the early years of marriage. The average age at which a woman had her last child in the mid-nineteenth century was 39, but fell to 32 by the 1930s, and to 28 for women born after the Second World War (Anderson, 1985). The reasons for this change inevitably are complex, but economic considerations seem to have played a central part (Banks, 1954). The general fall in the birth rate of course reflects the practices of the majority, and certainly there are variations. We know that ethnicity is relevant here, especially that mothers of Asian origin, and living in Britain, on average, bear more children than white mothers, although there is some evidence that this is beginning to change (*Social Trends*, 1988, p. 29, table 1.11).

The third element which needs to be added to this particular discussion is improvements in mortality rates and increased life expectancy, especially for women. For the majority of elderly people who have had children, this means that they can expect to live to an age when they can know several succeeding generations of their own family.

When we put all these changes together, we see that the same changes which have re-formulated the shape of the life span for individuals have also created kin groups in the later part of the twentieth century whose character is distinctive in a number of ways. These changes have clear implications for family support, both in relation to the need for support and the capacity to provide it. As I noted in chapter 2, it is only relatively recently that most people could expect a period in later adult life when they are free from responsibilities for young children: a situation brought about by a combination of increased life expectancy and the compression of childbearing into early adult life. These changes have been particularly profound for women (Titmuss, 1958). The life pattern in which a woman has her last child by the age of 30, then has up to 30 years more in the labour market, followed by 15 or 20 years as a retired person, is a distinctive feature of recent generations.

The same changes also have had a profound effect on relationships between generations. Because people in the twentieth century have had most of their children earlier, and also have lived longer than previous generations, there is a much greater chance that they will know personally their own grandchildren and even great-grandchildren. Anderson has calculated that, by the 1970s, the following pattern had become the majority experience: last child was born within seven years of marriage; that child married by the time the parents were in their early fifties; last grandchild was born before the grandparents reached the age of 60; great-grandparenthood an increasingly common experience. The grandparents of the interwar period were the first generation of whom the majority could expect to know personally all their grandchildren, and by the 1970s, both women and men could expect to live long enough to see all their grandchildren married, if they married at the median age (Anderson, 1985).

Patterns of overlap between generations differ somewhat for different members of the same kin group, with the factor of birth order being the most significant. Here again, the twentieth-century pattern seems to have consolidated into one where brothers and sisters experience relationships more similarly than did sibling groups in earlier generations. In the very different demographic conditions of the nineteenth century, with larger and more spaced families plus higher mortality rates, older children were much more likely than younger ones to overlap with their parents in adult life, and younger children, especially those who married late, were far more likely than older ones to be in the parental home at a time when one or both parents needed their direct support (Hareven, 1978). By contrast children in more recent generations are likely to have been born within only a few years of their brothers and sisters, and early in their parents' long adult lives. All of them are far more likely to experience relationships with their parents as adults, and none is likely – except in statistically unusual circumstances – to remain unmarried in the parental home at a time when their parents need physical care. Some of this possibly may be modified in the future if we get a significant growth in the number of children born in second marriages, where at least one of the parents is in early middle age.

*Consequences for support in families*   Clearly these changes have profoundly affected significantly the shape of the kin group within which the majority of people have to work out notions of responsibility and duty, and also have affected both the need for support and the capacity to provide it. For example, it is now commonplace for three adult generations to coexist, and this has created the possibility of what Brody (1981) has called 'women in the middle'. These are women in the second of three adult generations with responsibilities in both directions, supporting elderly parents on the one hand and adult children in the early phases of child rearing on the other, and being net givers rather than receivers in any calculations about the balance of support. More generally, the coexistence of three adult generations over a long period of time creates a far wider range of opportunities for exchanges of different kinds, and makes long-term reciprocation a realistic possibility.

My point is not that this is what actually happens in the majority of cases: my review in chapter 1 shows that frequently it is more complex in reality. The point is that these possibilities exist for large numbers of families in a way that simply could not have happened under the different demographic conditions in the past. How people respond to and handle these new demographic conditions is a separate and important question which bears empirical investigation. There is certainly some evidence which suggests that the changed generational overlap may not lead to increased reciprocal support in practice. Anderson (1985) has argued that these very changes have actually reduced rather than extended the basis for reciprocity, because of the timing of typical life-cycle events for each generation. He argues that in earlier generations it was possible for women to spend their whole adult lives caring for their own children and some of their grandchildren: the limited number of years after their own childrearing was ended would occur at the time when their own older offspring would themselves be bearing children, and thus there was a real possibility for reciprocal exchange of services. However, in the twentieth century, because women have been freed from their own child care responsibilities earlier, they have gone back into paid work at a time when their own grandchildren are being born, and by the time they themselves reach old age their children have re-entered the labour market. Thus two trends come together and militate against mutual support: at the time when they might assist in the care of their grandchildren they are not available, and when they need care in old age their children are not available. This is a very interesting line of argument which certainly is at least as plausible as the alternatives, but whether these kinds of changes really have occurred, and for what proportion of the population, itself is a matter which still needs detailed empirical investigation.

In terms of financial support between kin, a similar line of reasoning can be pursued. One could argue quite plausibly that changes in patterns of family formation have extended the range of opportunities for financial support, or alternatively that they have reduced the range of circumstances in which it can appropriately be given. In relation to the first account, one can point to the fact that more people live to see not only their children but also their grandchildren embark upon adult life. This extends the range of possible people in descendent generations who might be recipients of financial support in order to enable them to set up home, or start out in business, or pay children's school fees. Those three examples are chosen deliberately, since each of them is becoming an increasingly common experience in the British population. An alternative line of reasoning is again provided by Anderson (1985), discussing the issue of inheritance within families. He argues that the changes in generational overlap have had an impact upon the age and circumstances under which people inherit from their parents – not a universal experience of course, but one which again is becoming more common because of the increase in home ownership (see chapter 1). Anderson argues that, as late as the nineteenth century, children could expect that their father would die and that they would inherit when they were, on average, 37 years old. Since many people married later and carried on having children for longer, there was a good chance that this would happen when they were still in their childbearing and rearing phase. However, people born in the middle of the twentieth century can expect to reach an average age of 56 before both their parents are dead and therefore are well beyond the phase of establishing their own household, probably indeed after their own children have married. This, he argues, has served 'to transform the role of inheritance in the family's life cycle' (p. 76). As I noted in chapter 1, we have little systematic evidence which makes it possible to judge which of these accounts matches reality at the present time.

Looking at this set of interlocking changes associated with family formation and generational relationships therefore raises some extremely interesting questions about support between kin, which are very much ripe for empirical investigation.

### Household formation and composition

The term 'family formation' has been used so far to denote marriage and childbearing, but these events often are implicitly associated with another change: a move out of the parental household and the formation of an independent one. The relationship between these two events has never been neat and tidy however, nor is it today. I am therefore considering patterns of household formation separately, in this section looking principally at the transition of young people from the parental home to independent households, but also more generally at the question of who lives with whom.

The relevance of household formation and composition for the structure of family obligations has to be considered carefully. It is a mistake to assume that, simply because people live in the same household, they are giving each other practical or personal help. Clearly the relationship between co-residence and other types of support is not that simple, whether one is talking about historical or contemporary conditions (Anderson, 1980, p. 36). However, as I indicated in my historical discussion in the previous chapter, the composition of households does have some relevance for other patterns of family support, for two main reasons.

First, households are themselves economic units, at least in the minimal sense that the people in them share the basic resource of a roof over the head and facilities associated with it, although all members may not necessarily enjoy equal shares. However, most households, especially those which contain relatives who live together, are economic units in a much stronger sense than that. Wallman, in her (1983) study of eight London households sees them as 'resource systems', in which the members share, manipulate and maximize not only the material resources available to them, but also less tangible resources such as time, skills and knowledge. Evidence from Brah (1986), which I quoted earlier, confirms that this is true for young Asian people who are unemployed and receive support from the wages of other relatives in their households. R.E. Pahl's (1984) influential study of the division of labour in households makes it very clear that the economic circumstances of individual members has a profound effect on the living standards and lifestyle of all members of the household; so that, where no household members are in paid work, the whole system operates quite differently from cases where household members have jobs.

The second reason why household composition is relevant to patterns of family support concerns geographical proximity. A person who shares a household with another is the most obviously accessible to provide various kinds of support, and probably looks especially suitable for those kinds of practical support which may be needed on a daily basis. There is evidence that many people operate with a notion of a 'hierarchy' of responsibilities to provide care, and sharing a household with an elderly person pushes the co-resident up the hierarchy, whatever their genealogical relationship (Qureshi and Simons, 1987; Ungerson, 1987; and see chapter 1 for further discussion). Apparently there is an assumption made that the relatives with whom an elderly person lives are providing for their various needs. That expectation permeates the views of providers of state support services for elderly people, so that those who do live with relatives are less likely than those who live alone to receive home helps, meals on wheels, day care, and so on (Bergmann et al., 1978; Hunt, 1978; Bebbington and Davies, 1983; Charlesworth et al., 1984). Thus although sharing a household with a relative does not necessarily mean that you actually are providing other services for them, it is likely that other people will assume you are so doing. This in itself forms a part of the context within which actual patterns of support have to be negotiated.

*Young adults leaving the parental home*  I indicated in chapter 1 that sharing a home with relatives is quite rare in adult life now, except on a temporary basis. This applies to the white majority but less so to people of Asian origin in particular, where co-residence on a permanent basis is much more common. The norm for the white majority is for young people to leave the parental home at a relatively early age and on a permanent basis. Indeed, it looks as if the process of leaving the parental home is becoming compressed into a narrow age band, in a similar way to the age of first marriage.

Within this general picture of uniformity, there are some quite important differences by social class. Jones (1987) has shown that young people from working-class backgrounds are likely to leave the parental home slightly older than middle-class young people, and more of them leave because they are marrying. Young people from middle-class backgrounds are more likely to leave for reasons of education or employment, but it is also quite common for them to return to the parental home for a period after their first departure. Especially for those young people from the middle classes who go into higher education, there seems quite commonly to be a transitional phase in which the parental home is regarded as a base which they can fall back on when they need to.

Anderson (1985), on the basis of the analysis of General Household Survey data for 1979, has calculated that the average gap between a young person's initially leaving the parental home and living in an independent household of which they are the 'head' is now only one year. About three-quarters of 24-year-olds were living in their own independent households in this way at that time, whilst almost all 17-year-olds were living with parents.

The idea of moving from one's parents' household directly to form an independent household of one's own contrasts with earlier generations who, as I indicated in chapter 2, often had an intervening period where they lived in the household of relatives, sometimes also acting as servants, or with non-relatives as lodgers. There is some evidence that the opportunities to form independent households may be reduced in the future as government policies make it more difficult for young people to be independent financially unless they are in paid work. These are issues which I shall consider in chapter 4. But at the present time, it is much more possible than it was in the past (or than it is now in some other European countries) for young people to form their own households, even if they are unemployed (Murphy and Sullivan, 1986).

Extrapolating from these trends Harris (1983) has argued that the effect is to weaken substantially the basis of parent–child relations, which is the foundation of inter-generational relationships between kin. Living away from the parental home for a period before marriage and/or childbearing, he argues, creates a distance between parents and children which means that young people can establish a conjugal family completely independent of their parents' support and influence, and can bring up their own children without their own parents' active participation. If this continues over several generations, he suggests, the whole structure of parent–child relationships will be significantly weakened (p. 221). This is an interesting argument which, as Harris accepts, cannot be substantiated at the present time and which clearly requires empirical investigation if it is to get beyond the realm of speculation. But the general point certainly holds: the increased likelihood that young people will establish households independent of their parents at an early age, whilst it may be welcomed as proper by all parties, does nonetheless create different structural conditions for the development of patterns of support between parents and children in adult life. How people actually respond to that is a separate issue.

*Older people living with relatives*   I have concentrated mainly in this discussion upon the position of young people, but it is also worth giving a brief consideration to the position of older people in households shared with relatives. Wall (1984), reviewing the evidence on historical continuities and changes, concludes that the most dramatic change in the residence patterns of elderly people is that many more now live alone (or only with their spouse) than did so in the past, and that this change has occurred largely during the twentieth century. However, there are significant continuities with the past: it has always been more common for elderly women to live alone than elderly men, and a small but fairly constant proportion of elderly people have always lived in residential institutions. The numbers of people who live with kin other than their own children has also remained fairly constant; so the real change has come in the number of elderly people who live with their offspring. Wall considers various possible explanations for these changes and submits them to empirical scrutiny. He concludes that the most plausible explanation is that the general rise in living standards since the Second World War has actually made it viable for elderly people to sustain an independent household; and at the same time, it has meant that there are fewer economic advantages to children if they take in an elderly parent.

Again, we know all too little about the nature of the interpersonal processes which lead one family member to offer a home to another, and lead the other to accept, but it looks as if both older people and younger people have seized the opportunity to live in households independent even of their close kin when the economic opportunities have permitted. Indeed, I noted in chapter 1 that there is some evidence from Qureshi and Simons's (1986) study in Sheffield that material advantage to both parties is a key consideration when elderly people do share a home with relatives today. Apparently it is rare for them to move in with a relative simply to be cared for.

So far as structures of family support are concerned, the fact that people are more likely than in the past to live independently of their relatives does not imply that they are *not* giving each other quite substantial support. But it does remove some of the opportunities which present themselves when one is sharing a household, not least the pooling of resources for daily living. Whether the moral basis of family support, in terms of feelings of duty and responsibility, is also weaker when people do not live together is a fascinating question which must as yet remain unanswered.

### Divorce and remarriage

The increase in rates of both divorce and remarriage in the later part of the twentieth century is well known and well documented. But what are its consequences for relationships within the wider kin group, and for structures of support and concepts of responsibility in particular? We move here into an area where very little empirical evidence exists, but which clearly raises important issues for any understanding of family obligations in contemporary Britain.

To begin with the basic picture of divorce and remarriage: since the early 1960s, the divorce rate has risen from just over 2 per 1,000 of the population to 12 per 1,000; or to express it in a different way, one in three of all marriages contracted currently is likely to end in divorce. Rates of remarriage have also risen, so that second marriages (that is, remarriage for at least one partner) now account for about one third of all marriages currently contracted, compared with only about 15 per cent in the 1960s. In about half of the second marriages, both partners have been married previously, and these instances represent about one in eight of all marriages. (For more extensive discussion of the policy implications of these figures, see Rimmer and Wicks, 1983; Parker, 1985.) There are some regional differences in divorce rates although little is known about the reasons for this. There are also social class differences in divorce and remarriage, using social class in the conventional sense based on occupational criteria. Taking men only, men in social class I are more likely than average to marry and less likely to divorce; for men in social class V the reverse is true. Once divorced, men in the higher social classes are more likely to remarry, and to do this more quickly, than men in the lower social classes; for women, the pattern is reversed (Haskey 1983; 1987b; 1988).

One of the most visible effects of these trends is the creation of single-parent households, and much public debate has been directed towards this. In fact in absolute terms the increase is not as dramatic as is sometimes supposed: households headed by one parent constituted 4 per cent of households in 1971 and 8 per cent in 1981 (Parker, 1985, p. 16). If we take only households with children, 10 per cent of all children live in a household headed by a lone mother, and 1 per cent are living with a lone father (Haskey, 1986).

Survival as a single parent with children, a situation much more common for women than for men, is one circumstance which might rather obviously create a greater need for support (financial, practical and emotional) from other members of the kin group. As I noted in chapter 1, there is evidence to suggest that a number of people who are separated or divorced, both women and men, return to the parental home at least for a while. The people most likely to return seem to be those who would have most difficulty in getting independent housing, so this does seem to be one way in which being separated creates a need for family support, at least at first (Sullivan, 1986). People who have custody of children are in a better position than single divorced adults to get local authority housing, although even then there is no guarantee. In her small-scale study of young Asian people who are unemployed, Brah (1986) quoted examples of a divorced Asian woman with children who had been obliged to return to the parental home whilst she waited for a local authority house, and who felt very unhappy about the renewed dependence which this represented. Thus separation and divorce do seem to be situations in which people commonly need to mobilize family support, but this may well be done with some reluctance.

Another possible consequence of these trends which has direct policy implications, and which has been the subject of some investigation, is the question of whether the experience of divorce and remarriage reduces the likely supply of women who might care for elderly relatives. There are several aspects to this. Parker has argued that as increasing numbers of women are single parents, either they will take on paid work and therefore not have the time to be unpaid carers for their relatives, or they will not have a job, be living in relative poverty, and therefore not be able to sustain the additional financial expenditure which such caring inevitably entails (Parker, 1985, p. 15). This argument can get little further than speculation through lack of evidence, although there is some indication in Martin and Roberts's survey of women's employment that women who have previously been married (that is, the divorced, separated or widowed) are rather less likely to be caring for a dependent relative than women who are currently married, or those who are single (Martin and Roberts, 1984, p. 112).

The issue of remarriage is also relevant here, and in particular the extent to which it changes the shape and constitution of an individual's kin group. The implications of that go much wider simply than the supply of carers, of course. The most direct change comes in the substitution of one set of in-laws for another. Or is it a straightforward substitution? As I indicated in chapter 1, we have very little up-to-date evidence about how people relate to their 'first' in-laws when they remarry – an issue which can arise also in the case of people who have been widowed. I suggested that what we know about in-law relationships generally would indicate that the severing of ties is most likely, once divorce or death has removed the person who formed the link between the parties.

However, the precise effects of divorce and remarriage upon in-law relationships, and upon kin relationships generally, remain unknown in any systematic way. One might surmise – it can be little more than that – that the increased likelihood that anyone will divorce and remarry at some stage creates a structural context which could serve to accentuate the importance of the family of origin. Certainly it cannot be supposed that adults normally will stay within a kin group whose composition will remain stable over an adult lifetime. However, that part of their kin group which includes their family of origin will remain the more constant element. It is certainly a possibility that such structural conditions are conducive to enhancing the family of origin as the stable element in kin relationships, but whether this is actually happening at the present time can be no more than speculation.

## Conclusion

I have considered in this chapter a range of social, economic and demographic factors which together, I have argued, shape the structural context within which family support is worked out. I have tried to emphasize the point that these cannot be seen as 'determining' patterns of support in any direct sense, still less directly determining beliefs and values about family responsibility and duty, but that they set the limiting conditions within which individuals work out what they are going to provide for each other.

These are limiting conditions in the sense that they help to shape both people's need for support from their relatives and their capacity to provide it. If you are an only child of elderly parents, the nature of your decision about whether to offer to care for them does become different from that faced by someone who has several brothers and sisters. If you have lived into ripe old age, and have both adult children and grandchildren, you do have a different decision about how to make your will than someone who expects to die at the age of 50, before some of their own children are grown up. If you are an unemployed single parent, the options for forming relationships of reciprocal support with your relatives are much reduced by comparison with someone who has a reliable income and no children. Each of these three circumstances has become a more common experience than it used to be in Britain, because of the distinctive economic and demographic conditions which have prevailed in the second half of the twentieth century. In each case we can see that external factors make a difference to the kind of obligations the individual will develop within their family; but it is much less possible to predict *what kind* of difference it will make.

How people actually handle this type of situation and 'make their own lives' within the circumstances created by these limiting conditions is a central issue in the later chapters of this book. At this point, I simply want to emphasize that they do form part of the picture which we must grasp, if we wish to understand how family obligations operate in contemporary Britain – but they are *only* a part.

# 4

# Contexts: law and social policy

## Introduction

The commitment of all major political parties in recent years to 'supporting the family' is a curious mixture of the benign and the sinister. On the one hand, it is difficult for anyone, especially any politician, to be against this general aim. The family, like virtue, is something that we all are in favour of – except some feminists of course, who have been the only people in recent public debates to say openly that there are good reasons to see the family as a harmful institution. On the other hand, it is seductively easy to de-code the phrase 'supporting the family' and to show that it really means 'pushing onto relatives certain responsibilities which really should be borne by the state.' Clearly governments have a vested interest in defining what structures of support should exist in families, and how people should think about their family responsibilities. At the same time they do have to tread carefully because there is a strong political and cultural expectation that these matters will be reserved to the privacy of family life, free from external interference.

This chapter is concerned with examining how these matters have been worked out in the British context, looking in particular at how the law and social policy have been used to shape the obligations which people acknowledge in practice. As in the previous chapter, I am concerned here with the external contexts within which individuals work out their own relationships. Whilst still bearing in mind Giddens's warning that external social structures should be seen as facilitating human actions, not just as constraining them, in this chapter the emphasis is upon the constraints which are imposed by governments' legal and other regulations. In a sense it is the whole point of creating such regulations that individual actions should be made to conform with official concepts of the proper way to behave, as I indicated in the introduction to this book. At the same time, it becomes apparent that governments are not always successful in their attempts to shape people's private behaviour, for a variety of reasons. The completely sinister view of what 'supporting the family' actually means is not correct, if it implies that we all end up doing what the government wants us to. We do not; in any case 'what the government wants us to do' is not always very clear.

In addition to any direct attempts to encourage people to take on responsibilities within their own families, public policies are also important in framing the context of family obligations through alternative sources of support which they may or may not provide. For example, I indicated in chapter 2 that the introduction of old age pensions, in the early twentieth century, was an important move which ensured that the principle of the financial independence of older people was accepted in public policy. Although state pensions have never been provided at more than a minimum level, the fact that it is just about possible to survive on them creates a climate, in respect of financial transactions between generations in families, which is very different from a situation where older people have no other sources of financial support – as in fact is the case for some elderly people of Asian origin living in Britain. Pensions notwithstanding, I still may choose to give money to my elderly parents on a regular basis – but I do not have to do it, in the same sense that I might feel I 'have to' if it is a matter of basic survival, and they do not have to accept it.

I begin the discussion by outlining briefly how the law has been used in codifying obligations in families, then move on to look more broadly at social policies, in order to tease out assumptions which are made there about family support and its basis. The chapter ends by drawing these strands together in a discussion which is central to the concerns of this book: What kind of impact do public policies really have upon the structures of support which people develop in their own families? Do they ensure that people give support which otherwise would not have been offered? Do they also affect the way people think about responsibilities and duties in families? Do public policies shape our 'sense of obligation' as well as the patterns of support which we develop?

## Legal definitions of family obligations

Beginning at the most general level, I shall consider first the ways in which family obligations have been codified in the law in Britain. The extent of this in fact is quite limited now although it was more extensive in the past. Nonetheless the law provides an important public and explicit statement about the nature of responsibilities in families which 'ought' to be honoured.

*How has the law been used to codify family obligations?*

*The Poor Law*   For the majority of the population the main way in which the law has embodied the concept of family obligations was the Poor Law, with its concept of 'liable relatives'. This ceased in 1948 except for obligations between spouses, and of parents for immature children, but before that date the obligation to maintain one's relatives extended beyond these relationships.

The origins of this codification of family obligations through the Poor Law lie in the Elizabethan law of 1601, and the definitions laid down there remained essentially unchanged until the mid-twentieth century, although there was certainly variation over time in the way they were enforced. The aim of this law was to enable the public authorities to recoup the costs of maintaining paupers by claiming it from liable relatives, who were assumed to be naturally bound to offer support through the normal obligations of kinship.

It can be seen immediately that the codification of kinship ties in the first instance was intimately bound to the need to keep down public expenditure, and this has remained an important motivation even when legal support for family responsibilities has been presented as purely a moral matter (Crowther, 1982). Indeed, the Poor Law itself can be seen as not simply a law about poverty, but a law *for* the poor in a much stronger sense. As McGregor puts it, it was a mechanism for governing a class, not merely for handling poverty (McGregor, 1973). When the Poor Law was revised in 1834 under pressure of the changed circumstances of industrialization, the definition of family obligations essentially was unchanged, but its effectiveness in governing a class and in keeping down public expenditure was strengthened. The explicit aim was to produce 'self-sufficiency' among the population, but it can be argued that in practice this meant 'class-sufficiency' based on enforceable kinship obligations (Humphries, 1977). At the same time, the 1834 legislation did accept collective responsibility for the poor – in the form of the parish authorities – as a 'last resort', albeit by providing a safety net which was designed explicitly to deter its use by making it both materially and morally unattractive.

In the twentieth century, the most important application of the principle of family obligations through the relief of poverty came in the operation of unemployment assistance during the 1930s. At this time large numbers of men who hitherto had considered themselves respectable and hardworking were deprived of any income earned through wages. The particular circumstances of this period meant that limited attempts to replace that principle of 'assistance' (the Poor Law principle for the relief of poverty), with the more dignified and less stigmatizing principle of 'insurance', soon became inadequate because of the large numbers of people reliant upon insurance funds who very quickly exhausted their entitlement to benefits. Their only redress was to the safety net of the Poor Law, which the government of the day was unwilling to allow because of political reasons, especially the fear of social unrest. As a consequence of the financial crisis in 1931, a modified system for financial support of the unemployed was introduced based upon a means test, a form of rationing with which some Poor Law authorities had experimented previously in a limited way. The means test entailed taking into account the income of other members of the household when assessing the amount of benefit which an unemployed man would receive (for a detailed discussion of how this operated, and its social policy implications, see Deacon and Bradshaw, 1983, pp. 14–29). Thus an additional principle was added to the Poor Law concept of liable relatives, namely of mutual financial support between people living in the same household. This explicitly included not only spouses, but also other wage earners (most commonly adult children) who – it was assumed – pooled their resources with their parents.

*Inheritance laws*   The Poor Law is an example of external structures, in this case legal structures, rather obviously designed to constrain and to restrict people's choices. Laws governing inheritance also codify family obligations, but in this case we can see that the legal structures may facilitate people's efforts to shape their own lives as much as constraining them. It can be argued that inheritance laws developed historically to serve the needs of a quite different class from that with which the Poor Law was concerned, initially that class whose wealth was based in land and property, but then increasingly in the nineteenth century the developing entrepreneurial and business class (McGregor, 1973; Davidoff and Hall, 1987). I have already indicated, in chapters 1 and 2, something of the significance which we should accord to inheritance laws in understanding the operation of family obligations in the past and in the present.

The effect of English inheritance laws is to codify the people who may make financial claims upon a given individual, defined in terms of their relationship to that person, and arranged in a hierarchy of claims. They do not guarantee that a particular person will inherit a given proportion of an estate, since the law also pays great respect to the principle of testamentary freedom, that is, the right of people to dispose of their own assets as they choose. But they do represent underlying principles which can be mobilized in case of dispute, and are based upon notions about which are those obligations that a reasonable person ought to honour.

Those principles are most apparent where a person dies intestate, that is, without having made a will. In those circumstances, a surviving spouse has the strongest claims, but she or he is not entitled to the whole estate. If the deceased had children they are entitled to claim a share. If s/he had no children but siblings or surviving parents, they are entitled to a share in the estate. Where someone has made a will the right of testamentary freedom operates, but since 1938 there has been legislation which enables certain relatives (and occasionally non-relatives) to apply to the courts if they believe that the deceased failed to make reasonable provision for them. Principally it is spouses and children who are given such a right, although anyone else could apply if they can demonstrate that they have been maintained by the deceased before his or her death (Cretney, 1984, ch. 23).

*Other legislation* There are some other laws which, whilst not codifying a positive obligation to assist relatives, do have a bearing upon this more indirectly. One example of this is the Invalid Care Allowance, which was introduced in 1975 as a small financial benefit paid to certain relatives who had given up work to care for an elderly or infirm person (Groves and Finch, 1983). In a sense this represents an incentive or reward – albeit a very small one – for people who have acknowledged responsibilities for kin. Initially the relatives who could claim such a benefit were quite restricted and at that stage the ICA could be regarded as codifying the relatives who were 'expected' to provide such care. Its subsequent extension to non-related carers, and finally to married women (under pressure from the European Court in 1986) rather dilutes that.

A quite different example of indirect legal support from family obligations is through Income Tax, which has permitted a Dependent Relative's Allowance, to be claimed by a tax payer who financially supports a close relative. However, this was abolished in 1988. These were always very limited measures which represented some public recognition and 'reward' for acknowledging obligations to relatives, and the removal of the Dependent Relatives Allowance means that this recognition will be even more muted in the future than it was in the past.

More recent legislation which is relevant here is the Social Security Act 1986, in particular the provisions for a Social Fund. This provision replaced the previous system of single payments, which entitled someone who was already receiving supplementary benefit (that is the system of income support for people who are not in paid work) to apply for an additional sum of money to cover specific needs – for example, the purchase of a new cooker or furniture. Under the 1986 legislation the complex regulations for these single payments have been replaced by the Social Fund, out of which all such needs must be met. This fund will have cash limits set each year, and it appears to be the government's intention to allow people's needs to go unmet once the Fund is exhausted. Payments will be at the discretion of a Social Fund officer, but the legislation requires officers to take certain factors into account when reaching their decision. One factor is 'the possibility that some other person or body may wholly or partly meet that need' (Matthewman and Calvert, 1987, p. 50). At the time of writing it is not clear how this will operate in practice, but press reports and speeches in Parliament indicate that government ministers do envisage that the 'other person or body' will include relatives as well as charities. This opens up the possibility that claimants will be asked to get financial support from their relatives if they can. Is this re-establishing the concept of the liable relative in British welfare legislation? That remains to be seen.

Finally, it is worth mentioning in this context the proposed Community Charge, which is due to be introduced in Scotland in 1989 and in England and Wales in 1990. Although it does not specify legal liability between relatives (except between husbands and wives), this measure does have possible implications for financial support between persons who share a household. It entails a change in the law to alter the mechanism through which taxation is raised at a local level. It replaces domestic rates (paid to the local council and calculated on the basis of the value of the property) with a so-called poll tax, levied as a flat-rate charge against every individual over the age of 18, with a system of partial rebates for people who are not in paid work. Households which have to pay more under the new system than the old mainly will be those who contain more than two wage-earners. This means that households in which young adults are living with parents will be among those most affected, with many ethnically Asian households being especially hard hit, since they are the most likely to contain numbers of adults co-residing (Oppenheim, 1987). Although it is individuals who are liable to pay the tax under the Community Charge, it can be argued that parents of young adults in particular will find it difficult to insist that the full charge is paid by their children. This will apply especially to children who are earning low wages, since this is a regressive tax which bears heaviest upon those least able to pay. In those circumstances, the overall effect would be to put pressure upon parents to treat the charge as household expenses and possibly to provide an incentive for them to encourage their children to leave the parental home. However, at the time of writing, all this must remain at the level of speculation.

From this brief review it is possible to draw out some general points on two issues: the kind of obligations which are codified in law, and the people between whom such obligations are presumed to operate.

*What kind of obligations are codified?*   The laws which have codified family obligations have been concerned mainly with economic support. This is obvious in the case of inheritance, but the Poor Law was more complex, as was the administration of unemployment assistance. These also were concerned with economic support in the broad sense, but in neither case was there a straightforward requirement that money should change hands. Provided an elderly person or an unemployed man did not become a charge on public funds, the law did not intervene to direct liable relatives (in the case of the Poor Law) or members of the household (in the case of unemployment assistance) in precisely how they must fulfil their legal obligations to give support.

Some general points can be made about the type of family assistance codified in law. First, very little attempt has been made to use the law to enforce types of support between relatives other than economic, notably practical or nursing care for an infirm person. Assistance for the latter type of family responsibilities has come more indirectly through a range of social and economic policies, rather than through the law. Only in the case of the care of young children (not specifically considered in this book) has the law been concerned with the practical duties of relatives; in the case of the care of adults it has not.

Second, governments have used the law more readily to require *that* economic support be provided by relatives, than to specify *what* should be provided. In the case of the Poor Law and unemployment assistance, provided an individual was prevented from becoming a charge on public funds the law took no interest in how relatives achieved this. Only if that arrangement broke down was a 'price' given to the support of a particular relative – a situation paralleled today in arrangements for financial support between husband and wife (Cretney, 1984, ch. 25). One could express the same point differently, looking at it from the point of view of the dependent person, and say that the law has never given an individual the right to be supported by their relatives. The case of inheritance is a little different from this, to the extent that legal rules govern in more general terms the proportion of an estate which specified relatives are entitled to expect (ch. 23).

Third, the concept of the household as an economic unit is one of the assumptions built into the law about maintaining relatives. This was most obvious in the case of unemployment assistance in the 1930s, when the household formed the unit of assessment for the means test. The whole rationale for that implies that those who earn wages can maintain the fabric and the running expenses of a household, and those who do not earn wages can be expected to benefit from at least a minimal level of support. It is that kind of assumption which makes it possible to require legally that support should be given to relatives in one's own household, without specifying precisely what should be given. The same line was taken by the Poor Law authorities, who assumed that people were maintaining their elderly relatives simply by having them under their roof. The actual administration of the Poor Law often in practice equated 'household' with 'family' although this did not appear in the legislation (Crowther, 1982). Whether these assumptions held or hold good is a question which I shall consider later in this chapter.

*Between whom does the law specify obligations?*   It should be clear from the foregoing discussion that two different principles have been incorporated into legal definitions of who is responsible for whom in families. They are: the principle of liability defined by genealogical relationship; the principle of mutual support between adults who share a household. As I have already indicated, both were modified by gender. In relation to the first, although there have been some notable reductions in the range of obligations between relatives codified in law, especially since 1948, there is a clear continuity over time in the definition of who constitutes a liable relative. Under English law this has been confined to three generations, and included only spouses, parents and children.

The legal obligation to maintain has now shrunk to support between spouses, and for children under the age of 16. It could be argued that effectively it extends beyond this age if children are in full-time education in that, for example, the system of student grants which has been operating in Britain includes a means-tested parental contribution. However, this does not entail a legal obligation since, despite campaigns on the part of the National Union of Students, there is no legal requirement on most parents actually to pay their contribution, and it is well known that some do not. In any case, proposals to introduce a system of student loans rather than grants would reduce the significance of the parental contribution.

Obligations which are legally enforceable at the present time include therefore only two generations, but before the abolition of the Poor Law in 1948 they extended to the third generation, because obligation to maintain parents was included. This principle that only close kin were liable to maintain each other dates from the 1601 Poor Law, and the relationships specified laid more obligations upon older generations than upon younger, in that grandparents were liable to maintain grandchildren, but not vice versa. There was also a gendered distinction between children, in that all sons were liable financially to maintain their parents, but only unmarried daughters. The assumption here of course is that once a woman is married she becomes part of the financial unit headed by her husband, and therefore to include married daughters would imply a requirement that men maintain in-laws. Indeed, the whole structure of the law in relation to family obligations has always been, and to an extent remains, 'wedded to traditional notions' in terms of gender (Atkins and Hoggett, 1984, p. 161). In Scotland the definition of liable relatives was broader; it included reciprocal liabilities between grandparents and grandchildren, and extended the list of liable relatives to include brothers and sisters (for detailed discussion of these regulations see Wall, 1977; Quadagno, 1982; Crowther, 1982).

Other laws which bear upon obligations between adult relatives are framed in similar terms. The Invalid Care Allowance, when first introduced, was specifically designed to support single daughters who cared for elderly parents, although it was quickly extended to other categories of relative, and therefore represents an example of a legal entitlement which supports family responsibilities defined more broadly in genealogical terms. Inheritance laws again focus principally on the rights of spouses and children with parents, brothers and sisters being allowed somewhat weaker claims.

Where the law has specified which kin have obligations towards each other, a fairly consistent pattern emerges therefore. The structure of obligations essentially is confined to the husband–wife and the parent–child bond, and over time the range of people involved has shrunk from three to two generations. Certain zealous Poor Law authorities did pursue other relatives when – in the absence of closer kin – they tried to extract support from uncles, nephews, sons-in-law and so on. Such activities were wholly outside the law although considerable moral pressure could be put upon relatives who were strictly non-liable, for example by treating the shame of the workhouse as the only alternative. Indeed the majority report of the Royal Commission on the Poor Law, in 1909, endorsed the belief that non-liable relatives should be made to contribute support (Crowther, 1982). But for the most part the 'extended family', in the sense in which this has commonly been understood, has never really come into the picture in terms of legal definitions in Britain, especially in England.

Liability to maintain people within one's own household represents the major alternative principle for defining who is responsible for whom. Often it may overlap with people who would count as liable relatives on the first definition, but this does not happen in all cases, since a minority of people do live with other relatives including siblings, grandparents and sometimes more distant kin.

The operation of the household means test in the 1930s demonstrates that people do feel that such definitions are anomalous in reality. The partial re-introduction of this principle of household support in the Community Charge could produce similar anomalies. More generally, the idea that households should operate as mutually supportive units has considerable importance in the thinking which underscores contemporary social policy, as I shall indicate in subsequent discussion.

## How are legal obligations between relatives administered and enforced?

In practice the effect of any of these legal provisions upon people's lives depends upon when and how they are enforced. Enforcement has been variable in the past between individuals, between localities, and over time.

Local variation in the administration of the Poor Law was a well-known feature. Some authorities were much more stringent than others in their own provisions and in the extent to which they pursued liable relatives. It was indeed a recognition of this which led to attempts to tighten up the administration of the Poor Law through the 1871 Circular on Outdoor Relief, which laid a strong emphasis upon getting contributions from relatives when elderly people in particular were receiving outdoor relief, rather than being taken into the workhouse. For the next twenty years, considerable pressure was put on the Boards of Guardians by central government to tighten up on this (Quadagno, 1982).

As far as variation between individuals is concerned, there was a recognition that the liability to maintain a relative should not be unconditional. In particular, it was accepted that a person could, as it were, forfeit the right to maintenance through actions of their own which could be considered unreasonable. For example, an able-bodied person who apparently could be working to support themselves would not be entitled in practice to maintenance from their relatives; nor would a person whose conduct had been disreputable.

The actual mechanism for enforcing liabilities upon relatives – and for enforcing the rights of relatives under inheritance laws – is of course through the courts. Boards of Guardians did bring cases in which the courts required the payment of maintenance costs by liable relatives, but the amounts of money actually recouped through this process were very small (Quadagno, 1982). Crowther (1982) argues that this cumbersome and rather ineffective procedure provided the main incentive to introduce means testing, which represents a more efficient mechanism for extracting support from relatives, albeit indirectly. It is more efficient because it can operate with a less precise and therefore a more flexible definition of family responsibilities.

There is a sense therefore in which change over time in the legal codification of support between relatives has been moving in two apparently contradictory directions. On the one hand, the definition of liable relatives has become more restricted. On the other hand, the expansion of means testing, especially where it has included the use of the household as the economic unit for assessment purposes, has introduced a rather effective mechanism for defining family responsibility in practice. Although the household means test as such has not been used in the post-war period, it remains the case that in periods of economic stringency the state has 'an economic interest in defining the liability of relatives as widely as possible' (Crowther, 1982, p. 139).

Thus we can see that the effect which legal definitions of family responsibilities might have in reality at any point in time cannot simply be 'read off' by looking at what the law actually says. Especially where it overlaps with other economic and social policies, we have to judge the likely effect of the law upon people's lives in relation to this wider context.

## Family obligations: implicit definitions and assumptions

In addition to explicit assumptions about family obligations which have been given legal force there is a range of social policies which, whilst not codifying family obligations in quite the same way, do incorporate certain assumptions about who ought to be able to rely upon whom. I shall suggest that the same principles which have shaped the legal definition of obligation can be detected in other policies.

### What model of the family informs social policy?

In looking at the specific question 'What implicit assumptions are made in social policies about obligations towards relatives?' we need to consider the more general issue 'What model of the family informs social policy?' This latter question, which forms the background to the former, was first posed by the American sociologist Litwak (1965) who concluded that the 'modified extended family' was the dominant model in social policy in the United States. This means that policies are formulated on the assumption that family life consists of 'a coalition of nuclear families in a state of partial dependence' (p. 291). For example, public policies assume that each nuclear family should be housed separately and that individual nuclear families are entitled to aid from public resources. But it is also assumed that any such aid will be supplemented by assistance from relatives. It is the business of social policies to support people's inclination to remain in active contact with their kin, so that such aid can flow.

Litwak's analysis broadly still holds good for Britain in the later part of the twentieth century. The idea of the state and the family providing complementary sources of assistance for dependent individuals is common ground amongst all mainstream political parties in Britain, and can be seen most obviously in relation to the practical care of elderly and handicapped people. The idea of 'community care' which incorporates support from both relatives and public resources became very much the political orthodoxy in the 1970s and 80s, and the idea of complementary sources of care receives authoritative expression in documents such as the 1981 White Paper *Growing Older* (Cmnd. 8173) and the Barclay Report on the future of social work (National Institute of Social Work, 1982). The actual balance between these two sources of support is a matter partly of political persuasion and partly of pragmatic considerations. As we noted in relation to the financial support of individuals who are out of the labour market, in times of economic stringency state policies place stronger emphasis upon family support, in the interests of keeping down public expenditure, although of course some other overt reason may be given (Crowther, 1982). The same is true of relatives' provision of practical support. Around 1977 both the main British political parties began to place the idea of 'supporting the family' at the centre of the political agenda, and it is not difficult to detect the economic pressures which lie behind this. As the economic recession has bitten deeper, and a Conservative government committed to restricting public expenditure has been in power, the unpaid support given by relatives to frail and elderly individuals clearly has saved the Treasury very large sums of money every year. Indeed, it is possible to produce a calculation which demonstrates that this unpaid support for elderly people is at least equivalent in financial terms to the total expenditure on health and social services for the over 75-year-olds (Finch and Groves, 1980; Dale and Foster, 1986; Finch, 1986b).

Whilst Litwak's argument fits the British case fairly well, his analysis does however have one weakness, namely that it does not make visible the dimension of gender. In fact it would be more accurate to say that social policy is informed by a model of the 'gendered modified extended family' in which independent nuclear households, composed of a male breadwinner and his female dependent plus their immature children if they have any, are linked in a state of partial dependence upon each other. The nature of that partial dependence is governed by expectations that women should provide the unpaid labour entailed in caring for the sick and elderly. The assumptions built into social policy, concerning gender relations in the nuclear family household, were exposed initially and importantly by the work of Hilary Land (1978; 1983) and this point is now widely recognized. Work by feminists on the topic of community care has also exposed the gendered nature of assumptions about who will provide unpaid care for their relatives, and this also is now widely acknowledged (Finch and Groves, 1980; Walker, 1982; Dale and Foster, 1986).

This model of the 'gendered modified extended family' which informs social policy may or may not be an accurate reflection of the way that most people actually live; indeed there are good reasons to suppose that it is out of line with contemporary experience for large sectors of the population. The sizeable number of single-parent households headed by women is an obvious example (see chapter 3). In this respect the model of the family which informs social policy not only is out of line with the reality of many people's lives, but also can be seen to be ethnocentric, since a mother-headed household is a cultural norm for many people of Caribbean or African origin, where it can be seen as a sign of a strong family life rather than an undesirable modification (Brittan and Maynard, 1984, pp. 134–7). Ethnocentricity is evident also in relation to many kin groups of Asian origin living in Britain, where the degree of practical and financial interdependence is much greater than the concept of the modified extended family suggests (see chapter 1). As Crowther (1982) has noted, it is quite possible for the definition of 'the family' in social policy and the law to drift apart from people's experience in practice, or indeed with commonly held moral beliefs about what family life 'ought' to be like. This appears to have happened in certain ways at the present time, but there is as yet little sign that that model of the family which has informed social policy for some years is about to be revised.

### What assumptions are made in social policy about family responsibilities?

The concept of 'liable relatives' which was so explicit under the Poor Law, seldom makes a public appearance in contemporary social policy debate. For the most part loose phrases are used, such as 'family care' or 'the family supports its members', without specifying the nature of the genealogical relationships between which support might be expected to pass. However, contemporary policy makers appear to operate on the assumption that a latent structure of responsibility between relatives does exist and can be drawn upon, even when people are not actually doing much for each other in practice. But as Allan (1983) has warned, existing empirical studies of kin relationships indicate that it is really only relationships between primary kin, which are likely to contain a commitment of the order sufficiently reliable to provide consistent support. In practice that brings us close to the range of people who were considered liable relatives under the Poor Law. Interestingly, there is a sense in which the liability to support relatives economically has declined during the twentieth century, whilst the expectation that one will support the same range of relatives in more practical ways has been expanded in social policy. Of course the latter is associated more with women than with men.

The principle of mutual support within households, used in the law to define financial responsibilities, is less clear-cut in policies concerned with practical support. One might expect this, given the importance in social policy of the model of the family based around a coalition of households. In fact when it comes to matters such as domestic support for or personal care of a dependent relative, the assumption made in social policies appears to be that such assistance may be given across households, especially when they are geographically close.

The principle that the family is a unit which operates on the basis of mutual aid underscores much social policy thinking. The problem about incorporating such assumptions into social policy is the implication that members of the household or the kin group have an identity of interest. 'The family' becomes a collective entity which the state supports with certain resources, but it is then assumed that the principle of mutual aid will take over, so that the individuals contained within the unit will derive equal benefits according to need. Everything which we know about the distribution of resources within households would question that assumption (Pahl, J., 1983; 1984). The concept of mutual aid within families conceals, among other things, the unequal distribution of resources between women and men, and the claim that the family *is* the basic unit of mutual aid very easily becomes an assertion that it *should* be.

Rather than draw on an eclectic range of illustrations to demonstrate how these assumptions are translated into concrete policies, I shall discuss two specific examples, both of which concern relationships between parents and children, and both covering issues which are of contemporary importance in policy terms.

*The care of dependent elderly people*    Policies about the care of elderly people who are not able to manage independently on their own are of great contemporary significance because of the demographic trends outlined in chapter 3. They also provide a good case study for considering how assumptions about family obligations are built into social policy.

As I have already indicated, the legal liability upon children to maintain their parents financially was finally removed in 1948. This change, plus the expansion of welfare services in the post-war period, has led to a widely-held belief that children (and indeed other relatives) are no longer willing to accept responsibilities for supporting elderly people, which previously would have been taken for granted. This belief was beginning to find its way into social policy discussions as early as the 1950s, and its progress has been documented in a discussion by Means and Smith (1985). They consider the widely held belief (more common among Conservative than Labour politicians, but commanding wide credibility) that the establishment of the welfare state undermined the willingness of families to take responsibility for elderly people, and to provide various support services for them. The underlying assumption of course was that it should be the responsibility of women to stay at home and look after dependent people, although this was often not stated explicitly. The apparent consensus which emerged during the 1950s and has continued, (namely that elderly people should be living in their own homes wherever possible) masked considerable uncertainty about where the proper boundaries of family responsibilities and state responsibilities should be drawn (ibid. pp. 240–3). A belief that the sense of obligation within families had been undermined by the welfare state persisted, despite the evidence of empirical studies in this period which demonstrated clearly, first, that relatives did still provide services for elderly people on an extensive scale, and second, that their willingness to do so was not removed if the person was also receiving services from state or voluntary sources (ibid. pp. 248–51).

This analysis retains a strong resonance in the 1980s. There remains the belief in some influential circles that the welfare state has undermined family responsibilities (e.g. Anderson, Lait and Marsland, 1981; Anderson and Dawson, 1986), and current policies about the care of the elderly quite clearly are designed to extend the responsibility accorded to relatives. Evidence for this can be found in a series of policy documents published since the mid-1970s. Since the earlier ones have been reviewed extensively (e.g. Finch and Groves, 1980; Parker, 1985) I shall concentrate upon some evidence from more recent documents. These contain a clear message that care by 'family and friends' should be treated as the normal and desirable state of affairs, and that services should be provided by the state as a supplement to this care, or where it is not available. For example, the Audit Commission's (1985) report on managing social services for elderly people considers various categories of elderly people in need, but for each one it includes the phrase that services need to be provided 'for those without assistance from friends and relatives'. This report makes quite explicit that if local authorities wish to reduce their expenditure on such services, 'friends and relatives' provide a useful alternative,

If an authority decides it wishes to lower its level of community expenditure on those now dependent on the public sector, it needs to ensure it can mobilize support from friends and relatives and the voluntary sector to take on some of the tasks previously carried out by social services. (Audit Commission, 1985, para. 66)

The Griffiths Report (1988), commissioned by the government as a review of their community care policies, expressed unequivocally the view that 'families, friends and neighbours' should continue to be the cornerstone of support for people who cannot fully care for themselves,

Publicly provided services constitute only a small part of the total care provided to people in need. Families, friends and neighbours and other local people provide the majority of care in response to needs which they are uniquely well placed to identify and respond to. This will continue to be the primary means by which people are enabled to live normal lives in community settings. (Griffiths, 1988, para. 3.2)

The idea of 'mobilizing informal support' has become a common theme in the 1980s and it implies that there is a latent willingness, presumably based upon a residual sense of responsibility, which can be activated. This assumption is reinforced in reality by rationing the use of scarce public services and concentrating them upon people who have no relatives providing informal support. Priority is given especially to people who live alone in allocating services such as home helps, or community nursing (Bebbington and Davies, 1983; Salvage, 1985). Meanwhile people who live with relatives have little access to such publicly provided support. For example, the study sponsored by the National Institute for Social Work of people looking after a relative who was elderly and mentally confused (surely by anyone's standards among the most difficult group for whom relatives might be caring), found that 45 per cent of elderly people who were heavily incontinent were never visited by a community nurse, and that more generally their relatives were not receiving support services. More importantly, they had not been offered such services. For example, of those relatives who had never been offered the possibility of having the elderly person admitted to residential care for a short period to give them some relief, 83 per cent would have liked this possibility (Levin, Sinclair and Gorbach, 1983).

The message is clear. It is assumed that the state's responsibility essentially is discharged if a person lives with a relative. The question of *what* support is provided, or the quality of the care which an elderly person receives, is not a matter with which state services need seriously be concerned. This point was recognized in a report from the Social Services Inspectorate on procedures for admitting elderly people to residential care. In reviewing the admission procedures of a number of local authorities, they noted that whilst most asked the social worker to find out whether an elderly person had any care available from family and friends, only one asked for the quality of that care to be assessed, and only one asked for the needs of the principal carer to be taken into account (Social Services Inspectorate, 1985, Appendix, p. iv). Just as under the nineteenth-century Poor Law the state was interested in putting the responsibility for financial support upon the relatives of an elderly person, but not interested in what assistance that person actually received, so in the circumstances of the late twentieth century public authorities in effect place responsibilities for practical care onto families wherever possible, but take little interest in what that means in practice for the elderly person.

The effect is to put pressure to provide unpaid care on the two categories of people upon whom the law has concentrated in respect of financial support: people who share a household with an elderly person and those who would have been defined as liable relatives under the Poor Law, especially children. Their obligations in this respect are not enforced in law, although direct pressure may be applied by professional workers or officials (an issue to which I shall return). However, pressure also is applied more indirectly by the fact that, in many cases, there are likely to be few alternative services available to an elderly person who looks as if they have someone in either of these categories who 'could' care for them. This means potential carers in that situation face a set of choices which are shaped by assumptions made in social policy about what kind of obligations would be honoured by decent people. Equally, the choices open to elderly people become more restricted, especially for those who might wish to retain practical independence from their children or from other members of their household.

*Support for young adults*   My second example reveals similar themes to my first: a belief that there is a latent structure of family responsibilities which can be activated by policy interventions, the terminology of debate being rather vague ('the family' or 'family and friends'), whilst in practice the focus is on parent–child relationships; and the application of the principle of mutual support within households.

I have chosen the example of support for young adults again because of its contemporary importance in social policy. The reason why support for young adults – especially in relation to money and accommodation – is a live issue at the present time was initially a consequence of high rates of unemployment. Although parents have no legal liability to maintain their children financially after the age of 16, in view of relatively high rates of youth unemployment in the 1980s there was a concern on the part of government to reduce the likelihood that young people would become a direct charge on the state. This has raised more generally the question of how young people should be supported once they have left full-time education if they are not in the labour market, what are the proper roles of parents and the state in their support, and how this all relates to the process of becoming a full adult member of society. Debates about these matters incorporate various assumptions about family obligations and responsibilities, especially between parents and adult children.

I shall begin this discussion by looking at some of the actual directions which state policies have taken in the 1980s in respect of young people's support. High rates of unemployment form the backcloth to this, and it is worth noting how young people have been affected, especially those who leave school with few or no qualifications. In 1975, 60 per cent of young people who left school at 16 went into employment. By 1987 this figure had fallen to 17 per cent; and even one year later only 44 per cent had obtained jobs (Roll, 1988). Clearly most young people now cannot expect to support themselves independently on the basis of wages. So can they then be supported? The obvious alternative is the means of support which is available to unemployed adults – social security benefits. There is actually an historic resistance to 'allowing' young able-bodied people to live independently solely from state benefits. For example, when the Unemployment Assistance Board relaxed its regulations a little in 1936, there were accusations that the Board was 'allowing young people to settle down on assistance and thereby become unemployable' (Deacon and Bradshaw, 1983, p. 25). The social security system was never designed as a separate means of income support for young people and even at its most generous it does not enable young people to become independent of their parents after leaving school. For example, 16-year-olds have never been allowed to claim more if they lived on their own and independently of their parents than their parents were entitled to claim for them if they remained in the parental home (Cusack and Roll, 1984, p. 5).

It has never been easy for young people to use state resources to live independently and various policy changes under way in the 1980s are having the effect of increasing these difficulties. Four particular measures stand out, all of them introduced between 1984 and 1988. First, changes in the supplementary benefit regulations introduced in 1984 meant that 16 and 17-year-olds living in the parental home and drawing supplementary benefit, would no longer be paid an extra allowance to cover housing costs (Cusack and Roll, 1984; Roll, 1988). In other words, it was assumed that all housing costs were being covered by their parents.

Second, some further changes introduced in supplementary benefit regulations in 1985 affected young people's right to claim board and lodging allowances. The aim of this change was to prevent young people living away from their parental home claiming allowances for board and lodgings at the cost they were actually paying. This followed press publicity about young people allegedly living in luxurious accommodation in places like holiday resorts, at public expense. The total costs of such payments had been rising steeply, and this attempt to restrict public expenditure applied to young people under the age of 26, except those who have children or have some other special circumstance such as a disability. Soon after the regulations were introduced, further exemptions were announced, including an exemption for young people living in the parental home, who were allowed to claim board and lodging allowance (House of Commons, vol. 81, 1984–5, cols 780–90). The initial aim of the regulations can be interpreted as an incentive for young people to remain in the parental home and a disincentive to become independent whilst relying on state benefits; in a sense the exemptions strengthened that.

Third, a rather different but equally significant measure concerns students. Changes announced in 1986 would mean that students in full-time education could no longer claim supplementary benefit for the Christmas and Easter vacations, although their entitlement to claim in the summer was not affected. At the time when this change was first considered, a spokesperson made it clear that the government believed it right for students to be supported by 'their families' during the vacation, if not by their own earnings (*Times Higher Education Supplement*, 7 June 1986).

Finally, the newly re-elected government brought forward proposals in 1988 which can be seen as a logical extension of their previous measures. These entail the complete removal of entitlement to receive state benefit (in the form of Income Support) from all 16 and 17-year-olds, with some rather limited exceptions. This was linked with a commitment to ensure that all young people in this age group who were neither in employment nor in full-time education would be guaranteed a place on a government training scheme, which carried a small 'training allowance'. These schemes in fact have proved rather un-popular with many young people (Roll, 1988). The assumption again is that parents rather than the state should be responsible financially for their young adult children in the last resort.

The implications of all four measures clearly is to remove the financial support for young people, and indeed the provision of their accom-modation, from a cost on the state to at least a partial cost upon parents. Another way of putting the same point is that there is an apparent attempt to shift upwards the age of economic 'adulthood', that is the age at which it is possible for all young people to be independent economically, irrespective of whether they have a job. These policies rely on the assumption that parents are – or perhaps more importantly that they ought to be – willing to give economic support to their young adult children if that is necessary. Again assumptions about the parent–child relationship, always at the heart of the concept of liability between relatives in British social policy, surfaces in a distinctive form in the particular circumstances of the 1980s. The rationale behind this kind of thinking has been articulated by Marsland who has argued that it is inappropriate to treat young people as adults until they are in their early twenties; they should not be given the means to live independently of their parents; if they leave home to seek work this should be for short periods and they should return to the parental base,

Young people need the support of their families and the family is seriously weakened as an institution if it loses its responsibility for young people. But genuine family responsibility for young people is make believe unless at least some of the costs of their care are shifted back from the state to the family. (Marsland, 1986, p. 94)

The theme of interdependence within the household obviously is also important in respect of these policies towards young people. I have noted already that changes in the supplementary benefit regulations assume that young adult children resident in the parental home should have their housing costs borne by their parents. Changes in the housing benefit regulations, introduced around the same time in 1984 actually make assumptions of support in the other direction. This particular change in the way in which parents are assessed when they claim housing benefit means that, if their adult children are earning wages, it is assumed that they are contributing towards rent from the age of 16, and that 18 to 20-year-olds (who previously were expected to pay a reduced contribution) are assumed to be paying the adult rent contribution to the parental household. As Cusack and Roll (1984) found in their small study of the effects of these changes, there is room for doubt about whether young people earning wages in this age group actually are earning enough to make such assumptions realistic. More importantly from the point of view of the present discussion, this change comes close to the type of household means test which was so disliked in the 1930s. In general, regulations which govern benefits do assume the interdependence of adults in households which contain young people, and this implies the sharing of resources. Such assumptions have been reinforced by the changes which have taken place in the 1980s.

In respect of the care of elderly people I made certain arguments about the effect of social policy assumptions upon potential supporters. These can be applied also to the case of financial support for young adults, with one minor modification. In this example we find again that sharing a household implies that one will give assistance; and again we see that the concept of liability to give support is concentrated in the parent–child relationship, although with parents rather than children the targets in this instance. The effect in this situation also is to put pressure upon target individuals to offer assistance even though there is no legal obligation so to do, and the choices available to both parties are thereby restricted.

How do people really handle all this in practice? We can see the message contained in social policies; we see that they may make life a bit more difficult for the children of the elderly and infirm or the parents of unemployed young adults, but do people really knuckle under and do what is expected of them? After all, legal sanctions apply only in very restricted circumstances and even then it may be possible to avoid the full force of the law. What effect do these external structures really have upon human action in this instance? In what sense do the law and social policy 'shape' obligations in practice? These are the issues to which I turn in the last section of this chapter, and they represent an important underlying theme in subsequent chapters.

## Impact of the law and social policy in practice

I suggested earlier in this chapter that we cannot 'read off' the impact of the law upon people's lives simply by knowing what the law says about family responsibilities and family support, because the application of the law is variable in practice. This comment applies with even more force to the kind of social policies which I have been discussing in the previous section, which are more vaguely formulated than the law. At the same time, I have also argued that the law and social policy do have an impact on people's individual commitments to members of their families, and to the support which is offered or withheld. Certainly governments have believed consistently that they are able to influence people's behaviour in this way, as I showed in the introduction to this book. Historically in Britain, governments have felt that it was properly their role to use the law and public policies to ensure that the whole population acknowledges in practice those family responsibilities which they deem to be natural or proper.

There is little empirical evidence which really would help us to understand how strongly people feel that there is an 'official' expectation that they will support their children financially or care for their elderly parents. And if indeed we are conscious of that, there is little research evidence which shows whether most of us accept it as inevitable, try to find ways round it, or feel able straightforwardly to reject it. I shall use what we do know to develop some tentative conclusions about the impact of the law and social policy in practice under three headings: the effects of legal definitions and sanctions; interactions with state agencies and welfare bureaucracies; public morality.

## Legal definitions and sanctions

At the simplest level one might expect that the law and administrative regulations, which are backed up by sanctions enforceable through the courts, would determine the support offered to relatives most directly. People are obliged to comply with the law because sanctions are brought against them if they do not. Thus legal structures have the capacity to determine patterns of support pretty straightforwardly. However, there is a problem about that interpretation. We need to know – and probably have no way of knowing – whether a particular person gave money to their children *because* the law required it or whether they would have behaved in this way in any case. This example illustrates a more general problem of interpretation of evidence about the impact of legal rules and sanctions.

Therefore, before looking at the effects of legal sanctions upon structures of family support, we need to consider a prior question: does the law change people's behaviour, or does it simply codify the dominant norms which most people would in any case comply with? We need an answer to that question in relation to specific legal requirements because certain laws may align more closely with dominant beliefs than others. We also need to locate such discussions in historical time, since laws which codified the dominant norms of a particular period may drift out of line with them several decades or centuries later. For the most part the kind of evidence needed to make such assessments does not exist. However, there is a prima facie case for arguing that assumptions about family obligations do not always simply codify what is already happening. Historically the whole purpose of the Poor Law was to ensure that people did acknowledge certain obligations which they might *not* have done otherwise. Furthermore, it is worth noting the fact that the assumptions about family obligations embodied in the law have changed very little over several centuries, despite the massive economic and demographic changes which have taken place and have affected the shape of the kin group as well as the material circumstances of people's lives (see ch. 3). This suggests that significant gaps may well have opened up at various points in time between what the law has expected and what people regarded as realistic and reasonable, in relation to their own circumstances.

To help us to sort out some of these difficult issues I shall return to two historical examples which are well documented. The first is the application of the Poor Law requirement to support elderly parents in the late nineteenth and early twentieth centuries. Although there were no changes in the letter of the law at this point, there is evidence of a notable tightening in the way it was applied. Reviewing the evidence about how the Boards of Guardians operated in this period, Anderson (1977) argues that some put considerable pressure on people to take an elderly relative into their home and thereby to maintain that person, when the relatives actually were unwilling to do this and where consequently considerable tensions were created within the household. In his view the law was attempting to enforce a model of one-sided obligation, in a situation where people's relationships with their kin depended upon the balance of *mutual* support. The effect of the application of the law upon people who regarded its particular version of family obligations as unreasonable was to create an incentive for people to 'lose touch' with their elderly relatives and thus to be inaccessible to such pressure. Given this background, when pensions were introduced in the early years of the twentieth century (see chapter 2) the effect was actually to strengthen rather than to weaken family ties, argues Anderson. Pensions removed the element of compulsion to give financial support to one's parents, and therefore enabled people to bring their family relationships back into line with the norm of mutual interdependence. As Anderson points out, this rather undermines the argument that family affection necessarily results in material support, and that enforcing support through the law helps to encourage 'natural' affection.

My second historical example is the introduction of the household means test for unemployed people in the 1930s. Here the situation is rather different in the sense that we are looking at the effects of introducing a new set of regulations to suit the particular economic circumstances of the inter-war period. As I have indicated, this was a very unpopular measure, and there was considerable concern at the time about its effects on family life (see for example, Bakke, 1933; Pilgrim Trust, 1935; Hannington, 1937). A key issue was precisely the one which Anderson has identified in respect of the Poor Law; namely that where there is a legal requirement to maintain a relative, and where people regard this as unreasonable and outside the structure of family responsibilities which they endorse, they will take evasive actions which result in the weakening of family ties.

In this instance, it was the young adult children of the unemployed who were most likely to take such action. This occurred because the household means test operated in such a way that adult children living in the household and earning a wage were expected to support their parents. This was a situation which many fathers clearly found unacceptable because of the continuing assumption that the male 'head of household' should be the family breadwinner. There was particular concern during the whole period about men who were long-term unemployed, although as Hurstfield (1986) has shown, the effects of unemployment upon women were equally severe. Some of the Public Assistance Committees tried to get round the problem of adult men being supported by their children by so-called 'dignity money', which meant that they did not apply the means test to the full household (Deacon and Bradshaw, 1983, p. 17). However, the system operated in such a way as to provide an incentive for young people to leave the parental home, since both they and their parents would be better off if they did. Unless there was some 'good' reason (for example, young women going into residential domestic service), leaving home was regarded as 'collusive desertion' by the Public Assistance Committees. It was seen to constitute a serious problem and was a matter of substantial public debate at the time, although as Crowther (1982) has pointed out, we do not have the evidence available at present to know on how large a scale this collusive desertion occurred, and we certainly do know that many young people did not leave home. But as writers at the time were quick to point out, the logic built into the system gave an incentive for co-resident relatives of the unemployed to leave the household, which made a nonsense of the overt justification of the scheme, namely increasing family solidarity (Cole and Cole, 1937, pp. 213–16).

The importance of both these historical examples to the present discussion lies not so much in knowing precisely how many people lost touch with relatives, or moved out of the parental home in order to avoid legal obligations to members of their family, as in the underlying social processes which they reveal. They point to the conclusion that it is possible for family obligations, as defined by the law, to drift seriously out of line with what many people regard as acceptable and reasonable. When that does happen, a likely outcome is that at least some of the people affected will take action to distance themselves from members of their family and thus avoid their legal obligations. Far from the law encouraging the development and continuance of supportive family ties, it has the effect of weakening relationships in these cases. The contemporary relevance of this is obvious. It is pertinent to ask whether the current attempt, through various social policy measures to strengthen structures of support within families, is likely to have the same effect. This issue will provide an important underlying theme in subsequent chapters.

### Interactions with state agencies and welfare bureaucracies

If the law provides a rather heavy-handed, and sometimes counter-productive, instrument for reinforcing particular definitions of family obligations, are there more subtle and possibly more effective means available? Such means perhaps can be found in the actions and decisions of people who work in and administer social and welfare services. As I noted earlier, the definition of who 'counts' as a liable relative (in an implicit rather than a legal sense) is left vague in most policy documents. This places the onus upon people such as social workers, doctors and wardens of old people's homes to interpret official expectations in particular circumstances. Is it actually through these pressures that social policy has its greatest impact upon individuals, especially in contemporary circumstances, where the law itself plays a relatively small part in defining obligations between adult kin?

Especially in times of economic stringency, it is officials and professionals who have the difficult task of implementing twin policy objectives which are often contradictory: to ensure that all citizens have their basic needs for money, shelter and personal care met, and at the same time to keep down public expenditure. In these circumstances it is almost inevitable that their actions in practice will endorse a broad rather than a narrow view of family obligations, since support by family members is one obvious way of resolving these two objectives. Certainly we know that this process occurred historically when, for example, officials administering the Poor Law began to put pressure on widows and elderly people to go and live with their kin, thus operating in effect a form of household means test which was not envisaged in the Poor Law and requiring support from certain relatives (especially married daughters) who were not legally liable (Anderson, 1977; Crowther, 1982). The administration of the Poor Law through day-to-day dealings between officials and individuals ensured that social policy in practice had a rather different shape from that embodied in the law, and the effect of this was significant for far more people than the law itself, since relatively few prosecutions were brought.

Although we have rather limited evidence about parallel situations today, there is no reason to suppose that similar processes do not occur. Professional workers act as gatekeepers for a whole range of public services for which demand exceeds supply, and they have high levels of discretion about whom they respond to and how they respond (Foster, 1983, pp. 78–80). We have little systematic empirical evidence about how professional workers actually operate in terms of family obligations when they put that discretion into practice, but if we look at the collective outcome of their decisions, we can see a pattern whereby certain people are more likely to get public services than others, and these decisions would appear to have been made on the basis of assumptions about who can rely on relatives. In particular, people who live with relatives are much less likely to receive various support services than those who live alone, especially services which other household members are presumed to be capable of providing. The available evidence suggests that, where a person has a severe disability which requires specialized nursing care, then their household arrangements do not seem to affect whether that service is provided for them.

But for services such as meals on wheels and home helps it is very different, as I have already noted: an elderly person who lives alone is many times more likely to receive them than one who lives with relatives (Parker, 1985). The assumption, one must presume, is that relatives in the same household can and will do the necessary cooking and cleaning.

This evidence about the outcome of decisions made by service providers suggests that, in their difficult choices about how to allocate scarce resources, they do make use of ideas about what relatives can be expected to do for each other. These ideas reflect assumptions made at the level of policy-making about who should take responsibility for whom, especially that relatives living in the same household should be reliable sources of practical assistance. Supporting evidence for this conclusion can be found in some studies which contain data on how social workers and other professionals actually handle their clients. Qureshi and Simons, in their study of people caring for elderly relatives, demonstrate that in general people allocate responsibilities for the care of an elderly person according to a hierarchy of obligations defined in genealogical terms: spouse has the strongest obligation, then daughters followed by daughters-in-law, then sons, then other relatives. If a person shares a household with a relative, this pushes them up the hierarchy to a higher place than they would otherwise have occupied (see chapter 1 for further discussion). The authors of this study argue that such views were 'widely and strongly held', not only among elderly people and their carers but also among professional workers; although it must be said that their data come from interviews with carers and not with professionals. It was the experience of carers that people such as social workers, health service personnel and police officers do make use of this hierarchy of obligations in order to persuade them to give assistance to their elderly relatives 'irrespective of the actual quality of the relationship between them' (Qureshi and Simons, 1987, p. 131). The hierarchy of obligations used by professionals reflects again the principle of support by other members of the household, and also is a very clear expression of the notion of 'liable relatives'.

We must conclude that the gate-keeping activities of professional workers and officials do constitute a mechanism which potentially is significant in defining the range of choices open to individuals who need support, or their relatives who are targets to provide it. But undoubtedly the impact differs. For that fortunate sector of the population with sufficient resources to purchase private care for an elderly or handicapped relative, or indeed for themselves, official definitions of family responsibilities are bound to have less relevance. If I can afford to pay for my own sheltered housing and nursing care in my old age, I will never need to meet a social worker or a doctor who has the power to grant or withhold a service which I need, or who will try to persuade me of the importance of family responsibilities; more importantly for this discussion, neither will my relatives.

## Social policy and public morality

The effect of the law and social policies on shaping family obligations in practice may well be most significant when it is at its least direct. In a society where there are a range of different (and sometimes conflicting) norms and values about family life, social policies represent a very public statement of a particular position which can potentially be backed up by sanctions and therefore it is likely that they occupy a distinctive role in shaping what is often referred to as 'the climate of opinion' (Study Commission on the Family, 1982). In this sense, the effect of social policy upon family obligations spreads much more widely among the population than simply to those people who have ever had dealings with public bureaucracies.

How far and in what ways do the assumptions incorporated in social policy have an effect of this type upon family obligations in practice? That question requires empirical evidence of a kind which is difficult to obtain and little of which is currently available. It also requires that we develop a conceptual model of how commonly held values and beliefs have an impact upon personal relationships. I shall attempt to develop such a model in chapter 6.

To anticipate the discussion there, I shall argue that the concept of 'public morality' provides a useful framework for understanding these phenomena. Briefly, this analysis suggests that people's presentation of themselves and their families to the outside world is shaped by their understanding of what are the dominant and acceptable public norms of family life. Since it is always safer 'not to challenge or violate public morality' (Voysey, 1975, p. 42) most people will seek to present their family relationships in a way which is consistent with it. Examples of people presenting their situations in this way can be found in a number of small-scale studies of people who care for elderly or infirm relatives. Consider, for example, the following three quotations taken from Clare Ungerson's study of women and men caring for a close relative,

It's the most natural thing in the world to do; she's my wife.

To me you look after your mum and dad . . . I couldn't do this sort of thing for anybody. To me it's family. I'm a *daughter*. It's family isn't it?

I suppose I've got a conscience. And it's the way I was brought up – you have a duty to help your relatives.

(Ungerson, 1987, pp. 86–94)

In each of these cases, the carer presents her or his situation in terms which show a consciousness of how their own family matches up to the publicly endorsed concept of 'the family', and how a proper family operates ('she's my wife'; 'it's the family'; 'a duty to help your relatives'). The implication is not necessarily that some deception is practised in the presentation of one's family life to the outside world, but that the version of family life which is embodied in the practice of official agencies plays an important part in shaping how people think about their own family life, and hence in how they actually conduct it.

In this sense the law and social policies, and their application in practice, have a significant effect on the social construction of reality in a given society. They may well be the most indirect but also the most pervasive way in which these public institutions influence private relationships among kin.

## Conclusion

In conclusion we can say that the law and public policies do have to be taken into account as an important part of the context in which people work out their commitments to their own families. They have been so in the past and they are in the present, despite the removal of legal sanctions associated with the Poor Law which attempted to enforce family responsibilities. Those legal sanctions always have been supplemented by the activities of professionals and officials. They have tried to exercise the responsibilities laid upon them (including the responsibility of keeping down the cost of public services) by going beyond what the law required, and by putting pressure upon people to acknowledge a particular version of family responsibilities, which accords with publicly endorsed ideas about what a normal family will do for its members. These ideas still reflect quite strongly the two principles which have been used historically to allocate family obligations through the law and public policies: the principle of mutual support within households, and the concept of liable relatives, focusing principally upon the mutual responsibilities of spouses and of parents and children. Where we find examples of pressure being brought to bear through public agencies in this way, it suggests that public definitions of family responsibilities may change the patterns of support which relatives actually give to each other, but that they do not necessarily alter straightforwardly the 'sense of obligation', or privately held definitions of what it is reasonable to expect.

I have argued that we need to take these processes into account when assessing how family obligations operate in practice, but the emphasis in this chapter has been upon the need for a rather complex view of how people actually respond to pressure from these sources. At one level, I have argued that the expectations embodied in public policies can and do drift out of line with what the majority of people regard as reasonable and proper in relation to their own families. Where that happens, there is evidence that many people try to take evasive action. Some people always will be able to do that more successfully than others and the people best placed to take evasive action are those whose social and economic position is relatively privileged. But in general it seems that policies which attempt to enforce family obligations through direct penalties and heavy sanctions are not necessarily very effective and indeed may be counter-productive. At another level, however, I have indicated that these publicly endorsed concepts of family obligations have a pervasive and indirect effect upon the way in which people think about their own family relationships, and in the end this may constitute their most significant impact on people's lives. I have suggested that the concept of public morality is a good way of understanding this, and I return to that issue in chapter 6.

This line of reasoning directs us back to the issues which I raised at the beginning of chapter 3, and which have recurred throughout these two chapters where I have been discussing the external contexts of family obligations, namely the way in which we should conceptualize the relationship between external structures and human agency. My line of argument certainly is in line with the view of Giddens (1979) that we should not see social structures as simply external to individuals, and having the effect of constraining human actions, but as used by human agents in constructing their own line of action. Although I have emphasized the ways in which the law and social policies have the effect of restricting the range of choices open to individuals, we can also see that people operate within and around those restrictions in their attempts to construct their own lives, and especially their own relationships with relatives. In the next two chapters, the focus shifts from these external contexts to human agents, and the processes whereby we work out our own commitments.

# 5

# The proper thing to do

## Introduction

In this chapter I switch the focus of discussion away from the social contexts of family support and onto individual human beings, attempting to work out their relationships with their own relatives. The emphasis is less on patterns of support which occur in practice (although this discussion must always be grounded in concrete examples) and more upon the underlying 'sense of obligation'. In what sense can we say that any practical and material support which we give to our relatives in the contemporary British context is grounded in feelings of duty, obligation or responsibility? More generally, what place should we accord to morality in understanding family relationships?

I shall argue that we need a subtle and complex view of how individuals operate in their own social worlds if we wish to understand how duty and obligation work within families. The idea that people recognize easily what their responsibilities are, and that most then simply carry them out, is certainly too crude. Even in societies where rights and responsibilities seem more clear-cut than in contemporary Britain, the reality is not like that. It is useful perhaps to consider an example from such a society to illustrate the complexities which we have to handle. In her discussion of ethnographic data from Tunisia (to which I referred in chapter 1), Cuisenier discusses the issue of inheritance and in particular the custom that women do not actually claim their share, although they are entitled to inherit along with their brothers under Islamic law. When they make such claims customarily this is regarded as scandalous, although brothers have no right to deny them in law. Cuisenier cites the account of one of her informants who discusses this,

It isn't that we do our sisters out of their rights. God has given them their share and it's unlawful to refuse them. It's out of solidarity that a girl marries and goes to live with her husband; she will be sheltered from need and will stop being dependent on her family when she becomes dependent on her husband. It's quite right she should give up the idea of doing her brothers out of their share and so making them a bit poorer. (Cuisenier, 1976, p. 142)

What does this example tell us about rights and duties within families? First, it shows that legal rights and obligations are not the same thing as the moral obligations in practice: brothers have the legal obligation to share inheritance with their sisters, but they think it wrong that they should be expected to do so in reality. Obligations can look quite unambiguous to an outsider but in practice there can be considerable room for manoeuvre. Second, people do not operate in a vacuum when they think about obligations and duties within their own families; they make an assessment of what would be the proper thing to do by considering the social and economic circumstances of the individuals involved. In the above example, whether you really should have to share your inheritance with your sister depends on her circumstances and yours: a woman who can be presumed to have an alternative form of support cannot really expect to deprive her brothers, whatever the law says. We see people using ideas about justice and fairness which are related to the life circumstances of each family member, and which operate independently of legally codified rights and duties. Third, it follows from this that it is perfectly proper to take your own interests into account when considering your responsibilities to your relatives; although in the Tunisian example it looks as if it is fine for men to act in a self-interested way but less fine for women. This brings us to the fourth point: the gender divisions seem to be a crucial element here, as in so many other aspects of family life. Rights, duties and obligations work differently for women and men in practice, and this is considered to be quite proper: a woman who tries to contravene this will be regarded as acting scandalously.

Although the details of this case clearly are rather different from the British context, it is useful to consider such an example as a way of reflecting upon the questions which we should be asking about our own more familiar arrangements. Even in a situation where rights and duties seem more fixed, we see that they are open to considerable negotiation in practice and that the outcome of those negotiations will be an interplay between, on the one hand, ideas about moral obligations derived from the wider culture, and, on the other hand, very personal assessments about the circumstances of one's own relatives.

In this chapter and the following one I shall explore the question of how obligations and duties towards one's relatives operate in the British context. I shall look at the issue from two different angles which complement rather than contradict each other. I shall suggest that there are two different ways of looking at family obligations – as normative guidelines and as negotiated commitments – which together present a rounded picture of how people act towards their relatives in practice. The idea that family obligations can be understood as normative guidelines, the subject of this chapter, focuses mainly on how the content of obligations is defined, while the next chapter is concerned with how people put obligations and responsibilities into practice. Both discussions draw upon the descriptive accounts of support between family members given in chapter 1.

## The idea of normative guidelines

In previous chapters I have made extensive use of words like duty, obligation and responsibility to refer to those features of family relationships which I wish to explore. My choice of words is deliberate and reflects the language commonly used in everyday life – if not always the actual words, then certainly the ideas to which they refer. They are words which refer to a moral component in relationships and imply that what people actually do is governed quite significantly by beliefs about 'the proper thing to do'.

This is the place to explore more fully the meaning of such ideas. Although much of this chapter will be concerned with the actual content of the underlying principles upon which family obligations are based, I shall begin with a more abstract consideration of the words and the concepts which we need to develop this kind of discussion. The questions which I shall pose include: Can we say that there are moral rules which direct people towards the proper or correct way to treat their relatives? Is there a consensus about what constitutes correct behaviour? Can we explain people's actions towards their relatives by saying that they are following these moral rules? What is a 'moral' rule? Is 'rule' the best word anyway; would 'norms' or 'guidelines' be better?

In developing this discussion I shall draw upon a range of debates in philosophy and social science which consider questions about how far human actions can be seen as stemming from moral considerations, and whether these are produced by forces internal or external to the individual. Such complex issues merit more extensive treatment than I can give them here. They go to the heart of certain central questions which social theorists have tried to resolve, about how far human beings can be seen as taking autonomous, independent actions and how far we are constrained by social forces. As Philip Abrams put it in his discussion of the common ground between history and sociology,

[The problem] is easily and endlessly formulated but, it seems, stupefyingly difficult to resolve. People make their own history – but only under definite circumstances and conditions; we act through a world of rules which our own action creates, breaks and renews – we are creators of rules, the rules are our own creations; we make our own world – the world confronts us as an implacable and autonomous system of social facts. The variations of the theme are innumerable. (Abrams, 1982, p. xiv)

As I indicated in chapter 3, one of the most influential formulations of this issue in recent years is Giddens's discussion of the relationship between social structure and human agency. In that discussion, he accords a central place to norms and obligations in social life, which he sees as necessarily built into all human interactions. The social order, which facilitates human interaction, is built upon normative concepts: in a given set of circumstances some people have legitimate rights, others have obligations, and so on. But that social order has to be 'sustained and reproduced in the flow of social encounters' (Giddens, 1979, p. 86). Where people act purposefully and strategically in their encounters with others – for example if I try to ensure that my brother sees the financial support of our parents as his responsibility rather than mine – this represents, in Giddens's terms, an attempt to 'mobilize obligations' through the responses of other people. I am drawing on my understanding of the legitimate social order, and thereby helping to reproduce it, but in terms of direct consequences for myself I am making specific claims about which rights and obligations are going to be recognized in this particular situation.

I make no claims to advance these theoretical debates at a general level. But I find them helpful in suggesting ways in which we can understand how family obligations operate in reality. I shall draw on them in the course of this chapter and the next. To begin this discussion of the concepts of duty, obligation and responsibility in families I shall consider a number of contrasts which are built into relevant debates, under five headings.

## Describing and prescribing

The first set of contrasts need not detain us too long because the point is fairly straightforward, although it is important to make it explicit. The contrasts here are:

> Behavioural regularities vs Normative rules
> Is vs Ought.

The central issue to which these contrasts refer concerns how we interpret observed behaviour. If we observe as a matter of fact that most people do try to give assistance to their aged parents, should we conclude therefore that there is an underlying moral rule which prescribes that such assistance should be given? Put like that, it is obvious that observing a 'behavioural regularity' does not necessarily imply a 'normative rule'. There are other possible explanations of why people might assist their parents, for example that they do it because they hope to inherit goods or property when the parents die. In effect, I have been using this distinction between behavioural regularities and normative rules in earlier chapters when I have talked about actual patterns of support on the one hand and the 'sense of obligation' on the other. It is actually quite easy to fall into this particular trap of confusing the two in empirical research on family relationships, since it is usually rather difficult to get information directly about the underlying normative rules (if they exist), and in the absence of such information it is tempting for researchers to take the evidence of observed behavioural regularities to imply that certain normative rules do exist (Schneider, 1968, p. 6).

In moral philosophy similar issues are dealt with by developing the distinction between 'is' and 'ought' and through debates about whether 'ought' can ever be derived from 'is'. These debates as such need not be considered here. Understanding the 'ought' component in family obligations is not a matter of what is possible in terms of logical arguments, but whether in practice people do derive prescriptions about what 'ought' to happen from their observations about what generally does happen. Put like that, the matter is quite complex since one of the grounds upon which people justify their own actions is that they are only doing (or not doing) the same as most other people. Although probably most people would accept that a particular action is not *necessarily* right or wrong just because everyone does it, the fact that it is commonplace does change the nature of an individual moral decision about whether or not to do it.

The fact that people do sometimes derive 'ought' from 'is' in practice can be seen by considering the kind of decision faced by a daughter who has elderly and infirm parents and also a full-time job. In such circumstances it is known that many women consider giving up their jobs, and some decide to do so. If a woman does give up her job to care for her parents she will receive public endorsement for having acted appropriately, although the same would not necessarily apply to a son who made such a decision (Finch and Groves, 1980; Groves and Finch, 1983). Women who wish to stay in employment are vulnerable to pressure on the grounds that many other women do give up their jobs: it is the common response to parental need, therefore it is what a particular individual ought to do. Examples of women who have experienced such pressures can be found in Lewis and Meredith's study of daughters who have cared for their mothers. One said that she was 'adamant' about not giving up her job and thought that she was 'completely justified in standing my ground' when under pressure to do so, indicating by the strength of her language that she did find it difficult to resist the expectation that this is a reasonable thing to do. Another interviewee challenged the assumption that this is the kind of sacrifice which should be made by women rather than men.

My brother suggested to me. He suggested I give up my job. I said, why don't you give up your job? (Lewis and Meredith, 1988, p. 78)

Although not articulated directly by the interviewees in this example, one can see that the dilemma posed derives partly from the conflation of 'is' and 'ought'. Because many women *do* give up their jobs to care for a parent, it becomes easier for brothers, social workers, and whoever else makes an intervention in a particular case, to say that a particular woman *should* do so. Possibly in a logical sense 'ought' cannot be derived from 'is', but in reality people act as if there is *some* relationship between the two. The question of what precisely is that relationship in a given set of circumstances is one of the many interesting empirical questions which one can ask about family obligations in practice.

## The scope of normative guidelines

The contrasts which I shall deal with here are an overlapping set which derive in the first instance from moral philosophy:

Absolute vs Relative
Abstract vs Concrete
Universal vs Situational

The point here is really about the scope of normative rules or guidelines, and whether they can be said to apply equally in all circumstances. Would I be willing to allow my 25-year-old son to live rent-free in my house if he did not have a job? Only if he was trying hard to get a job? Would it matter to me how he lost his previous job? Or would I feel that children should be able to rely on their parents when they need to whatever other circumstances obtain? Again, I am less interested in the detail of philosophical debates than in using the contrasting concepts to help develop our understanding of how people perceive the nature of normative rules in practice. Do people espouse certain clear and absolute rules which they would consider it wrong to breach in any circumstances? (Whether in practice they do sometimes breach them is a separate issue to which I shall return.) Do people think about family obligations in terms of abstract principles, or alternatively as concrete rules about particular relationships? Do people consider that there are certain rules which apply to everyone in all circumstances, or that the right thing to do has to be worked out separately in each situation?

Empirical studies of family relationships do not give clear answers to these questions, since different writers interpret their findings in different ways. One strand of thought can be illustrated by work which derives from social psychology, in the tradition represented by Argyle and Handerson (1985). They review empirical material on family relationships taken from a number of different societies and use it to itemize 'rules' of relationships. They see the obligation to help kin as a strong example of such rules, and say that there are certain basic rules which seem to apply cross-culturally: you should be prepared to help kin when they need it, beyond the assistance that you would give to friends or neighbours; you should be prepared particularly to help your own children and your parents. Although in fact much of the data which they consider concerns what I have called behavioural regularities rather than normative prescriptions, Argyle and Henderson offer an interpretation which sees certain rules of kin relationships as widely (perhaps universally) applicable, and not depending upon the details of a particular situation. A similar line of reasoning, although with quite different intellectual foundations, can be found in the work of those socio-biologists who argue that the foundations of kin support are genetic and therefore universal (see chapter 7 for further discussion).

A contrasting approach can be found in the work of Douglas on the meaning and use of social rules. His view is that moral rules in social life are relative not absolute, and that the meaning of those rules can be understood only in relation to situations where they are put to use. Although he does not deny that people do understand moral rules in an abstract as well as a 'situated' sense, he argues that philosophers of all traditions have rather missed the point by analysing moral rules solely in terms of abstract generalizations. The point that they miss is that people's experience of moral rules in practice is essentially problematic: we regularly disagree with each other – perhaps even with ourselves – about the right thing to do in particular circumstances; we find it difficult in practice to work out what is the moral or ethical intent of someone else's statement or action (Douglas, 1971, pp. 135–9). This problematic nature of moral rules is an unavoidable and a necessary part of human societies for two reasons. First, the whole point about moral responsibility is that it must be possible for a person to take several different courses of action: for a decision to be a *moral* one, it has to be problematic. Second, the concrete situations in which decisions are located are themselves complex and changing, so decisions about the proper course of action cannot be pre-programmed (ibid. pp. 167–9).

One does not have to agree with the detail of Douglas's position to accept the force of his argument that, when we look at how moral rules operate in practice, we are struck by the importance of situation and context in understanding why particular rules or norms operate when they do. Philosophers in fact are not blind to these distinctions in quite the way that Douglas implies. There is a well established contrast in moral philosophy between 'autonomous' morality (which concerns matters of principle which are universal and generalizable) and 'social' morality which derives from the way that people live their lives. A key feature of the latter is that a particular action may not be considered wrong in itself, but becomes wrong because of the consequences which it has in particular circumstances (Baier, 1970).

The principle use of these debates in developing an understanding of family obligations and responsibilities, is to raise certain questions which require an empirical answer: How far do people treat moral issues in their family relationships as matters which have to be worked out in particular situations, rather than matters of generalizable principle? Are there any guidelines at all which are regarded as matters of general principle and not subject to pressures of circumstance?

### The source of the guidelines

The main contrasts here are:

> Individual morality vs Social morality
> Internal constraints vs External constraints

There is an obvious contrast in ideas about the source of moral rules which, to put it simplistically, is: Does each individual make up the rules for her/himself, or do we simply follow the rules imposed upon us within the society in which we live? Put like that, it seems obvious that there are elements of both the individual and the social in the way that people's moral actions should be understood.

That conclusion perhaps is more obvious to a sociologist interested in what happens in practice than to a moral philosopher, especially one concerned with the long-standing debates about reasoning and rationality as the basis for moral actions. Halsey, commenting as a sociologist upon that tradition, argues that although reasoning plays some part the values which an individual adheres to cannot be understood solely in those terms. Custom, convention and upbringing are other key elements, so that 'most people, for most of the time, take morals as given from their social surroundings' (Halsey, 1985, p. 7). Whilst Halsey is careful to point out that he does not imply any particular theory of social causation by this observation, the issues raised here do relate to the very long-standing debate in social science about how far individuals can be said to internalize social rules, and under what circumstances they can reject them – the issues which I referred to at the beginning of this chapter, quoting from Abrams and from Giddens.

Again, the main point which I want to take from these debates is not to argue conclusively for a particular theoretical position, but to indicate that they raise important empirical questions. In this case it can be expressed in the form: In practice do people go along with socially accepted moral rules in family relationships? In what circumstances do people want to derive their own guidelines on some other basis, such as rationality? When and where do conflicts arise between these two elements in morality, and how are they dealt with? I began to consider these questions in chapter 4, in relation to the impact of the law and public policies on the ways in which people think about their own family responsibilities. However, these are not the only source of the 'social' element in morality.

It is important also to link these questions to another: in practice how far do people perceive that clear moral rules exist which are socially derived? I shall return to this issue in the next chapter, but it is worth noting here that we do have evidence to suggest that people may not always have a clear idea of what is the socially approved moral position in many circumstances, or they may feel that different rules apply to different groups in society (say, different social classes). Bott, in her discussion of the norms of family life based upon intensive study of 20 couples, suggests that there are very few items which would count as what she calls 'norms of common consent', that is, prescriptive statements upon which most of her respondents do in fact agree. But there are many circumstances in which people's ideas about 'social norms' influence what they do. Her use of the term social norms refers here to items about which people *think* that there is agreement among the relevant social group. This does not mean that agreement *does* exist necessarily: often in fact it does not (Bott, 1957, p. 197). So when we ask questions about how far people's actions are shaped by considerations of socially approved morality, we need to understand what a particular individual actually perceives that morality to be – which may not be the same thing as a normative consensus on a particular matter which could be demonstrated empirically.

### Application of the guidelines

The next set of contrasts to which I refer concerns the application of rules or guidelines for conduct. I shall consider questions about application more extensively in the next chapter, but I raise them here in a preliminary way because questions of how the rules get applied affect our understanding of what we mean when we talk about moral rules, norms or guidelines. The contrasts which I shall consider are:

> Beliefs vs Actions
> Rules vs Guidelines

The idea of moral norms or rules encompasses both beliefs in an abstract sense and actions which are based on those beliefs. The relationship between beliefs and actions is particularly important if one is interested in how family obligations and duties operate in practice, and that relationship is not necessarily straightforward.

There are a number of reasons for this, the most important of which is that we need to select and apply relevant rules in any given situation. For example, I noted in chapter 1 that relationships between siblings in adult life seem to operate on the basis of reciprocity: when support is given, it must be repaid in a fairly obvious way. Suppose that I have a relationship with my sister where we have each given the other various types of assistance over the years. One day she arrives on my doorstep saying that she has been made homeless through non-payment of rent. Does the principle of reciprocity operate straightforwardly here, so that I offer her a temporary home whatever disruption it causes? Do I only offer it if I have plenty of space in the house? Do I have to consider how other members of my household will feel about it? Would it make a difference if she had been made homeless for a different reason, let us say, walking out on a violent marriage? In this example, the principle of reciprocity is only one of the possible guidelines for my action, and I need to decide whether it is the appropriate one in *this* set of circumstances. Moral philosophers commonly recognize that there is an important difference between endorsing or justifying a particular moral rule in general terms, and justifying a particular action based upon that rule (Rawls, 1967; Wallace and Walker, 1970; Warnock, 1971). We are not necessarily talking here about inconsistency between principles and practice: it is perfectly possible to agree with a rule in general terms, but believe that it is not relevant to particular circumstances, or to believe that it does not apply to myself for particular reasons. In addition there is the possibility that several different rules, all of which I endorse in general terms, could apply potentially to a given situation although each of them suggests a different line of action. Empirical evidence about family life suggests that situations do arise where people need to select relevant rules, sometimes where different rules conflict with each other.

The most obvious examples of conflicting rules concern situations where a person feels torn between their responsibilities to one person and equally pressing responsibilities to someone else. For example, one of the interviewees in Lewis and Meredith's study spoke very directly about the emotional difficulties she experienced in 'having to choose between one kind of duty and another kind of duty', in her case between her duty to her mother who needed full-time care, and her duty to her children who needed the income from her employment. Although on one level she wants to insist that the children should take precedence, it is clear also that she finds the conflicts very difficult to handle,

Someone said I should have given up my job and looked after my mother . . . I said, well I have three young children and if I give up work my children would miss a lot . . . [I had to] choose between one kind of duty and another kind of duty. That was very difficult. I had to choose to let her go [into a home]. (Lewis and Meredith, 1988, p. 78)

This is just one example which could be replicated across a number of studies.

In the next chapter I shall return to this issue of selecting and applying moral rules and I shall argue that it is central to understanding how family obligations operate in practice. I have mentioned these matters briefly here because they help us to sort out what we mean by 'rules' of morality. The considerations which I have elaborated above should, I think, lead us to reject the use of the word rules in a strong sense – that is, meaning clear and specific prescriptions for action, which remove the element of individual judgement from a situation by specifying in advance what is going to be done (Warnock, 1971, p. 65). The idea of rules in this sense is probably applicable, if at all, to a very restricted range of circumstances in family life; although in relation to any empirical example it is worth asking the question: are there *any* situations in which the honouring of family obligations can be understood as simply rule-following behaviour in this strong sense?

More promising in terms of its analytical potential is a weaker use of the concept of rules, which can be highlighted by the distinction between rule-governed and rule-guided behaviour. This is a distinction which derives from, for example, the writing of Douglas (1971) and has been usefully applied to family relationships by Sarah Cunningham-Burley (1985) in her work on grandparenthood. She wishes to retain the word 'rules' to denote that external constraints are important in a person's negotiation of the role of grandparent, but she argues that actions are rule-guided rather than rule-governed, because people elaborate and apply their own understanding of the appropriate behaviour for grandparents in concrete circumstances.

If the notion of moral rules is to be used in relation to family obligations, I suggest that it is usually most appropriate to use it in this weaker sense, in which actions are seen to be 'guided' by rules, but not 'governed' by them. It could be argued that the use of the word rules is not really appropriate, if people in practice have to take an active part in actually working out what to do in specific situations. Indeed, I think that there is a case for suggesting that the concept of 'norms' is more appropriate than rules, in that it refers by implication to behaviour which is expected, but not required in quite the same sense that a rule requires compliance. Also the concept of norms places the issue firmly in the realm of moral values and beliefs. Alternatively, it could be suggested that, since behaviour for the most part is rule-guided not rule-governed, the rather weaker concept of 'guidelines' for action might be appropriate, making more explicit the idea that people do have a good deal of flexibility about how these guidelines are applied. In fact my own preference is for the use of the term 'normative guidelines', and that preference is strengthened by a consideration of the type of guidelines which operate in the sphere of family obligations.

### What type of guidelines are they?

In this final set of contrasts, and building upon the preceding discussion, I shall consider the nature of the rules or guidelines about family obligations, especially the question: What kind of advice or prescriptions are contained in these guidelines? The contrasts with which I am working are:

> Rules vs Principles
> General advice vs Detailed prescriptions
> Hierarchy of priorities vs Parallel sets of values

I have already noted, for example on the basis of Bott's (1957) work, that in family life there appear to be very few issues upon which there is a clear consensus at a general level about the right thing to do. It follows from this that there are few guidelines of the type which give detailed specifications for appropriate action. This conclusion is borne out in the empirical work of Firth, Hubert and Forge on middle-class family relationships where they show that the concepts of duty and responsibility are very important in the way that people understand their own family relationships. However, as they put it, whilst there are general standards of conduct which apply to kin relationships, there are no rules about putting into effect these notions of responsibility, so that an individual has to make choices about how to respond when a relative needs specific assistance (Firth, Hubert and Forge, 1970, pp. 451–2). A more recent empirical illustration of the lack of detailed guidelines for appropriate action can be found in the work of Allatt and Yeandle (1986) on the family relationships of young people who are unemployed. They argue that a central guiding principle upon which parents in these families operate is the idea of 'fairness', a principle which is deeply embedded in family life, but which needs to be brought to the surface and re-interpreted to suit the particular circumstances. In particular, parents regularly had to reconsider questions of how much money should be taken from and given to a young employed member of the household, so that the situation could be demonstrated as complying with the principle of fairness to all parties.

The general point I would take from these empirical examples is that the nature of the advice available to an individual in these guidelines about family relationships and responsibilities remains at the most general level, and in no sense does it give detailed specifications for action. Further, the guidelines seem to be less to do with specifying what actual actions are right or wrong, and more concerned with giving criteria which can be used to work out what would be right or wrong in particular circumstances.

This second – and very important – point can be developed further by introducing the work of some feminist writers who have considered the differences between women and men in the way they handle moral claims upon them. From the perspective of a moral philosopher, Noddings has argued that women do not approach moral problems in the same way as men: they do not order priorities hierarchically and they do not discuss such issues in terms of abstract principle. Rather, when faced with a moral dilemma, women tend to ask for more information about the situation and see it as a concrete problem to be resolved, not as an abstract dilemma to be settled by reasoning. Noddings is careful to point out that she is not suggesting that women are unable to arrange principles hierarchically or to derive logical conclusions, but that 'they see this process as peripheral to or even irrelevant to moral conduct' (Noddings, 1984, p. 96). Drawing rather similar conclusions, but arriving at them via her empirical work as a social psychologist, Carol Gilligan (1982) has argued that women's approach to morality is different from men's and specifically that the idea of moral 'rules' really does not work for women. Women's morality, she argues is situationally and contextually based and they are much less likely than men to fall back upon moral rules of a generalizable and abstract kind. When faced with moral dilemmas in which there are conflicting claims or considerations, men and boys tend to respond by developing a set of rules which will secure a just or fair outcome, and this often entails prioritizing claims. Women and girls, by contrast, will try to resolve the situation in such a way that no one gets hurt, if necessary themselves making a sacrifice rather than expecting that of other people.

The question of whether men's and women's morality in fact does differ in these ways is a question which requires further empirical work and I shall pursue that later in this chapter. I raise the distinction here, however, to highlight the general point that the nature of the advice contained in guidelines for moral action is such that it leaves room for women and men to take quite different messages from it, and to make use of the guidelines in quite different ways. The feminist philosopher

Jean Grimshaw who builds upon the work of Noddings and Gilligan, makes a useful distinction between rules and principles which, in my view, considerably advances the argument at this point. In her usage, a 'rule' is a guideline for conduct which eliminates, or at least minimizes, the need for reflection and judgement in particular situations; whereas a 'principle' specifically invites reflection rather than blocking it. Principles, she suggests, are best expressed in the form 'Consider . . .' (the effect which your actions will have upon other people; whether other people's needs should outweigh your own etc.). In her view, the contribution of Noddings and Gilligan would be assisted by making this distinction (Grimshaw, 1986, p. 207).

It seems to me that this distinction between rules and principles is very useful and applies much more generally than to the question of gender differences. In using the concept of 'normative guidelines' I wish to imply hereafter that guidelines should be understood as principles rather than as rules. This definition supports other lines of argument which I have been developing in this discussion. Warnock, for example, suggests that acting upon moral beliefs is not a case of accepting moral rules, but more of 'recognizing or accepting some range or variety of reasons for judging' the appropriate course of action (Warnock, 1971, p. 70). Douglas, who comes from quite a different intellectual tradition, nonetheless reaches rather similar conclusions when he writes, 'social rules are the criteria that normal members of the society are expected to make use of in deciding what to do in any situation for which they are seen as relevant' (Douglas, 1971, p. 141).

To summarize, this perspective suggests that we might expect to find that the principles reflected in normative guidelines about family obligations have the following characteristics: general rather than detailed; concerned with criteria for judgement rather than specifications for action. In other words, it makes sense of available empirical data to say that these guidelines are concerned with *how you work out* the proper thing to do in given circumstances, rather than *specifying what* you should do. It is important to have further research which tests this analysis systematically.


### Normative guidelines for family obligations

In the second part of this chapter, I move on to consider what the normative guidelines for working out obligations to kin actually are. I shall be building upon the preceding discussion about the nature of such guidelines and how they operate, both in this chapter and the next. I have chosen to focus here upon five normative guidelines which I consider the most important ones in relation to family obligations, on the basis of existing evidence.

### The principle of selection: i) who is this person?

In deciding whether to offer assistance to a particular person, or in working out whether I can expect that person to offer assistance to me, a prime consideration is my relationship with him or her, in both senses of that word. On the one hand, there is the question of where we each stand in a genealogical sense; on the other hand, there is the question of how well or badly we get along on a personal level. This distinction between the structural and the personal relationships – of course intimately intertwined in practice – is a longstanding one in social science even if it is not used as much as it should be in contemporary writing on the family, as Bulmer (1985) has suggested. I shall argue that my 'relationship' to other people, in both senses, underscores some of the most important normative guidelines for support between kin. I begin in this section with the structured elements of relationships, arguing that the principle of selection operates, so that my obligation to give support to a relative is stronger or weaker, depending upon that person's position in my kin network. When faced with a concrete decision about whether to give assistance, the first question to be asked is: who is this person?

The necessity for making this kind of selection flows from the fact that the rules of British kinship are 'permissive' not 'obligatory' (Allan, 1979), which means that an individual is obliged to select which shall be honoured. However, the selection should not be wholly open and idiosyncratic. There are guidelines for working out whose claims are strong and whose weaker. The clearest empirical support for this idea in recently produced work comes from Qureshi's study of the family care of elderly people, where the data demonstrate a 'hierarchy of obligations', as I indicated when I discussed this study in chapter 1 (Qureshi and Simons, 1987; Ungerson, 1987).

Most of the existing empirical evidence does not give such clear guidance on the prioritizing of claims as does this work. There is a problem common to many studies in this field, in that an insufficiently clear distinction is made between 'is' and 'ought', so that much of the evidence is actually about what happens in practice rather than the moral question of what ought to happen. In so far as any hierarchical priorities are established clearly, they usually focus upon the nuclear rather than the extended family. That is, one's spouse and immature children always 'count' as the closest circle of family between whom assistance should be shared (Firth, Hubert and Forge, 1970). These are the relationships which are not my specific concern in this book, but they are an essential part of the total picture when one is considering the broader issues of obligations to kin and how they are prioritized.

*Genealogical principles* In chapter 1, I reviewed much of the evidence necessary to answer questions about how the principles of selection operate. I suggested that in the context of the white majority in Britain, kin relationships can be seen as a series of concentric circles, of which the outermost circle is not relevant for a kin support discussion since it contains relatives with whom one has no contact, although their existence is known of, and usually their names. Some obligations seem to be acknowledged in respect of kin in the two other circles, with obligations to people who fall in the inner circles being more extensive than to those in the outer. The identity of kin falling into these inner and outer circles cannot be predicted solely on the basis of genealogical relationship, but apparently people always count their spouses and children as part of this 'close family' and most people count their parents. It is quite common to include grandchildren, but less common to count grandparents as close kin (Bott, 1957; Firth, Hubert and Forge, 1970; Morgan, 1975). The situation of various ethnic minority groups living in Britain is different, with a greater likelihood that more people will be included in the inner circle, extending quite often to cousins and in-laws.

So far as evidence on the dominant culture of the white majority is concerned, there seem to be various principles of selection which have the effect of designating the relatives to whom one has the strongest obligations. First, there is the principle that one's own kin are favoured over one's spouse's, despite the fact that this kinship system is bilateral in the sense that married couples recognize the relatives of both *as* kin. But when it comes to matters of duty, with the exception of the spouse themselves, obligations seem to operate most strongly in relation to one's own direct kin, both ascendent and descendent (Argyle and Henderson, 1985, p. 223). Assistance may be given to the close relatives of one's spouse, but there is some evidence that this is seen as helping your spouse to meet his or her own obligation, as I indicated in chapter 1. After the death of a spouse people feel a less clear sense of obligation to the spouse's kin (Firth, Hubert and Forge, 1970, pp. 95–111). The second underlying principle of selection is that lineal links are stronger than lateral ones (La Fontaine, 1985, p. 54). Most obviously this means that duties towards one's parents and children are much stronger than towards brothers and sisters. Although quite a lot of assistance passes between brothers and sisters in practice (especially between sisters), there is not the same underlying sense of obligation as occurs in assistance between parents and children (Argyle and Henderson, 1985, p. 220). The third principle which one can see in operation is that lineal ties of obligation apply particularly to one generation in each direction, but much more ambiguously thereafter. There may be an obligation to keep in contact across three or four generations, but less of a clear obligation to give assistance (Bott, 1957; Schneider, 1968).

Finally, there is the principle that people in the same genealogical position should be treated similarly. The best example probably is siblings, so that most obviously in the case of inheritance, there is an expectation that all children will be treated 'alike'. As I noted in my discussion of inheritance in chapters 1 and 2, this idea is of early nineteenth-century origin and grew to serve the growing entre-preneurial classes. The early, aristocratic tradition was to favour one child, typically the eldest son, over the rest. It may be that fragments of this can still be traced in British kin relationships, but for the most part the idea of equivalent treatment for people in equivalent positions seems to hold good. However, there sometimes is room for ambiguity about whether two positions are indeed equivalent, for example whether grandchildren should acknowledge equivalent obligations to their maternal and parental grandparents. Remarriage and the introduction of step relationships into a kin network also can produce ambiguities about whether the step-relative counts as equivalent to the corresponding blood relationship, as I indicated in my discussion of these issues in chapter 1.

Collectively these principles seem to define which genealogical relationships imply the stronger obligations and which the weaker, although they are principles which leave room for competing obligations even within the inner circle of close kin. Where such conflicts occur there seems to be a tendency to favour the marriage relationship and the decendent generation (that is, spouses and children) but there are no clear-cut rules and these are situations which commonly are treated as tricky to resolve. I shall draw an empirical example of such a situation from Mansfield and Collard's (1988) study of the early years of marriage. It is an example which concerns the anxieties of a young wife that her husband was continuing to give his own mother a considerable amount of emotional and moral support in a way which he had done before their marriage. She was especially worried about the way her husband had been used as his mother's sole support during the time when she thought that an unmarried daughter was pregnant, an anxiety which she had not mentioned to her own husband. The way in which the interviewee talks about this makes it clear that she found the situation very difficult to handle, that it was very difficult to tell her husband that he should *not* be supportive to his mother, but nonetheless she felt a conflict of interest with her mother-in-law which should have been resolved in her own favour:

We had an argument about it – that was when I sort of had a go at him, saying that his mother would have to learn to – she would have to go to his father, you know, she couldn't keep coming to Keith all the time. (Mansfield and Collard, 1988, p. 96)

In this case, although there is an expectation on one level that the parent has less strong claims to support once their child is married, it is also clear that making such principles stick within the inner circle of kin is not a straightforward matter.

It is also important to note that boundaries are not fixed and it is quite possible for people who normally would be regarded as distant to get redefined as close kin. The effect is to create stronger mutual obligations than one would predict just from their genealogical position. There are two particular circumstances in which this commonly arises, one of which is the sharing of households. Evidence from recent studies of the care of elderly people suggest that they expect to, and do in practice, turn in the first instance to other members of their household when they need practical support (Wenger, 1984; Qureshi and Simons, 1987).

The other situation in which more distant kin get drawn into the inner circle is through a process of substitution, as I indicated in chapter 1. Again, the evidence for this comes mainly from studies of elderly people. Where they have never had children, for example, or where their children have already died or perhaps have emigrated, there seems to be a tendency for close bonds, involving obligations to provide assistance, to be formed with more distant kin such as nephews or nieces who, as it were, take the place of a child (Allan, 1983; Wenger, 1984). In such situations it may not be obvious to an outsider why, for example, one particular niece has taken on a great level of responsibility for an elderly aunt than have others although there is some evidence that this may be a consequence of their respective positions in the kin network as a whole. Firth, Hubert and Forge (1970, p. 390) give the example of one of their interviewees who felt some responsibility for her mother's sister, because when her own parents had been alive they had been close and had taken some responsibility for the management of the aunt's affairs. Once her parents were dead, the niece felt that she 'inherited' that responsibility. In this kind of example, it seems that a commitment to give support is really explained by the existence of a third person, who forms the genealogical link between the two parties. Assistance is given 'for the sake of' or 'in the place of' that third party, in a rather similar way to the support which passes between in-laws (see chapter 1).

*Gender as a cross-cutting principle*   In this discussion about principles of selection my emphasis has been upon genealogical relationships. But there is also the issue of gender, which appears to cut across the other principles. So, for example, we need to modify the observation that the parent–child relationship forms the clearest case of family duty, by distinguishing between sons and daughters, and between mothers and fathers. The precise form which 'duty' takes in these cases will also vary with ethnicity (as indicated in chapter 1).

The question which I am concerned with here is not so much about patterns of kin support in practice, but whether it can be said that women have a clearer, or a different, sense of obligation towards their relatives than do men. This theme comes across strongly in Ungerson's study of a small number of women and men who were caring for an infirm relative. In a discussion entitled 'Men's love, women's duty' she argues that the distinction between love and duty is the key distinguishing characteristic between men and women, when they explain the reasons why they are providing personal care for a relative. Whilst women sometimes talked about love and affection as well as duty, 'the word "duty" never crossed the lips of any of the men.' The women meanwhile quite often spoke in terms like 'one has a responsibility to one's family' or 'you have a duty to help your relatives' (Ungerson, 1987, pp. 91–4). This kind of evidence supports Graham's

(1985) observation that a sense of responsibility forms the 'central motif' of women's accounts of caring for their relatives.

Ungerson's work is relatively unusual in that she makes visible these questions about obligation and duty, and treats them separately from support which is actually given. In many other studies there are problems about using the data in a discussion about responsibilities and duties, because the fact that support passes is taken to mean that a sense of obligation is present. In other words, there is a tendency to derive 'ought' from 'is' in an inappropriate way. However, Ungerson's study is on a very small scale and clearly there is a need to test out her analysis on a larger population. More generally, we lack up-to-date studies of the kind needed to answer the questions raised in this section. Contemporary research is needed to answer questions such as: Do the principles of selection which I have outlined still hold? What variations have resulted from Britain's having become a multi-racial society? Are there really strong gender divisions in the ways in which the selection principles operate? How do those vary within ethnicity, and possibly with other characteristics such as social class, or employment status? Research capable of answering such questions would have to be designed in such a way that answers about principles of responsibility and obligation are not simply 'read off' from examples of support.

### *The principle of selection: ii) how do I get on with this person?*

At a commonsense level the quality of the relationship between two people is an obvious criterion for selection. The idea that anyone would give significant social or practical support to someone for whom they had hostile – or even neutral – feelings seems inherently implausible. It probably strikes us as unremarkable if people say that 'getting on well' with an infirm person provided their motivation for offering personal care, as did some of the interviewees in Ungerson's (1987) study.

On the other hand, if there are normative guidelines about giving support to relatives, and especially if there are 'rules' about such matters, then the whole point about them is that the decision is to some extent removed from the feelings involved in an individual case. The role played by the quality of the relationship in the question of selecting whom to support is likely to be quite complex and implies consideration of two issues: Does the quality of a relationship override the principles of selection which are derived from genealogical relationships? If it does not override those principles, does it at least modify them? A different way of expressing the same issues would be: Are there guidelines about *how* you should take the quality of the relationship into account when deciding whether to offer support to a relative, or in working out whether it is appropriate to accept support from them?

I shall begin this discussion by drawing a distinction between feeling close to someone and giving them practical support. Stated in this way, it is obvious that the two do not necessarily go together, although in practice many studies of kin relationships have treated them as if they did, especially studies like Young and Willmott's (1957) which have emphasized mother–daughter relationships as the main channels of practical assistance within families. However, more recent studies which have tried to distinguish between the two have found that relationships in which a great deal of practical support is being given are sometimes characterized by emotional closeness and warmth, but sometimes not. For example, Cornwell's study, in the same area of London as Young and Willmott's but two decades later, found that 'Some relationships are based upon shared skills and practical activities and that is all; others involved some degree of emotional intimacy and the mothers and daughters are each other's confidante; still others are based simply on family loyalty and a sense of duty' (Cornwell, 1984, p. 112).

In the rather different context of a study of the carers of elderly people in Sheffield, Qureshi (1986) found that although 72 per cent of carers said that they felt emotionally close to the person for whom they were providing personal care, the rest did not. Qureshi concluded that levels of 'liking' had little effect upon whether a person was or was not giving practical support, especially to a parent. Lewis and Meredith, in their study of daughters who had cared for their mothers, felt that feelings of affection and duty were usually present together, and indeed that their interviewees held these feelings 'in delicate balance' (Lewis and Meredith, 1988, p. 28). Conclusions about the comparative unimportance of emotional closeness are borne out by studies of people not necessarily involved currently in practical support, especially the work of O'Connor and Brown (1984) on women's close relationships, to which I referred in chapter 1. This study shows that levels of intimate confiding to other people are not necessarily related to on-going practical dependency.

From this kind of evidence, it seems that the quality of the relationship, especially between parents and children, plays a relatively small part in determining whether support actually is given. However, (following the principle that 'ought' should not be derived from 'is') there is a separate question about whether the quality of the relationship is something which should be taken into account in defining who has obligations to whom. One possible interpretation of the data on parent–child relationships is that on the whole the normative prescription to give assistance is so strong between parents and children, that the quality of the relationship is not allowed to override it. Unfortunately most of these studies do not separate out the normative element in a way which would make one confident in drawing that conclusion. We still lack the systematic evidence which would tell us just how poor the parent–child relationship has to be before the usual normative guidelines cease to operate; or conversely whether a particularly good parent–child relationship means that assistance should be offered beyond the normal 'call of duty'.

The same problem arises with support passing between other relatives, although because there is more variation in these it is a little easier to pick up hints about how normative guidelines may operate. I think that one can make a case for the quality of the relationship operating as a 'defining in' criterion; so that, although normally one might not be expected to give extensive practical support to an aunt or a sister, if your relationship with her is particularly close and warm, then you should be prepared to give that support and she has the right to expect it. For example, the evidence reviewed by Argyle and Henderson (1985) on relationships between siblings suggests that these do not demonstrate the same strength of obligation as in parent–child relationships, but that this can develop if there is a close relationship between a particular pair of siblings. Conversely, if someone has a rather poor relationship on a personal level with a particular brother or sister, there seems to be nothing like the same kind of pressure as one finds with parents and children to overlook personal dislikes and to give them assistance if they need it. Examples of this can be found in the study by Firth, Hubert and Forge of middle-class kinship. They cite several instances where relationships between siblings had become difficult after disputes over inheritance from their parents, and where little contact had been retained. In one such case, an informant told the researchers that he felt his own brothers and sisters had mostly behaved very badly and that he would be very reluctant to either give or ask for assistance from them, apart from one brother of whom he was particularly fond (Firth, Hubert and Forge, 1970, p. 376).

To take this argument one step further, I would suggest that the quality of a personal relationship between two individuals may operate at a normative level so that a good relationship 'defines in' that person to a structure of obligations, but a poor relationship does not necessarily 'define out'. This latter point applies to parent–child relationships with particular force, but the 'defining in' process may operate there also. A study in the United States by Hoyt and Babchuk (1983) brings out this point rather well. They studied a sample of 800 adults and asked questions about close and confiding relationships within families. They found that people are highly selective, even within the close kin group, about those with whom they are especially intimate, and although adult children (where they exist) are a popular choice as confidants, most people singled out *certain* adult children but not others. On the basis of this evidence (and indeed of commonsense observation), we can conclude that even parent–child relationships vary in their degree of warmth and intimacy. So any tendency to 'define in', that is to strengthen ties of obligation on the basis of good quality relationships, probably applies to parents and children as well as to other kin relationships.

At the most general level, therefore, I would conclude that the quality of a relationship between two individuals does not determine the strength of obligation to provide support in any simple way. The clearest statement of this particular normative guideline is in the form:

'You should be especially willing to assist people to whom you feel close'. But the opposite is not implied where relationships are of poorer quality. In those circumstances, the normative rules based upon genealogical relationships would seem still to apply, although we really know little about how far this has to be pushed before the quality of the relationship becomes the most significant normative consideration.

### Reciprocity, exchange and mutual aid

In my discussion of historical studies of family support in chapter 2 I indicated that the concept of reciprocity has been an important one which historians have used to understand the dynamic of aid passing between members of a kin group. Along with the concepts of duty and obligation, the idea of reciprocity is associated distinctively with family relationships in many people's minds, and some writers take the view that it has considerable explanatory power (Morgan, 1975, p. 81; Bulmer, 1987, p. 161–2). It can be argued that it underlies certain other principles which operate in family life, such as fairness (Allatt and Yeandle, 1986).

Studies of family relationships sometimes fail to see its significance because they focus upon issues like 'dependency' which imply one-way support, whereas it is possible to demonstrate that even elderly people who are themselves receiving significant support from family members often are also giving assistance as well (Wenger, 1984). The importance of reciprocity is indicated by Pahl's study of household work strategies, based in the Isle of Sheppey. In discussing 'informal' labour (which could be paid or unpaid, but which is outside the formal economy) he shows that such exchanges between kin, neighbours and friends happen most frequently where people are able to reciprocate in some way, and he notes that typically people claim they do more for others than they receive in return, indicating 'the general concern of people not to appear too dependent on others' (Pahl, R.E., 1984, p. 250). I cited a number of other examples in chapter 1 which illustrate the importance often accorded to the two-way nature of support.

The idea that the giving of goods and services ought to be a two-way process in families is the central one which I shall discuss in this section. I shall consider how far this provides a normative guideline for use in particular circumstances. I shall introduce this by referring to three overlapping but not identical terms: reciprocity, exchange and mutual aid. Of the three, mutual aid is a term perhaps best used purely descriptively, to indicate that in practice the flows of aid in families are in several directions. Especially if one takes a fairly long-term perspective, it would be difficult to say that certain individuals are net givers and others net gainers overall. I shall not review the empirical evidence which supports that conclusion here; indeed I have already referred to a good deal of it in chapter 1. My main concern here is more with explanations of *why* aid in families is mutual, what is the basis of that aid, and how far we can say that the principle that aid 'should' be mutual is a central normative guideline in family life.

*Social exchange*   In this context, the concepts of exchange and reciprocity offer rather different ways of understanding the basis of mutual aid. In my view the concept of exchange is the less satisfactory of the two, for both empirical and theoretical reasons. The basic idea of exchange is a simple one, implying that people assist others and get something back in return, although it is often difficult for a researcher to identify what is actually being exchanged. One problem is that exchanges of help take many different forms and some of them may be subtle and indirect (Sussman, 1965). Similar problems are created by the fact that people may not necessarily be able to say whether a particular object or service which they give to a relative counts as part of an on-going pattern of exchange or not. In his study of three-generation American families, Hill draws an important distinction between exchanges, gifts and loans, and demonstrates that people categorize their actions between these three differently in different situations (Hill, 1970, p. 69). A researcher still may wish to treat gifts and loans as part of an exchange, but then the rules which govern these particular types of exchange need to be elicited.

A further empirical problem, which also leads us into more theoretical considerations, is that exchanges can be of different types, and are not necessarily of equal value, as the concept of 'exchange' implies. Thus at the very least we have to be able to identify different types of exchange, along some kind of continuum of equal and unequal benefits. Gouldner, in his classic discussion of the norm of reciprocity, argues that most exchanges are in fact unequal in terms of their value, but that there is some normative pressure to create an equivalence if not equality. As he puts it, there should at least be 'tit for tat' even if there is not 'tat for tat' (Gouldner, 1973, p. 244).

Attractive though this argument is, it may apply with less force to family relationships than to other situations of social exchange, since one of the key features of these relationships is that there is less likelihood – or even possibility – that people will end the relationships if the terms of the exchange are unsatisfactory. As Argyle and Henderson (1984) have pointed out, social exchange theory seems rather an inadequate basis for understanding social relationships where, as a matter of empirical observation, people do seem to stay in some relationships even when they are not getting much out of them.

There also is the question of whether a person's economic or social circumstances change the nature of the exchange in which they are involved. For example, does a person who has a low-paid job, in a kin group where the others are economically secure, get different terms of exchange? Or does that person get excluded from certain types of kin exchanges (or even from all such exchanges) because their capacity to pay back is at a level lower than the rest? Evidence about the relationship between kin and support class position suggests that people probably are not cut out completely in such circumstances, certainly not from exchanges of practical support. That conclusion is supported by the evidence of Goldthorpe and his colleagues (1980) on men who have been socially mobile. As I indicated in chapter 3, in families where men's class position (measured by their occupation) has risen above that of their parents, this seems to have little effect on the likelihood that they will turn to kin for practical support. Economic support may well be different, however. Studies of men who are unemployed (reviewed in chapters 1 and 3) suggest that some worry about becoming 'too dependent' on relatives, especially on parents, and this could be interpreted as being unable to sustain their own position in patterns of exchange. On the other hand, unemployed people do make great efforts to reciprocate and examples have been quoted elsewhere of various types of support – economic as well as practical – being given by the unemployed to their relatives. The evidence is inconclusive, therefore, on this question of whether a person's economic or class position changes the nature of exchanges with their kin. It seems fairly clear that disparities in social and economic position do not cause kin exchanges to cease in any simple way. However, possibly they may change the terms under which those exchanges are conducted. That conclusion must be tentative for lack of systematic evidence. The main point which I want to make here is that the concept of exchange seems insufficiently subtle to deal with these issues.

Essentially the argument against exchange theory as a way of understanding the basis of mutual aid in families is that it is too simple to capture the complexities of the flow of aid, especially over long periods of time, because it implies that people exchange equivalent goods in pairs. This does not mean that it has *no* relevance; indeed it may be very appropriate to understanding certain kinds of short-run exchanges, which is precisely the way in which Anderson (1971) used it to interpret his historical data on family relationships (see Bulmer, 1987, pp. 165–8, for an elaboration of this point).

*Reciprocity*   The concept of reciprocity, it seems to me, is a more useful one, but to exploit its potential we have to understand it in quite a subtle way. The particular development of the concept of reciprocity which I find most useful in understanding family support comes from the work of anthropologists, who make the perspective of time, and flows of assistance over time, central to their analysis. Levi-Strauss (1969), in his discussion of the structures of kinship, develops the idea of 'cycles' of reciprocity which involve a number of people and which give shape to exchanges over a long period of time. The concept of cycles of reciprocity has been developed and applied mainly by anthropologists who were studying societies other than Britain. But a good deal of the British literature on kin support could be reinterpreted in these terms. An example would be Grieco's (1987) work on the use of kin networks to gain employment. She shows that, when one person gets a job through the sponsorship of a relative, this creates a strong obligation to reciprocate by giving equivalent assistance to other members of the kin network. The importance of this can be seen in the way that it underscores a whole system of chain migration linked with employment, which provides us with a good illustration of the practical consequences of cycles of reciprocity in the British context. Grieco is clear that the basis of the obligation to reciprocate is membership of the kin group where one has been a beneficiary, and that this overrides a number of other considerations, including personal preferences. She cites three cases of people who gave a home to a relative, whom they did not particularly like, because they felt that this was part of the pattern of reciprocity in which they were involved (pp. 88–9).

Sahlins developed a similar idea by drawing an important distinction between 'balanced' and 'generalized' reciprocity. Balanced reciprocity entails direct exchange, where the balance is created by returning the equivalent of the thing received, without delay. Generalized reciprocity, however, does not imply immediate or equivalent reciprocation, and indeed there may be *no* specific expectation of a counter-gift. A gift may eventually be reciprocated, but there is no specific expectation as to when, where and how. Situations of generalized reciprocity can tolerate a one-way flow over a long period of time, whereas balanced reciprocity requires a two-way flow over a fairly short time-scale (Sahlins, 1965, p. 147–8).

Putting together these ideas, it seems to me that we have a model particularly useful to understanding support within families, where it is embedded within relationships which, by their very nature, tend to last a very long time. It is a model in which some support may be reciprocated over the short-term in a way which looks like an equivalent exchange; but other types of support may not be seen as part of such a system at all, or may create an expectation that the giver will eventually get something back in some other time and place as yet unspecified, and possibly from a third party. On this basis, we can generate some very interesting empirical questions about the normative basis of reciprocity in families: Under what conditions do people feel a pressure to reciprocate in the short term? Are there particular relationships which will tolerate a one-way flow over a long period of time, and what kind of pressure is there for eventual reciprocation? In family relationships, do people operate with an expectation that there may never be direct reciprocation, but that they will eventually 'be repaid' for their generosity by receiving support from someone else?

When we distinguish in this way between observed patterns of mutual aid and the normative basis of reciprocity as it applies within families, it is actually difficult to answer these empirical questions for lack of data which make that specific distinction. In chapter 1 I reviewed evidence which is relevant here. Existing evidence points to a possible conclusion that genealogical distance is a key factor in whether there is pressure for short-term reciprocity, with husband–wife and parent–child relationships being those most likely to be able to tolerate a one-way flow for quite long periods (Allan, 1983). One can argue that the normative expectations of obligation and duty built into these relationships (which I explored earlier in this chapter) makes generalized reciprocity possible in ways which would not apply to most other relationships, with a generalized duty to support one's parents, for example, acting as some kind of guarantee that reciprocal assistance will be provided at some stage in the future.

At the same time, it is possible to argue that a structure of generalized reciprocity, once established, has the effect of strengthening the relationships within which it is embedded. This case is argued by Gouldner, who refers to the norm of reciprocity acting as 'a kind of all-purpose moral cement', because in the time lag between one part of the exchange and the other there is a period of indebtedness, in which both parties have a disincentive to break off the relationship or let it deteriorate. Also the knowledge that one is locked into a relationship (or set of relationships) in which there is a commitment to give support acts as a kind of insurance policy for the future. Especially if the normative pressure to reciprocate is diffuse and generalized, Gouldner argues, pressure can be applied 'to countless ad hoc transactions, thus providing a flexible moral sanction for transactions which might not otherwise be regulated by specific status obligations' (Gouldner, 1973, p. 249).

*Calculations and balance sheets*   It seems to me that these are important insights into the ways in which norms of reciprocity operate within family relationships, and that they give rise to a further series of questions about how people actually use the model of reciprocity in daily life. I will consider that issue through the concepts of calculations and balance sheets. The basic issue is expressed in the following questions: How do people calculate their own and other people's position in structures of reciprocal support? Is the idea of a 'balance sheet' appropriate? How frequently does that balance sheet get revised and on what criteria?

Again, it is difficult to answer these questions on the basis of existing evidence, not least because it is very difficult to get access empirically to the kind of calculations which people may make in part unconsciously (Leira, 1983). Firth, Hubert and Forge (1970, p. 449) suggest that everyone keeps a 'mental ledger' of services and gifts exchanged between kin, but that these are mostly concerned with what they term 'petty services': visiting, exchanging Christmas cards, giving a lift in the car. The more substantial types of support come into a different category. Bulmer (1987) regards the idea of a lifetime balance sheet as an appropriate way of conceptualizing the nature of social care within families especially, but he does not attempt to provide empirical evidence which would support that. Gouldner (1973) has produced an interesting argument that the kind of calculations which people make about long-term reciprocity depend very much on the past conduct of the people concerned, drawing a distinction between conduct (the basis of the norm of reciprocity) and a person's social status (the basis of duties or obligations). On this argument, a person's credit or debit is calculated mainly in terms of their moral worth, based on judgements about how they have behaved in the past.

I am attracted to both these ideas, but they do require empirical confirmation. We need to know what kind of balance sheet people actually keep, and how far the conduct of their relatives (good or bad) towards themselves or other people alters their calculations about where each person stands in the long-term structure of reciprocity. The kind of questions which I have in mind are: If my father is violent towards me, does that absolve me from any pressure to reciprocate, whatever else he may have done for me in the past? Or does it mean that I am not completely absolved, but I only have to do the minimum? If he is violent not to me but to my sister, does that absolve me as well as her? I use the case of violence to bring out the point in a clear-cut way, but of course there are very many less dramatic examples which could be used to illustrate the same issue. Indeed the question of *what* actions might count is itself an empirical question. There is also a question about whether women and men calculate such matters differently, which seems very likely given the evidence I have already cited about gender differences in evaluating moral claims.

In concluding this discussion of reciprocity as a normative guideline in family relationships, I suggest that it should be regarded as a principle which is separate from the principles of selection, but linked to them. Building mainly upon Gouldner's work, I would suggest that the question 'What has this person done, for me and for other people, in the past?' gets set alongside the question 'Who is this person?' when people are working out whether they ought to give assistance to a particular relative. It means that the guidelines about what should be given and to whom are less fixed in advance of concrete situations than they might appear if one considers solely obligations to particular people. Conversely, the norm of reciprocity helps to fill out the guidelines based upon obligation to particular people: the latter may tell you *whom* you should assist, but the principles embodied in reciprocity help you to decide *what* you should do or give.

## The balance between dependence and independence

Family relationships provide the setting for some of the most obvious and extreme situations where one human being is dependent upon another for basic comforts and survival. Physical dependence characterizes the family relationships of the very young, and those who are severely incapacitated. Economic dependence again applies to young people and in a very large measure to women. On a descriptive level, we might wish to say that dependence of one person upon another – not always mutual or symmetrical – is a prime characteristic of family life. However, at a normative level the picture is more complex. As I indicated in chapter 1, available evidence suggests strongly that it is seen as desirable and proper for family relationships to demonstrate a balance between dependence and independence in relation to the support which kin give to each other. This balance can be seen as part of a broader normative expectation that there should be a combination of intimacy and distance in kin relationships, especially those outside the nuclear family unit which are my particular concern in this book.

This desired balance between dependence and independence obviously links quite closely with the norm of reciprocity which I considered above. The norm of reciprocity implies that it is desirable for all people to give to others as well as to receive from them. The capacity to give to others is seen by some writers, most influentially in the work of Titmuss, as an essential part of human social life (Titmuss, 1970; Arrow, 1975). The implication of this line of reasoning for family relationships is that a state of affairs where one person is dependent upon another, unless perhaps it lasts for a very short time, is inherently undesirable. Rather than relationships of dependency strengthening family ties, they may actually weaken them because people's concept of the proper balance has been violated; conversely, where that balance is achieved, kin relationships are likely to be stronger (Anderson, 1977; Pinker, 1979, p. 13).

The particular balance of dependence and independence which is regarded as proper and desirable in exchanges between kin has been characterized by Litwak as 'partial aid'. Writing mainly about the United States, he argues that in an industrialized and democratic society, people expect to receive only part of the services which they need from kin, and the rest from formal organizations. Since this is the expectation, no family member is in a position to provide the entire service needed, and therefore no one can 'ask for complete subservience' from a relative, although people do sometimes overstep the mark and fail adequately to respect this norm of partial aid (Litwak, 1965, p. 310). This analysis potentially is a fruitful one, and I shall try to develop it in the context of data available about contemporary British society.

*Young adults and their parents*    The most obvious empirical examples of how this normative guideline applies concern relationships between generations. First, in the case of young people I have already noted that it has become less common in the twentieth century for young people to share their parents' home after marriage, except in the case of some people with minority ethnic backgrounds (see chapters 1 and 3 for further discussion). That particular form of dependence seems to be not only uncommon in practice, but also is regarded as normatively undesirable, at least for the white majority. For example, in Bott's study, where the data were collected in the 1950s, she was able to demonstrate that one of the few norms of family life upon which most people were agreed, is that each elementary family unit should be financially independent of relatives and have its own dwelling (Bott, 1957, p. 197). Interesting confirmation that this expectation still applies is to be found in McKee and Bell's study of households affected by male unemployment. In discussing the support received by such households from other kin, McKee argues that, in effect, the proper balance between dependence and independence was preserved through sustaining the position of the unemployed person in patterns of reciprocal exchange. Although gifts from kin (especially parents) were welcomed on one level, at the same time, 'Unemployed households were not always in a position of receiving or depending upon others for resources but sought actively to reciprocate in kind. Unemployed households fought against dependency and against the stereotype of "always being on the receiving end" ' (McKee, 1987, p. 115).

The clear message that, once married, young people should be independent of their parents in terms of housing and finance, does not mean that they are expected to cut themselves off completely from their parents after marriage – far from it. It appears that the desired relationship is a very subtle blend of dependence and independence which people often regard as quite difficult to accomplish successfully, although they have a fairly clear idea of what they are aiming for. Diana Leonard Barker (1972) in her study of young people in South Wales in the early 1970s, has produced some very valuable data about how young people's relationships with their parents change in anticipation of marriage and after the event. The picture which she paints is of parents, especially mothers, working very hard to produce the desired balance through a process of 'spoiling and keeping close'. Whilst encouraging their children to become independent in various ways in the period before they left the parental home, mothers also 'spoiled' them with gifts and services. The effect was to 'keep them close' in emotional and practical terms when they had moved into the more independent state characterized by marriage and a separate home.

These data now are somewhat out of date, and there is a real lack of equivalent studies which would enable us to see how the desired blend of dependence and independence for young people has changed in the circumstances of the 1980s, and what are the processes by which it is achieved. One important exception is the study reported by Allatt and Yeandle (1986) of young unemployed people, where it is clear that parents find it difficult to construct the 'proper' forms of financial support for their young adult children, when at one and the same time those children are significantly dependent upon their parents for economic support, yet at a stage in their lives when it is felt that they 'ought' to be achieving a measure of responsible independence. It seems that the idea of an appropriate balance of dependence and independence is still highly relevant.

*Older people and their children*   The second illustration of the idea of a 'proper balance' concerns elderly people. Of course it is quite incorrect to assume that elderly people are necessarily dependent upon their families or anyone else just because they are old. As Wenger (1984; 1986) has demonstrated forcefully, many people even in the over-80 age groups are competent and able to live independently, even if they have some physical impairment. Nonetheless, extreme old age in particular is a time popularly associated with greater dependence upon one's relatives, and at a normative level there appear to be some very strong expectations about what the desired balance should be. In particular, it is the norm of *in*dependence which comes across most strongly in contemporary work, with the present generation of elderly people strongly valuing their autonomy (Wenger, 1984).

Sixsmith (1986) has provided some very interesting data which underline the importance of retaining one's 'own home' as both a symbolic and a practical expression of this autonomy. His data show that the strong value which elderly people place upon independence is partly a matter of freedom and lack of control (you can do what you like, no one else tells you what to do) and partly a matter of not putting oneself in a situation where further reciprocal obligations are created which possibly cannot be fulfilled. Sixsmith reports that the phrase 'you are not beholden to anyone' was commonly used by older people when talking about why they valued their independence, and it seems to me that this is very revealing. It suggests that the acceptance of support (whether from a relative or from another source) could have the effect of disturbing the desired balance of dependence and independence, by putting the elderly person in a client status which they would be in no position to counteract through the giving of equivalent gifts. This is not to suggest that *no* support can be accepted from relatives, far from it. But older people seem concerned to ensure that any support given can be defined as part of an on-going pattern of *mutual* aid, rather than as assistance which places them in a position of dependency.

The argument about achieving the proper balance, and not being put in a situation where you are defined as dependent upon others, does make sense in relation to the evidence reviewed in chapter 1 about flows of support between generations. Since there seems to be an expectation that older generations will give support to younger, and that people in the ascendent generation will continue to be net givers throughout their lifetimes, it is a particularly sensitive issue for older people to be in a position of dependency. This whole line of argument of course could be tested empirically and one might expect to find that people who have more resources which they can give to relatives, especially through the medium of inheritance, would be less worried about 'becoming beholden'. If that is the case, it implies that the possibilities for achieving the desired balance vary according to a person's social class and economic position: older people in comfortable economic circumstances are more restricted, partly because they may need to rely on relatives less anyway (being in a position to purchase domestic nursing support) and partly because when relatives do help, that assistance can be reciprocated in some form.

*Achieving the proper balance*  How is this balance achieved in practical terms? In particular, how does it get translated into normative guidelines for use in family relationships? First, there are matters outside the control of the individual which may make it more or less easy. The actual level of physical or financial need is one of those. But also, the level of provision of public services is an important factor which either facilitates or obstructs the desired balance. In terms of financial provision, the fact that older people now have their income support provided by the population as a whole, through means of taxation, rather than by direct dependence on relatives can be seen as a feature which greatly assists the 'independence' side of the equation (Anderson, 1977; Kreps, 1977). As I suggested in chapter 2, the introduction of old age pensions at the beginning of the twentieth century marks an important step in the public recognition of elderly people's desire for economic independence. So far as practical assistance is concerned, that depends very much on the level of public service provision, which may not always be adequate to facilitate the kind of family support which people desire. For example, an important study undertaken in Scotland by West and his colleagues (1984) asked about the balance of family support and different types of professional support which people thought desirable in a range of different circumstances, concerning the care of people with different types and degrees of disability. It is clear from this that the preferred balance in each case accorded family members some role in the care of the disabled individual, but not the main responsibility. This fits well with the arguments which I have been developing about a normatively desirable balance between dependence and independence in kin relations, but the actual provision of services in many areas is well below that which would be needed to achieve that balance in most cases.

The other dimension of how this balance is actually achieved in practice concerns some rather complex issues about how people actually negotiate their relationships with their relatives – a matter which I shall discuss in the next chapter. For the moment, it is sufficient to indicate that the normative guideline about balancing dependence and in-dependence seems to be in the form of general, rather than detailed advice (I have already argued that such guidelines are like this). You may know in general terms what you are aiming for, but how do you weigh up the balance of support given and received in a particular case to make sure that you are not overstepping the mark and in effect making the other person too dependent? Is it important that assistance should be given in the right *way*, possibly as gifts in kind which can be defined as 'presents', rather than money? The difficulties in actually working this out are illustrated to some extent in Qureshi's (1986) study of old people and their carers in Sheffield, where she shows that there is considerable variation in old people's response to offers of assistance, ranging from 'eager acceptance' of dependency, to a 'determined refusal' of help. In the latter case, relatives sometimes found this difficult to understand, especially since accepting the elderly person's desire to retain their necessary independence, as they themselves defined it, might mean that they put their own lives at greater risk (ibid. p. 175).

As a normative guideline, achieving an appropriate balance between dependence and independence clearly involves some complex and sensitive calculations by a relative who is deciding whether or not to offer a particular form of assistance. Considering this particular guideline also makes it clear that choices about whether to give support to a relative may well concern issues of when you *should not* do this, as well as questions about how much you are prepared to give.

### The expectation of patterned change

The fifth and final normative guideline which I shall consider here concerns the way in which patterns of support between relatives change over time, particularly with regard to the expectation that they 'ought' to change. Family relationships, especially those with one's family of origin, are long-lasting by definition. The underlying principles upon which kin obligations operate include a recognition that it is proper for the balance of giving and receiving to change its character and its direction over time, in ways which are patterned and predictable. The most obvious example is that young children are net receivers of support from their relatives, but that the balance of giving and receiving should be much more even when they become adults.

Central to the norm of patterned change is the idea that there is a 'proper time' for certain changes to occur in the balance of support between relatives, the most striking example of which is the idea that there is an age or stage in a person's life when they should no longer be dependent upon their parents for financial support, for accommodation and for basic daily needs. Other possible examples would be: it is appropriate for a woman to help with the care of her grandchildren if she herself has retired from paid work, but not if she is in her early fifties and has a good job; it is appropriate for a daughter to give up paid work to care for an elderly parent if she herself is quite near to retirement age, but not if she has many years of working life still ahead of her. I offer these as examples of the kind of thing which I mean by norms about the 'proper time' for obligations to be honoured: unfortunately we do not have sufficient data of a quality which could establish whether those particular normative guidelines are significant in practice.

However, there is evidence in general terms that people do operate with normative concepts of patterned change in family relationships. I shall consider this by comparing two rather different types of explanation which social scientists have offered for these phenomena. One type of explanation sees the underlying dynamic of patterned change as natural or biological, the other sees it as social or cultural.

*Life cycles*   Those explanations which rely on nature or biology work with metaphors dependent upon the idea of a cycle: life cycle, family life cycle, developmental cycles. The basic idea behind the concept of the life cycle is that people's lives are divided into stages in a relatively predictable way, and that if we look at a whole family in these terms, we see a pattern of people growing up, producing children, growing old and dying in such a way that the cycle repeats itself, and at any given point in time we can predict where the group as a whole is 'up to' in terms of their relationships with each other. I do not propose to consider this idea as such here, since good discussions are available which indicate that one needs to be very wary of using biology as the main basis for any explanation of social relationships (Morgan, 1975). I shall simply take up one element in these ideas as they relate to obligations: the notion that when a person's parents become old and perhaps incapacitated, there is a natural reversal of roles so that the child takes responsibility for the parent. Some versions treat this literally as a role reversal in which the parent 'becomes' the child. Rejecting this notion, but offering a version which equally depends upon the idea of a natural progression based upon the psychological development of the individuals concerned, Blenkner (1965) argues that normal healthy adults in middle age need to resolve a 'filial crisis' in which they have to learn to accept that their parents are no longer a solid support, and are beginning to need significant support themselves. Blenkner argues that adults in this situation finally have to turn away from their own adolescent rebellion in order to turn back to the parent and to construct a new filial role in which they allow themselves to be depended upon.

The kind of process which Blenkner elucidates has resonance in many other studies and does seem to be one of the important ways in which people anticipate a change in their relationships with their own parents, and eventually with their children. I would question, however, whether an explanation based on biology or individual psychology is adequate for understanding this process. Certainly we have to take account of the culture of the particular society being discussed, in this case of dominant British and American culture, which does not place particularly high value on older people and puts them in relatively powerless social positions. A different way of looking at the same process comes much closer to my interest in the norms of family obligations, and this is the idea that people expect the balance of support to change over their lifetime, especially between parents and children, so that the support which was given to their children while they were young is, as it were, stored up in the form of a debt to be repaid when they themselves are old (Anderson, 1977; Smyer, 1984).

A rather less complimentary way of expressing the same point is that in effect people take out an insurance policy through the support which they give to their younger relatives. This has a certain plausibility, since the evidence of transfers of financial support, particularly between the generations, suggests that the flow of such transfers is normally one way from older to younger generations, and that old people continue to be net providers of financial support until they are quite well advanced in years (Sussman, 1965; Cheal, 1983). Sussman has argued on the basis of this evidence that 'the pattern of actual giving to children is one

subtle way of buying kinship insurance during the period of old age
and senescence' (ibid. p. 80). Qureshi (1986) reports that elderly people
and their carers do frequently talk about children repaying the care that
their parents had previously shown to them. The idea of the insurance
policy as a way of conceptualizing patterned change in family support
does seem to have some merits, but also some limitations. Like other
models of family life which incorporate the idea of a life cycle, it implies
that the future needs occur at life 'stages' which are relatively
predictable and obviously there are many reasons why this is not so: a
person can become disabled in middle age, well before they 'really
should' need physical care; or the child whom one had assumed would
provide daily support can move to the other end of the country. To
make the ideas of the insurance policy stick in relation to family support
one has to assume that it is an 'all risks' policy and with very few
conditions written in small print. This does not really accord with
evidence of how people conduct their family relationships, especially in
relation to the importance of reciprocity, and to achieving the proper
balance of dependence and independence.

*Normative timetables*   I would take the view that those explanations of
the dynamics of patterned change which emphasize the social and the
cultural are more satisfactory than those which emphasize the biological. I find the concept of normative timetables a particularly useful
one, which helps us to analyse the social and cultural dimensions of
patterned change.

The particular example of normative timetables which I shall use here
is the idea of the 'proper time to marry'. Leonard's (1980) study of
young people in South Wales, where the fieldwork was done in the late
1960s, indicates that very strong and well understood norms operated in
this regard: women should become engaged at about 19 and marry at
21; men should become engaged at 21 and marry at 22; a woman should
marry a man about two years older than herself. Leonard notes that
practice did conform to these norms very closely, and that people would
use devices such as varying the length of courtship to achieve the
desired outcomes. In a different study, undertaken in the early 1980s
and in London, 25 emerges as the proper age to marry, both for women
and men. Mansfield and Collard asked the couples whom they
interviewed to describe an 'ideal' marriage and those who mentioned
age in this context saw 25 as the right time. It marked the end of youth,
an appropriate time to settle down, but also it was a point at which
there had been an opportunity to live as an independent single person
and to have 'been around'. Interviewees used phrases such as '25
seemed a good age – you've been around' or 'see the sights, have a good
time and then settle down about 25'. Many people retained this idea
that the mid-twenties is the proper time to marry even though they
themselves had married sooner (Mansfield and Collard, 1988, pp. 57–9).
Like the respondents in Leonard's earlier study, these young people

had a clear sense that there *is* a proper time to marry, although they named a slightly older age.

It is difficult to be sure precisely why 25 emerges as the proper age to marry in this study, whereas for Leonard's sample it was 21–22. Regional differences in ideas about the proper time to marry is one possibility, since one study was based in South Wales, the other in London. Some class differences in the sample is another possibility, although Mansfield and Collard found that experiences of early marriage were not class-specific. Difference over time possibly is the most plausible explanation, since there was a gap of about 12 years between these two studies. This would suggest that ideas about the proper time to marry – and about normative timetables more generally – do change over time. The idea that the details of normative timetables change over time is entirely plausible if one looks at relevant historical material. In his classic study of family formation and limitation practices in the nineteenth century, Banks argued that the Victorian middle classes held a very clear notion of the proper time to marry, although this was defined less in terms of age than in relation to the income and resources which a man would need if he were to set up a home of an appropriate standard. Only when he had such resources should a man contemplate marriage, but then it was positively desirable for him to do so (Banks, 1954, pp. 43–7). Although age is not the major criterion of the proper time to marry in this example, we know that the age at which the majority of the population does marry fluctuates quite significantly over time and we should expect prevailing normative timetables to reflect this. I noted in chapter 3 that the middle years of the twentieth century have been characterized by an average age at marriage which has been both more uniform and also lower than previously, with some evidence that average age has been rising more recently. It could well be that the time difference in the two studies which I have been discussing has picked up on this shift, as it is reflected in changing normative timetables which prescribe the proper age to marry.

I have used the illustration of the proper time to marry because it is well documented in normative terms; however, it is obviously not of the most direct relevance to issues of family obligations. More central would be questions like: Are there normative timetables which indicate the proper time (whether defined in age or some other criteria) to stop supporting your children financially, to start supporting your parents practically, and so on? One way to investigate this empirically is to look at situations where people perceive that things are happening to them or to their relatives at the 'wrong time', or that the proper sequence of events has been reversed. We get hints of the importance of these feelings in shaping family relationships in some of the data on divorce. As I indicated in chapter 1, apparently it is a fairly common pattern for people whose marriage has ended to return to their parents' home for a while after they leave their former marital home, but usually this is regarded as a rather tricky situation. The problem is that they appear to be returning to a situation of being dependent upon, and under the authority of, their parents, in a way which should be characteristic of an earlier phase in their lives. Both parents and child are going backwards, as it were, and this is experienced as problematic. As one of Burgoyne and Clark's interviewees put it,

I were made more than welcome at me mother's . . . open arms actually . . . but I felt a bit sorry for me parents . . . I know your parents bring you up and that, but why should they have my troubles? You know what I mean? They've brought their family up and got them off their hands, they don't want another one on their hands. (Burgoyne and Clark, 1984, p. 81)

The feeling that your parents might reasonably expect to have 'got you off their hands' at a particular time seems to me to express very well the feeling that the normative timetable has been breached. Although there is a sense in which parents never relinquish final responsibility for their children, and always can be called upon to give support if necessary, at the same time there is the feeling that everyone can reasonably expect to be rid of major responsibilities at some point. Equally, adult children can reasonably expect not to have to depend upon their parents. The feeling of going back to an earlier stage, which divorce seems quite often to create, breaches this in a fundamental way and shows us something of the importance of normative timetables when people try to shape their own family obligations.

In searching for a way of developing our understanding of these processes, it seems to me that the historical work of Tamara Hareven (1978) comes closest to illuminating these issues through her analysis of the relationship between 'individual time' and 'family time'. I have spelled out elsewhere the relevance which I believe this has for a contemporary understanding of family obligations (Finch, 1987c). Briefly, Hareven argues that the timing of transitions for individuals between different statuses (into marriage, into retirement and so on) can be treated in the twentieth century as largely an individual matter; but in the past, when economic and practical co-operation with the kin group was more crucial to survival, people could not consider individual timetables in isolation from family timetables, and needed to synchronize them carefully. I find Hareven's analysis very illuminating but would question her assumption that things are completely different in the twentieth century. There is also the dimension of gender which needs to be made visible. However, in my view, the idea of normative timetables helps us to generate some interesting empirical questions about contemporary family obligations. *Do* people still feel under any pressure to schedule their own life changes with reference to the needs of their kin; if so, which kin? Under what conditions does this happen or, conversely, become irrelevant? Do women feel under more pressure than men to bring their individual time into line with family time? Also there are important issues about how much this varies for different ethnic and cultural groups in our own society. As Hareven pointed out, in the North American context in which she was working, Irish family time differs from French-Canadian or from native American family time.

This discussion of patterned change as a normative guideline has been rather speculative – perhaps more so than the other parts of this chapter – for lack of contemporary evidence which addresses family relationships in this way. But I would argue that existing evidence gives enough hints to be able to say with some confidence that the expectation of patterned change is an important element in family obligations, even if we know rather little about precisely what expectations people have. In terms of a guideline for action, the form which it takes is something like: consider what stage the relative who needs support has reached, and what stage you yourself are at, and whether this is the proper time for *you* to be giving *them* support.

### Conclusion

In this chapter I have tried to find the answers to the questions: Do people have a sense of 'the proper thing to do' in terms of giving support to their relatives? What *is* the proper thing to do? I have suggested that these issues are relevant for understanding family obligations in contemporary Britain, and that people do have a sense that moral or normative considerations are an important feature of family life.

The discussion here is incomplete in the sense that I have concentrated upon the content of moral norms, leaving to the following chapter a consideration of process issues – how those norms are put to use in a particular situation. Yet obviously this is something of a false dividing line, especially since I have argued that the circumstances of a particular case are seen as a proper and important consideration in respect of family support. These two chapters therefore need to be considered as complementary, and some of the questions which I have raised here will be given further consideration in the following pages.

I have argued that although normative guidelines are an important feature of how people understand obligations and duties to their relatives, they are guidelines of a particular type. I have not been able clearly to identify clear rules for *what* you should do (such as, 'Children should never refuse assistance to a parent' or 'You should put the needs of your children before those of your parents'). Partly this is because we simply do not have contemporary empirical studies which address these issues in sufficient detail and it could be that there is in fact general consensus among the population about statements of this type. But I have suggested that the existing evidence points to a rather different conception of moral rules as a way of understanding family obligations – namely as principles or guidelines. I have suggested that these express the criteria one should use in deciding what to do, rather than specifying precisely what one should do. I have argued that one can identify five normative guidelines of this type which can be expressed thus:

- Consider who this person is; what their relationship is to you in genealogical terms.
- Consider whether you get on particularly well with this person.
- Consider the pattern of exchanges in which you and they have been involved in the past.
- Consider whether receiving assistance from you would disturb the balance between dependence and independence in this person's family relationships.
- Consider whether this is the proper time in both your lives for you to give this type of assistance to this particular person.

I offer these as my own evaluation of the normative guidelines which operate in relation to family support, but I have emphasized throughout the discussion that there is a significant lack of evidence upon which to base firm conclusions. In that sense my analysis is tentative, although fruitful in the sense that the task of evaluating existing evidence and conceptualizing the nature of these guidelines has led to a series of questions which give direction to future research.

# 6

# Working it out

---

### Introduction

In the last chapter I argued that foundations of support within families cannot be understood simply in terms of norms of duty or obligation. When people give support and assistance to their relatives they are not acting simply in accordance with pre-ordained rules, but are engaged in a process of actively working out what to do. This chapter focuses upon that process of 'working out'.

Moral rules or norms are not wholly irrelevant to this process. Indeed one of the most interesting issues that we need to understand is how people make use of the general normative guidelines (in the sense in which I used that term in chapter 5), in the process of working out what to do for and with their own relatives. Thus a number of questions which my discussion of normative guidelines has already raised will be further explored in this chapter. Does my concept of guidelines hold up when we look at evidence about how people work out what to do for their own relatives? Can we detect processes of application and selection of guidelines? How do people deal with conflicts between different guidelines in a particular situation? How far do people base their own actions upon what most other people do? More generally, how important is it to work out what is the socially acceptable morality in a given situation? I do not pretend to be providing a definitive answer to any of these questions but I shall try to take them further here, on the basis of existing empirical evidence.

I shall centre this discussion around two concepts which I find useful in developing an analysis of family responsibilities: negotiations and public morality.

## Negotiation

In much of my discussion in chapter 5 I implied that people 'take decisions' about whether to give assistance to a relative in particular circumstances. However, the idea of taking decisions, with its implication that someone consciously and rationally weighs up the pros and cons, is almost certainly inappropriate for most situations which concern family obligations. The concepts of bargaining and negotiation seem to me to be more fruitful in this context. I shall outline briefly the main characteristics of these concepts in general terms.

### *Concepts of bargaining and negotiation*

The concept of bargaining is the less useful of the two, although it directs us to consider certain important issues when seeking to understand how people work out what kind of support is to be given to which relatives, and on what terms. In their work on the social psychology of bargaining, which is based on data generated in experimental settings, Rubin and Brown offer the following definition of bargaining in social life: 'the process whereby two or more parties attempt to settle what they shall give and take, or perform and receive, in a transaction between them' (Rubin and Brown, 1975, p. 2). In their discussion of various facets of bargaining, these authors make two points which seem of particular relevance to support within kin groups. First, they indicate that bargains are made in situations where there is some conflict of interest between two or more parties. Bargaining procedures are mechanisms through which either a compromise is reached, or the interests of one of the parties are subordinated to the others'. This directs us to analyse family bargains in a way which makes explicit the interests of each party. Second, they point out that bargaining can involve more than two people. If it does, that opens up the possibility of coalitions between different parties, whereby two or more join together to increase their bargaining strength. Again it seems important to acknowledge the possibilities of coalitions within families, and to understand when and how they operate in the process of working out structures of support.

Despite these useful insights from the literature on bargaining, it has a significant limitation in terms of analysing family life: it implies that such transactions are conscious and explicit. As I have already argued, the idea that family life is characterized by conscious and rational weighing up of choices and carefully planned actions seems inappropriate. The concept of negotiations seems to me to be particularly valuable precisely because it does not imply those things. Negotiations can be implicit as well as explicit, and need not necessarily be conducted at the level of conscious strategy. As defined by Strauss (1978), one of the most influential writers on this topic, the process of negotiation' constitutes one of the possible ways of 'getting things done' in social life. Other possible ways of getting things done include coercion, persuasion and manipulation. This seems to me to have particular relevance to the study of family relationships, where the process of negotiation itself may be intertwined with coercion, persuasion and manipulation. Looked at in this perspective, negotiations need not imply that full agreement is reached and all parties go away satisfied at the end. Negotiations may be conducted partly *through* these other means.

Further, I find the concept of negotiation particularly useful when it is linked to the idea of commitments. The concept of negotiated commitments represents an alternative way of understanding family obligations which contrasts quite sharply with the idea of following moral rules. By this, I mean that gradually, over a period of time, an understanding emerges between two people that there are certain things which they would do for each other if necessary. Such understandings can be arrived at without being discussed directly, and of course there is room for *mis*understandings in what Strauss calls these 'silent bargains' (p. 225). Commitments arrived at are not necessarily a private matter between two parties. They may be well understood in the kin network as a whole, so that when the situation actually arises where, for example, an elderly person needs to be cared for, it is 'obvious' to everyone that a particular child (of course usually a daughter) will be the person who will do this. Obligation, duty and responsibility, as understood in this sense, are commitments developed between real people, not abstract principles associated with particular kin relationships (Morgan, 1975, p. 79; Finch, 1987c).

Although I shall elaborate the relevance of this analysis to family support and the concept of obligation later in this chapter, I shall give one example here, to illustrate in a preliminary way how the idea of negotiated commitments can apply. My example is taken from Ungerson's (1987) study of people caring for infirm relatives, and concerns the case of Miss Nicholson, who was caring for her elderly mother. The account which she gives of the arrangements for her mother's care provide an illustration of negotiations, in this instance between herself and her sister and her brother. It had been agreed that the two sisters would share the care of their mother on an equal basis, taking half a week each, and the other Miss Nicholson travelled 100 miles from her home every week to take her share. Neither of the sisters was in paid work at the time this arrangement was negotiated although one took a part-time job subsequently. This arrangement had been negotiated formally and agreed explicitly with their mother. The brother called regularly at the house to see his mother and made arrangements for her to go into a residential home in the summer to relieve his sisters, but did not give any other practical assistance. Apparently it had never been suggested that the brother should play a more direct role in his mother's care but he had been, as Ungerson puts it, 'broker of the family's caring resources', in that he had been involved in the explicit negotiations which set up the arrangement described and had been the one delegated to talk to their mother about it (Ungerson, 1987, p. 40).

In this example it can be seen that the concept of negotiation is an apposite way of describing the way in which family support was worked out. Also it can be seen that the outcome of those negotiations clearly was influenced by factors outside the immediate situation, especially related to gender. Ungerson does not spell out the details, but fairly obviously the sisters looked more 'available' than the brothers since they were not in paid work, and the cultural expectation that caring for a mother is an appropriate task for a woman no doubt also was relevant. In this kind of example we can see the ways in which what I called the 'external contexts' of support (in chapters 3 and 4) do shape the course of negotiated commitments which develop between kin.

### External structures and interpersonal negotiations

The importance of bringing external structures into the picture becomes apparent when we consider the intellectual tradition from which the concept of negotiation is drawn, namely symbolic interactionism.

The idea of negotiations as I am using it here draws upon the particular understanding of social life developed within that tradition, which emphasizes that human beings are active in constructing the social world around themselves, but that they cannot do it alone. The process of participation in social life is concerned centrally with negotiating the social meaning of activities in which you are involved, in the sense of developing shared understandings of what a particular situation is about, and what each person involved in it expects of the others. Such ideas have been used to some effect in sociological studies of marriage relationships (e.g. Askham, 1984; Burgoyne and Clark, 1984), following the influential work of Berger and Kellner (1964); also in a less explicit way in studies which have looked at how the domestic division of labour is negotiated and renegotiated in situations of male unemployment (McKee and Bell, 1985; Morris, 1985). I am suggesting that they are also extremely fruitful in considering the particular aspect of family life with which I am concerned: obligations to provide various types of practical and material assistance.

It was a common criticism of early symbolic interactionist work that it ignored the existence of social structures. The implication was that human beings are free to create their own lives through interactions with other people, without acknowledging that certain choices inevitably are constrained, or that people enter negotiations with varying degrees of power deriving from their position in the labour market, their ethnicity and so on. More recent symbolic interactionist work has responded to these criticisms by making more explicit the issues of social structure. Strauss, for example, has developed the concept of the 'negotiated order'. By this he means to suggest that all social order has a negotiated element, even in the most repressive circumstances. But at the same time, the negotiations in which human beings engage are never completely open-ended because they always take place 'under specific structural conditions'. These conditions determine who negotiates with whom, when negotiations take place, and so on. Working at producing social order under specific structural conditions is a continuous process, and any change in the structural conditions requires the negotiated order to be 'reviewed, re-evaluated, revised, revoked or renewed' (Strauss, 1978, p. 5). This line of argument comes close to Giddens's analysis of the relationship between social structure and human agency, and indeed Giddens's discussion is influenced by ideas drawn from the symbolic interactionist tradition. Both Strauss and Giddens emphasize the importance of seeing the impact of social structure in small-scale interactions between individuals; and both insist that human beings do have the capacity to 'make their own lives', rather than simply being restricted and constrained by external structures.

This kind of approach to understanding the relationship between social structures and human actions relies a good deal on the idea of 'shared understandings' or 'shared meaning' to make the links between the two. People learn from their past experience of living in a given society how to interpret other people's behaviour and how social life works customarily. When approaching a new situation, certain elements will be 'taken for granted' by all parties. Although these taken-for-granted elements *can* be challenged and even changed, for the most part they are not, since constant challenges disrupt the flow of interaction and prevent the parties from 'getting things done' (Douglas, 1971, pp. 171–82). This means in practice that situations and relationships are not infinitely negotiable. We could apply this kind of analysis to the case of the Nicholson siblings which I discussed above, for example. It would imply that the siblings entered the negotiation about how to care for their mother with certain understandings which were shared between the three of them, and which each had learned through membership of British society in the late twentieth century. These would include: most people, both sons and daughters, acknowledge some responsibility for their parents in old age; daughters commonly are thought to be the people most suited to provide nursing care, for their mothers especially; men do not give up their jobs to care for a parent. There also may have been shared understandings which were specific to this kin group and which had developed between them over the years; for example, (to be entirely speculative) that their mother had made many sacrifices for her children and deserved to be repaid. The three siblings in this example negotiated an arrangement which was unique to themselves, and suited their particular circumstances, but also was consistent with these shared understandings. These are not so much moral rules, concerned with determining how someone 'ought' to behave, as common perceptions of 'how the world works'. Any of them *could* have been challenged but none was; our analysis would regard that as fairly predictable. Anyone else who was aware of what was being negotiated (for example social workers, or other kin) would be likely to endorse the outcome which was consistent with those shared understandings.

It can be seen from this discussion that (to use the terms I used in chapter 5) the process of selecting and applying normative guidelines should not be seen as individual activity, but as a process of developing shared understandings with other people in a particular context of kin support. In working out what constitutes the proper thing to do in a particular set of circumstances, people have to engage in a co-operative task, although of course it may not always be easy – or even possible – to reach agreement.

The procedures used to accomplish this are subtle and seldom explicit, being conducted by means of nuance and implication in words and through gestures and actions. Each individual needs to be able to deploy what Cicourel refers to as 'interpretive procedures' which enable us to identify the relevance of a particular normative rule to a given situation, to shape our own behaviour accordingly, and to evaluate the situation after the event in the light of those particular normative meanings (Cicourel, 1973, p. 32). Douglas, talking about the same processes, spells out some of the ways in which the relevance of a normative rule to a particular situation is established: by making analogies to other situations which could be said to be similar; by selecting certain rules which enable you to achieve the purpose in hand, but choosing not to apply others which could be relevant; by constructing plausible accounts of what you are doing through appeals to abstract principles like truth, reason, and so on (Douglas, 1971, pp. 214–15). The process of applying these rules also can lead to the rules being modified. Both Douglas and Cicourel are keen to emphasize that the rules themselves are subject to change over time, and it is precisely this process of applying them to particular situations which develops and changes them: people feed back the understandings which they have developed in particular situations into their more generalized understanding of social rules.

### *Shared understandings: the products of negotiation*

This means that each negotiation has several products, as it were. One may be a negotiated commitment to provide a particular relative with a particular kind of support. Another product is these shared under-standings of what is the proper thing to do in particular circumstances. These are carried forward to form part of the background against which the next application of a particular normative guideline will take place. Although this kind of analysis can apply to any social group, and more diffusely to a society as a whole, there is a case for arguing that it has particular relevance for understanding family relationships, because families typically are composed of people who meet in face-to-face situations, perhaps very frequently, but certainly over long periods of time, so that there is plenty of opportunity to develop, elaborate and negotiate shared understandings of what is considered to be the proper thing to do in *this* family.

Empirical evidence to support this line of analysis can be found in work from a rather different intellectual tradition, arising out of laboratory work in social psychology. Reiss (1981) has put forward an argument supported by empirical data, which suggests that family groups (by which he means adult kin, as well as nuclear family-households) develop over time a shared set of 'family constructs' which embody common beliefs and expectations about the social world. These beliefs, he argues, about how the social world is ordered and the place of family members within it, can vary quite markedly in different families, and are quite stable over time, and across generations. They are constructed and reinforced by family members actively adapting to external circumstances and thereby creating new, shared ways of viewing and handling the social world. Reiss's work is interesting in the context of this discussion, not so much for the detail of his experimental work, but because it indicates that it is possible to find empirical confirmation in various different ways for the idea that kin groups in particular develop shared understandings of the meaning of each others' actions, and those of people outside the group. It means that one can suggest with more confidence that the concept of negotiation, through which shared understandings are developed, *is* valuable in the analysis of the obligation to give assistance with families.

If we accept that this line of analysis is fruitful for understanding family relationships, we are still left with a problem of who counts as 'the family' or 'the kin group', between whom shared understandings or shared constructs develop. Are we talking about just the inner circle of kin? Or is the wider kin network – at least those with whom contact is maintained – drawn into a common set of understandings through their various interactions with each other over the years? In their celebrated discussion of marriage and the construction of social reality, Berger and Kellner (1964) suggest that when each couple marries they need to set about the task of constructing their own social reality with its own shared meanings, which are different from those in their family of origin. If this analysis is correct, it would imply that shared under-standings about family support normally would be restricted to the very narrow kin 'group', consisting of a married couple and their own unmarried children. Many of the examples which I have quoted elsewhere in this book suggest that it does extend wider than that, certainly that when adult children marry they do not abandon the shared understandings which they may previously have developed with their parents and their siblings, nor is marriage a barrier to the further development of such understandings. For example, in Lewis and Meredith's (1988) study of women who had cared for their mothers, there does not seem a significant difference between those who had married and those who had remained single, in the way that they and their mothers had defined filial responsibilities.

Essentially the question of who 'counts' as kin group for this purpose
is an empirical one, to which we probably would get different answers
in different families. In some cases, because interactions concerning
matters of support have taken place only between very close kin in
genealogical terms, we will find that the group which has developed
common understandings is very small. In other cases it may be wider,
either because support is shared more widely in a particular kin
network, and therefore a wider range of kin has been involved in active
negotiations, or because of overlapping membership of different sectors
of the kin network. As I have indicated previously, any kin network is
composed of interlocking sets of 'inner circles' of kin, and any
individual may belong to more than one circle. Suppose, for example,
that I belong effectively to two inner circles, one consisting of my father
and my two brothers, the other consisting of my children and
grandchildren. Of course my own children acknowledge my father and
my siblings as their kin and vice versa, but effectively they are in each
others' outer circles, whereas I am in the inner circle for both. I am
suggesting that, in this situation, we should expect to find that I have
developed shared understandings about family support and assistance
with other members of both inner circles. These may not take exactly
the same form, but it is unlikely that I will hold them completely
separate. My own understanding of how the world works and should
work is likely to spill over from one to the other. I suggest that this is an
important reason why we should expect shared understandings to
include quite a wide range of kin in some instances, although certainly
at this stage this is no more than an hypothesis which needs to be tested
empirically. It does seem important however that any research which
seeks to understand the processes of negotiation between kin should
not assume from the beginning that it is only worth studying a narrow
range of relationships.

## Public morality

This discussion of shared understandings leads directly into the second
set of ideas which I believe are useful for understanding how
obligations to give support are worked out in practice. These can be
summarized under the concept of 'public morality', which directs our
attention towards the audience people are addressing when they work
out the proper course of action. This audience is composed partly of the
others involved directly and partly of people outside the situation,
whose view of it may nonetheless be important to the participants. The
question of precisely which audience or audiences a person sees as
relevant needs really to be considered in relation to specific situations:
it cannot, for example, be assumed that on every occasion when a
person has to decide whether to lend their children money they are
playing to the same audiences. However, we can anticipate, as I shall
spell out below, that in the case of negotiations within the family the

audiences will be both internal and external to the kin network. The importance of the audience response in influencing what people actually do is an issue raised by the concept of public morality. It also enables us to tackle questions about how people identify what would be a socially acceptable response in a given situation, and how they orient their actions towards that.

The origins of the concept of public morality can be found in the work of Douglas and arise directly from his discussion of using social rules, to which I have already referred. Douglas argues that when people present their actions to strangers, and especially when they have to give a very public account of themselves which is 'on the record', there is a strong tendency to present actions in a way which appears innocuous, drawing upon 'a least common denominator morality which is the public morality – a communicative strategy designed to offend the fewest possible people' (Douglas, 1971, p. 243). These ideas were taken up specifically in relation to family issues by Voysey in her study of families with a handicapped child, a situation where people often have to give an account of themselves and their family relationships to public welfare agencies, as well as being faced with the more general problem of how to present to the outside world a family situation which deviates from the norm. Voysey demonstrates that the response of parents to this situation is commonly to present their family arrangements as 'just like' an ordinary or normal family, drawing upon the public morality of family life which not only is the least common denominator morality, but is also endorsed by official agencies (Voysey, 1975, pp. 40–3).

It seems to me that this analysis can be applied to obligations between kin. In a sense I have already discussed what this least common denominator morality consists of in chapter 5, when I considered what are the normative guidelines applicable to support between relatives. At this point I am interested not so much in the content of this least common denominator morality, but in the effect which it has upon the processes whereby people work out what to do in practice. The argument essentially is that a person's understanding of what will offend the least number of other people plays a central role in the way that negotiations are conducted. Far from normative guidelines simply being followed, or even selected on the basis of personal preference, people's actions towards their relatives are influenced significantly by considerations of how they will appear to other people. The key issue is: How can decisions and actions be presented in a way which others will find sufficiently acceptable, so that personal reputation and social identity are not undermined?

This focus upon the accounts which people are able to give of their actions is quite close to the earlier work of Wright Mills (1940) on the sociology of motivation. Mills argues that there are certain circumstances in which considerations of how I might *present* my actions are so important that they determine what I actually do. As Mills puts it, the question 'If I did this, what would I say?' looms very large, and I may choose to take a particular course of action precisely because it offers a socially acceptable answer to that particular question and therefore justifies my position (Gerth and Wright Mills, 1954, p. 116; see Finch, 1987c for further discussion). The importance of the 'account' which I give of my actions is recognized also by Giddens, in his discussion of the relationship between social structure and human agency. Acknowledging that all human interaction is dependent upon the reaction of other people to an individual's actions, he argues that the 'accounts' which people give of what they are doing (that is, how we explain what we have done and the reasons for it) is tied intimately to being 'accountable' for actions (that is, accountable in the sense of being held responsible) (Giddens, 1979, pp. 85–6). Although Giddens does not use the concept of audience, his analysis is very close to that of Douglas and Wright Mills at this point.

## External audiences

In relation to family obligations, who are the relevant audiences likely to be? I have already suggested that these are likely to include both other members of the family and people outside the family group. To take first the external audience, this raises the question of the public reputation of the family group as a whole. In situations (such as those studied by Voysey) where the family has literally to give an account of its provision for a handicapped and infirm member to representatives of public agencies, it is not difficult to identify who is the relevant audience. This helps us to understand some of the processes whereby the external constraints of law and social policy (which I discussed in chapter 4) affect the kind of assistance which is offered to kin.

More generally, how important is family reputation as a consideration when people are working out whether to offer support to their relatives, or whether to accept support offered to them? The idea that family reputation has to be guarded jealously comes across strongly in the literature on Mediterranean societies, where the concepts of honour and shame apply to the kin group as a whole as well as to individual reputations (Peristiany, 1976). In films and novels this is popularly portrayed by the expectation that young working-class men of Mediterranean (often of Italian) origin will maim, rob and murder other people who have damaged the reputation of their own family. Despite these images of violent male bravado, in these societies it is often women who play the key role in maintaining group solidarity and sustaining the honour of the family members. Goddard (1987) shows how this operates for working-class women living in contemporary Naples. She suggests that the significance of women's role in the maintenance of family reputation can be seen in the way that women are confined within the family and excluded, for example, from working for wages. This is the consequence of women's key role in maintaining the boundaries of the kin group and sustaining its solidarity, in a situation where the honour of the kin group is the basis of the social organization of everyday life. A rather similar argument can be made in relation to restrictions imposed on women in many Islamic societies, for example the custom of purdah, which has been continued in adapted form by some groups who have migrated to Britain. In confining women to a world entirely separate from men's, it can be argued that the purdah system ensures that women do not threaten the honour of the kin group which is founded on male pride and reputation (Saifullah Khan, 1976).

This particular concept of family reputation has not been part of white British culture, but that does not mean that reputation is unimportant. Certainly historical evidence suggests that it has been significant in tight-knit local communities and can be crucial in, for example, access to jobs. Such a situation is described graphically by Roberts in his account of working-class life in Salford in the early twentieth century, where literally everyone knows everyone else's business. The public reputation of each family was well known, and the position of each was either sustained or undermined through local gossip, which could make a crucial difference in securing work (Roberts, 1971, pp. 43–6). Looking at historical material from England in the sixteenth and seventeenth centuries, Chaytor (1980) argues that women play a pivotal role in this kind of gossip.

In the later part of the twentieth century, it seems that a good family reputation still can be the means by which people get jobs, as is apparent from Grieco's study of the use of kin networks in employment (discussed in chapter 1). She shows how families guard jealously the reputation that they are all good workers and keep up pressure on each other to perform to high standards, citing the example of one kin group who were clear that they would only secure jobs for those relatives whom they believed would be good workers (Grieco, 1987, pp. 31–2). Evidence from people responsible for recruiting workers confirmed that they did indeed pay attention to family reputation (p. 88).

However, in many cases it is not so easy as in these examples to identify the relevant outside audiences to whom an account of family obligations needs to be presented. Indeed it may more often be a case simply of anticipating how you would present an account if necessary, rather than actually being called upon to do it. Knowing what other people *might* say about you can be a powerful control in its own right, and people know what others might say through hearing what they *have* said on similar occasions. Matters concerned with duty and obligation in families certainly are the kind of situations where people do feel able to make strong moral judgements about others' lives. Consider, for example, the potentially powerful social control exercised over someone who knows that their neighbours are given to commenting in the following terms about a daughter who appears to be available to assist her elderly mother, but is not doing so,

I'd be ashamed . . . it's a disgrace. We all think in the road it's a disgrace. (Lewis and Meredith, 1988, p. 23)

At the most general level, it is possible to argue that people do take account of 'public opinion' when they take moral decisions, rather than run the risk of becoming a less socially acceptable person should their actions come to light (Sprigge, 1970). It is also apparent that situations can arise where members can become disadvantaged by being associated with a family whose life does not live up to the least common denominator morality – a process of labelling which is well known in studies of deviance. The respectable and economically secure middle classes are by no means immune from such pressures. As Turner has put it in his work on American families, the pressures upon family life in middle-class circles are such that they produce 'concerted patterns of acting *as if* each family were actually performing its appointed functions and adhering to its accepted roles' (Turner, 1970, p. 223, my italics). Who precisely forms this important audience, before whom people feel constrained to give an 'as if' performance, is a question which requires empirical investigation. The answer is likely to vary from situation to situation, even when the circumstances are similar in other respects.

## Internal audiences

The second type of audience to which people must play is the internal one: other family members, including both those who are involved in the negotiations in question, and those who are not. It is clear why this internal audience is important: unless an individual is going to withdraw from the kin group completely, the commitments which they negotiate in one set of circumstances, and the personal reputation which they acquire as a result, is going to affect future relationships and their position in future negotiations. The internal audience for the management of family obligations is not necessarily a group of passive bystanders: even if they are not directly affected by these negotiations they are needed to approve the action, to confirm that it is an acceptable application of the normative guidelines, and thus to play an active part in constructing social identity and personal reputation. The question of who counts as 'they' is an empirical one, to which we probably would get different answers in different situations.

One obvious example of the importance of internal audiences concerns situations where one person acknowledges an obligation to a relative, because of pressure put on by a third party or 'for the sake of' that third party. Parents and spouses are the most common third parties in this context. Firth, Hubert and Forge quote several examples of respondents who kept in touch with an aunt or cousin out of 'duty' to their own parents, rather than to the more distant relative. Parents sometimes played a more active part in this, as in the case of one respondent whose mother invited him to her house when she knew that a particular aunt would be visiting her, thus ensuring that some contact was maintained with her son (Firth, Hubert and Forge, 1970, p. 440). Similarly there are cases where people maintain reasonably cordial relationships with a parent-in-law 'simply out of loyalty to their spouse' (p. 417). It also can work the other way round. In the same study we are given an example of a woman who had stopped visiting her mother-in-law with whom she had very little in common. Her husband was sympathetic to her position and had played a key role in enabling her to establish her justification for ceasing contact (p. 111). In these cases the close kin are acting as the internal audience in front of whom an individual must play out their relationships with more distant kin. It is obvious in these examples that the desire to satisfy these audiences does exercise some constraints over individual actions. Although, as I indicated in chapter 1, relationships with the wider kin group typically are not expected to be close for most people in British society (at least for the white majority), and are characterized by the freedom to choose the level of contact and support which each shares with the other, in practice we are all less free to choose to ignore our more distant kin than this implies, because we have to have an eye to the reaction of kin to whom we are closer, in both senses.

The importance of third parties in managing the negotiation of relationships is explored in an interesting and rather different way by LaGaipa (1982), in his discussion of rituals associated with dissolving personal relationships. He argues that in all situations where relationships are changing, other people in the relevant social group need to be involved, not only in giving personal support to the participants, but also because the normative rules which govern human relationships are potentially threatened at the time of such changes. The role of third parties is to enable change to be managed without challenging the groups' prevailing norms about what constitutes a good or an appropriate relationship.

LaGaipa's arguments can be applied to the negotiation of family obligations, although we always have to leave open the question of precisely who constitutes the kin 'group' for this purpose. As I argued above, we probably should expect that the inner circle of close kin does constitute part of the relevant audience, but that it is not necessarily restricted to them because of interlocking allegiances within the wider kin network. It seems to me that other members of the kin network are likely to form the key audience of interested parties, especially necessary to an individual whose actions are an apparent breach of the normative guidelines – leaving their children out of their will, refusing to have an elderly parent to live with them, and so on. In those circumstances, even if the person concerned can construct a plausible account of why this is really quite consistent with the normative guidelines, it is to no avail unless other people involved in the kin group (and therefore part of the same set of reciprocal relationships) are prepared to accept their account as valid and legitimate, and thereby to sustain the personal reputation and social identity of that person as an acceptable partner in future negotiations. Other people have to both believe your story and accept it. On the basis of their data on middle-class kin relationships, Firth, Hubert and Forge (1970, p. 449) conclude that typically people show 'very great sensitivity' to the possibility that they are being 'up-graded or down-graded' by relatives, because of their performance in relation to family obligations.

The concept of personal reputation is a useful way of developing a discussion of the importance of internal audiences. When I use the idea of reputation, I mean something rather different from the public persona which some individuals also may have. I refer rather to the social identity which that person has as a member of a particular kin group – as a good son, a caring aunt, as a person who can be relied upon to turn up in a crisis but is not much interested in relatives otherwise, as someone who is never prepared to give or lend money, and so on. The concept of family reputation is, in my view, potentially a fruitful one and can be linked usefully to questions about how such information is shared within family groups. Some anthropologists have noted the importance of the concepts of honour and shame as important ways in which personal reputation becomes publicly identified. Whilst, as I noted above, these processes are particularly characteristic of certain cultures, especially Mediterranean cultures, they also are found in many other situations where small groups of people interact with each other in a face-to-face way (Peristiany, 1968). There is a possibly interesting application to family life. How far do people covet a family reputation of always acting honourably? What are the processes through which such a reputation is established or undermined?

In relation to this latter question, work of other anthropologists on gossip and scandal suggests some further lines of enquiry, especially in so far as gossip about an individual performs the important social function of 'maintaining the unity, morals and values of social groups', especially of small groups (Gluckman, 1963, p. 308; see also Rosnow and Fine, 1976). Gossip accomplishes this because even the process of criticizing certain individuals at the same time entails asserting and reinforcing shared values about the proper thing to do. This suggests to me that gossip within families (as well as outside them) possibly provides one of the processes through which personal reputations are shared and carried forward over time, thereby reinforcing the shared understanding of normative guidelines within a kin network, as well as giving continuity to the personal reputation of individuals.

Examples of situations where people have not succeeded in maintaining their reputation with the audience composed of other kin can be found in the study of middle-class kinship by Firth and his colleagues, especially in situations where there has been a dispute over inheritance. For example, one of their respondents told the researchers that his mother had brought him up to see his two aunts as 'black figures', because she resented the rather large share of her deceased husband's estate which went to them. Another respondent expressed forcefully his dislike for his father's sister, whom he believed to have deprived his father of his rightful share of their parent's will, saying that by her actions the aunt had deliberately 'put a dagger in (his father's) back' (Firth, Hubert and Forge, 1970, pp. 375–6). In both of these cases an individual's negative reputation in the family had been formed by incidents that had happened over 20 years before, and had been sustained by a younger generation who were only very small children when those incidents occurred.

These classic 'black sheep of the family' examples do have to be treated with some caution however. It is notable that people report that other people are black sheep, not themselves, and without data from all the members of the relevant kin group we cannot be sure how widely this view is shared. As most studies of family relationships rely on one person as informant, such data usually are lacking. However, we should note that the two examples given above concern the negative reputation of someone who normally would fall in the outer circle of kin (an aunt), disapproved of because of her actions towards someone who normally would fall in the inner circle (a parent). Thus when we talk about the kin network forming an internal audience for actions, and the reputation of an individual being formed as a consequence, we may really be talking about a situation where someone has to play to several different internal audiences, against the background of a somewhat different personal reputation with each – potentially a very tricky act to bring off.

However, the responses of these internal audiences are not entirely idiosyncratic and infinitely variable. Although kin groups may have developed their own set of shared constructs (in Reiss's (1981) sense), they do not have infinite flexibility in defining certain actions as proper and others as improper, but are in some way constrained in their own definitions of social reality by shared understandings with people outside the family. Thus the public morality is important not only in the public domain, but in the private one as well. The very fact that it is the lowest common denominator morality, likely to offend the least number of people, makes it potentially very useful because one can justify an action to the internal audience on the grounds that it is what everyone else does, or expects. It is through these processes that we can understand how public policies and the law can have an impact upon both the support which people offer their relatives in practice, and upon the ways in which they think about duties and responsibilities to specific kin. As I argued in chapter 4, the impact of these may be more significant at the level of public morality than through the direct application of sanctions and control. It certainly affects many more people.

## The process of negotiating commitments

I have argued that the concept of negotiated commitments is a useful way of analysing the processes through which people work out the 'proper thing to do' for their relatives, and that these processes of negotiation can be located in the broader social context through the concept of public morality. Working out what constitutes the proper thing to do does not entail following rules in any simple sense. It is a matter of negotiating with other parties a set of commitments to particular individuals. To take an hypothetical example, I do not assist my daughter by giving money to pay her rent simply because this is the proper thing to do for *a* daughter. I do it because I have developed a set of commitments to *my* daughter, and to other kin, in which this has been defined as the proper thing to do. The process of developing those commitments has not been a matter for me alone. I have arrived at them over a period of time by reaching shared understandings about what constitutes appropriate reciprocal support in our family. But we did not begin from scratch and we monitored the reactions of others inside and outside the family, and most importantly each other's reactions, as we went along. Of course we had to work within the limitations of our respective economic situations: you cannot promise more than you are able to give. The commitments which we have arrived at now are not static. They will be confirmed, renewed and renegotiated as our relationships develop over time.

This is the kind of account inspired by the analytical framework developed in my discussion so far. In this section I take it further by looking at the processes through which sets of commitments are developed in families. My discussion depends on an analysis of the available empirical evidence and, because this is often patchy and probably out of date, my conclusions necessarily must be tentative. I begin with a discussion of how commitments are negotiated when a particular need arises, and then move to a consideration of how commitments develop over time.

### Negotiating specific commitments

The argument which I am developing implies that whenever an individual has a particular need – for a loan of money, moral support in times of personal crisis, a roof over their head for the next six months, and so on – this triggers a process of negotiation with one or more of their relatives who may be in a position to supply that need. Many instances will not have this 'crisis' character, because it will be possible to anticipate that the need for support will occur at some point: you can see that your son's marriage is going to end, that your sister will return from abroad with nowhere to live, that your daughter is not going to generate enough capital to get on the first rung of the housing ladder. In these circumstances negotiations about what support relatives might offer probably will begin in advance. Through what means do such negotiations occur?

*Defining 'need' and 'capacity'*   Building on a distinction which I have used before, I suggest that negotiations proceed by developing shared definitions of what constitutes a 'need' for support and who has the 'capacity' to provide it. Both are negotiable, but such negotiations have to proceed in a way which takes account of the kind of structural conditions which I discussed in chapter 3 – the economic position of both parties, the range of commitments to other kin which each will have, how many relatives there are in total who 'could' contribute some assistance. The outcome also will be influenced by the public morality of family obligations and by specific cultural practices concerning kin relationships. For example, if my cousin is in need of money I am much more likely to be defined as having the 'capacity' to provide it if our family background is Asian, than if we are part of the white majority.

Taking the first definition of need, we can see that what counts as real or legitimate need is clear-cut in some situations, but in many it is not. For example, there is evidence that the past conduct and reputation of that person who needs support will make a difference to whether their need will be defined as legitimate, or at least as a need with which they can legitimately expect relatives to assist. The study by Firth, Hubert and Forge found that even in parent–child relationships, a parent's past conduct towards their children can mean that children do not accept the parent's need as one where it is legitimate to expect their children to respond (Firth, Hubert and Forge, 1970, p. 110). In these examples it is the fact that the person previously has contravened the moral order which leads relatives to define their need as 'not legitimate' in terms of family obligations, rather than the question of how well they get on with each other in an emotional sense – an issue to which I shall return later in this chapter.

These instances suggest quite clearly that the 'need' for support from relatives is socially defined and therefore subject to negotiation, not simply a matter of a person's physical condition or the state of their bank balance. The social definition of need can lead to withholding support which might otherwise have been given, but also it can work in the other direction: giving support which is not strictly needed. There is an interesting example of this in Daatland's study of the assistance given to elderly people in a Norwegian town by family, friends and volunteers. He argues that the support which people received was more easily explained by the need to sustain and develop social relationships, than by the physical needs of the elderly person. This led in some cases to the provision of support which was not actually necessary, because the parties involved 'defined their responsibility and contribution according to what ought to be done (i.e. the social relations) rather than what needs to be done (i.e. the care needs)' (Daatland, 1983, p. 8).

If the need for assistance is subject to social definition and negotiation, so too is the capacity to provide it. It can be demonstrated that inability to provide support is one of the major justifications which people give when they are not fulfilling an obligation which they might have been expected to honour. Some of the most interesting examples concern in-law relationships which, as I noted in chapter 1, have an element of ambiguity not present in the same way in relationships with one's family of origin. The study by Firth and his colleagues offers several examples where people try to claim that they cannot give their in-laws moral or practical support, through lack of time or because the absence of warmth between them would make their support pointless or ineffective (Firth, Hubert and Forge, 1970, pp. 111–12). They seem to be making substantial efforts to avoid presenting their lack of assistance as 'I do not want to.' It is in circumstances like this where people have difficulties in establishing a claim that they 'cannot' provide support, that we see the significance of such matters being socially defined.

A final point about the social definition of the need for support and the capacity to provide it concerns gender. The social definitions of what counts as both need and capacity are gendered in character, and this means that women and men have a differing chance of having their accounts accepted by others. The point about capacity to provide support being related to gender is well recognized, especially the capacity to provide personal care for a handicapped or infirm relative, where women are defined culturally as being more suitable and able to provide care than men (Finch and Groves, 1980; Equal Opportunities Commission, 1982; Ungerson, 1983; Graham, 1983). Women are also regarded as more available for such tasks. In her small-scale study of carers, Ungerson uses her detailed data to show, for example, that the role of paid work is sharply divided by gender when there are negotiations about providing personal care for a relative. The place accorded to work in the pattern of men's lives is such that there are clear 'start-up' and 'cut-off' points, and only after the phase of paid work has run its normal course are men available to provide personal care (which in their case almost always is for their wife). For men, work has the effect of 'blotting out' other demands, but not for women, who experience demands from various sources throughout their lives and attempt to juggle them and fulfil as many as they can (Ungerson, 1987, pp. 66–81). Ungerson's evidence reflects both what women do in practice, and what is regarded as proper for women to do, in a normative sense.

Thus women are defined as having a 'capacity' to provide care which is beyond the capacity of men. This means that when men engage in negotiations about whether they are going to provide personal care for a relative, they are much more likely than are women to be able to get other people to accept the claim 'I am not able to do that.' A woman who produced precisely the same reasons as a man (I'm no good at looking after people; I have a job; I've never been close to my father) is much less likely to have those reasons accepted as legitimate.

The point that the 'need' for support also involves gendered definitions is less widely accepted, but may be equally important in understanding the negotiation of support between relatives. Although we lack clear evidence, there are hints in the available data that the need for both practical and financial support is defined in gendered terms. We know that there is a long-standing expectation in British culture that women can manage on less than men – that they can live on less food and a poorer diet, less money, and so on (Oren, 1973; Graham, 1984; Charles and Kerr, 1988). Conversely, there is the expectation that men need to have 'extras', especially personal spending, and this expectation is reflected in evidence that money is actually given for this purpose by relatives in situations of male unemployment (Morris, 1983). It seems to me that there are enough hints in the existing data to suggest that both in terms of material resources and personal or domestic support, women and men are widely defined as having different needs and that this is likely to have an effect when commitments between kin are being negotiated.

In negotiations over specific instances where support may be given by a relative, I suggest that what is being negotiated is the need of one person for support and the capacity of the other to provide it. I am aware that any people might talk about 'willingness' to provide support rather than 'capacity', but I believe that the whole process is better understood as one where the final word is 'I cannot do this' rather than 'I don't want to do this.' Available evidence suggests that people do in practice tend to frame their accounts in terms of capacity rather than willingness. Also the perspective of public morality suggests that most people, for most of the time, are engaged in an exercise where they wish to affirm their continuing adherence to a set of values or normative guidelines, whatever their actions in particular cases. Hence the phenomenon, which was observed for example by Bott (1957) where, after having taken a particular course of action, people will reframe their understanding of the proper way to fulfil a particular obligation, so that the definition encompasses what they themselves had done. It seems to me that the concept of being willing or unwilling to honour a particular obligation fails to capture this, because it implies that people can readily acknowledge the existence of a duty but choose to ignore it. That misses the point that it is important for people to sustain their reputation as moral beings if their own position in the social world is not to be undermined.

*Negotiating skills*   The actual processes whereby people conduct negotiations with their relatives are bound to be subtle and often unspoken. Looking at it from the perspective of symbolic interactionism, one would expect that such negotiations would depend upon people conveying their meaning and intentions through gestures, cues and hints, which they can expect their relatives to understand because they have developed shared concepts of the social world over a long period of time. It is interesting also to speculate how far the capacity to do this differs for women and men. The evidence that women are more actively involved in their kin relationships than are men (see chapter 1), suggests that women have more opportunities to develop such shared understandings with other women relatives. Moreover, as some feminists have pointed out, women actually play a more active role in face-to-face relationships in families than do men, taking responsibility for keeping conversations going smoothly, for example (Fishman, 1978; Mason, 1987). All of this suggests that women may be able more easily to engage in the actual process of negotiating commitments to relatives than are men, because they have more of the relevant skills; by the same token of course they may be more likely to end up with a more extensive set of commitments.

I am suggesting that negotiating commitments with relatives requires one to deploy a repertoire of skills and knowledge. Partly this entails the use of commonly understood gestures and actions in order to convey the appropriate meaning, but also there is the use of what Harre (1977) calls maxims – rules for how one should present oneself appropriately in particular circumstances. In relation to negotiating commitments with relatives, these would include such matters as when you should ask for help and when you should wait for it to be offered, the way you should express your request and so on. Partly it is a matter of technique, of knowing how to deploy the etiquette of family obligations, but it is also related quite closely to matters of fine judgement. For example, the issue of when you should offer support and when an offer might be inappropriate is not just a question of knowing the rules of etiquette, but also of a careful application of the normative guideline that each person needs to be able to maintain a balance of dependence and independence in their family relationships (see chapter 5).

An example which illustrates this point very clearly can be found in Bell's (1968) study of middle-class families, which focuses principally upon relationships between parents and adult children. As I noted in chapter 1, his data offer a number of examples of financial support passing from older to younger generations in these families. One such example illustrates well the delicacy of the negotiation processes involved. It concerns a young man who was an architect, who wanted money to buy a partnership in a practice, and eventually obtained it from his father-in-law,

I told him I was considering changing my job like I said. I didn't ask but to tell the truth I hoped. He said 'How much?' and I told him and he said he would see. Eventually he gave it to me, called it a loan but said I needn't pay it back. But I am though – five pounds a month so I don't feel obliged to him. (Bell, 1968, p. 92)

The way this account is presented is fascinating because it makes plain several important procedures used in the negotiation, and demonstrates how skilful one needs to be if it is to prove successful. The son-in-law made it clear that he needed money, but did not ask for it directly, so that his father-in-law was left some choice about how to offer it. The father-in-law did not respond immediately, so that eventually when he came back this clearly was an 'offer' of money, rather than a response to a request. The money was 'called' a loan but the father-in-law made it clear that it was really a gift, a transaction between close relatives not a business deal. However, the son-in-law regarded it as important that he treated it as a loan and repaid it. Bell's analysis of that is that in this situation these were ways of resolving the conflict between the norm of independence and the reality that the son-in-law was partially dependent. In the terms which I have been developing in this discussion, procedures of negotiation were deployed very skilfully to ensure that the desired balance between dependence and independence was preserved for both parties.

The skill and judgement involved in the actual process of applying normative guidelines should not be underestimated, but at the same time it would be wrong to suggest that each situation is negotiated in a vacuum, with the parties having to work out from scratch how to conduct themselves. Established procedures for action can be called upon, and it may be useful to think of these in terms of rituals, in the sense that LaGaipa (1982) has discussed the rituals for withdrawing from personal relationships; that is, rituals are patterned actions which have symbolic significance, and which enable changes in relationships to be managed satisfactorily. We know rather little specifically, either about the appropriate rituals for negotiating whether to give support to a relative, or about the part played by third parties in that ritual, and this could be a fruitful line for future research to pursue.

*Power and negotiations*   Finally in relation to negotiating in specific commitments, there is the important question of power relations. As I noted above it is a classic criticism of interactionist work that it ignores power, although this is addressed in later work (Strauss, 1978). Certainly in family relationships one cannot assume that each party to the negotiation begins from an equally strong position. Any empirical study which seeks to understand how commitments are negotiated needs to try to uncover how far the differential power position of the participants shapes the direction of the negotiations and their outcome. We know from the long established literature that power in family relationships is likely to be a mixture of different elements (Parsons and Fox, 1968; Cromwell and Olson, 1975; Scanzoni; 1979). In part it is a question of how power relations within the kin group have built up over time which is a particularly difficult issue on which to generate empirical data. The researcher probably has to rely on the retrospective accounts of the participants, and they simply may not be able to remember the series of events which the researcher would regard as crucial to understanding the development of power relations. Such difficulties were encountered by Ungerson in her work on caring for elderly people. She wanted to understand how the situation came about where one relative was defined as the main carer for an elderly person and found that her interviewees told her consistently that everyone else who might have been an alternative carer had a legitimate reason for saying 'no'. She suggests that one way of interpreting this is that 'those who said "no" simply had more power within their family to be effectively negative.' If this is conceived as a battle between opposing interests, the eventual carer was the one who had lost (Ungerson, 1987, p. 143).

This is an interesting interpretation and I think that Ungerson is right to point to the exercise of interpersonal power within negotiations. But my own interpretation would reject that idea of a 'battle' of interests. On the basis of my previous analysis I would expect it to be both more subtle and more prolonged than that analogy implies. I would take seriously the respondents' interpretation that everyone else had legitimate reasons to say 'no'. On the basis of the analysis which I have developed here, I would deduce that negotiations had been going on implicitly for a long time within the group of close kin who might be potential carers for a particular elderly person, and it is in the course of those negotiations that individuals would have been attempting to wield whatever power was available to them, in order to define themselves out of the running. By the time the elderly person actually needed to be cared for, I suspect that the shared understandings which had been developed in this kin group ensured that the eventual carer did feel quite genuinely that no one else was available. Therefore it seems important to look for the exercise of power in negotiations over a long period of time, and not just when specific decisions have to be made. In that context, one can look also for alliances and coalitions being formed to increase the power of some parties relative to others, which is a classic part of interpersonal bargaining strategy (Rubin and Brown, 1975).

Why are some individuals more powerful than others in these situations within kin groups? There are a number of likely reasons, and the particular blend needs probably to be uncovered for each individual case. The impact of external structures upon negotiations becomes very apparent at this point. Let us suppose that I have three sisters, one of whom has been physically handicapped from birth. In our family we have developed a commitment to ensure that she is always well cared for, and an understanding that the other three sisters will take equal responsibility for that. A point is reached where my elderly parents can no longer manage to care for her physically and she needs someone else permanently on call to feed and bath her. Two sisters have well-paid jobs and they suggest paying privately for a nurse to come in regularly. I am attracted to that idea, but my economic circumstances mean that I could not pay my share. The only way in which I could fulfil my commitments is through my own labour, but my sisters, whose economic position is much more favourable than mine, have a wider range of choices available. Whilst in this situation my sisters would not necessarily wield power over me, my point is that they *could* do so by insisting that they are fulfilling their part of the bargain in one way and I must find a way of fulfilling mine. Their relative power in that situation, and my relative powerlessness, derives from our different locations within the economic structures of the wider society. As Giddens (1979, p. 88) puts it, building on the classic analysis developed by Max Weber, power in social life should be understood as the differing capacities which human agents possess to achieve defined outcomes.

Gender is a very important element in this context, specifically the exercise of patriarchal power, the power of men over women. The negotiation of support within families can show very clearly that men are able to allocate certain tasks to women – such as domestic support or personal care – without there being any equivalent power on the part of women to allocate tasks to men (Rose, 1981; Stacey, 1981). The evidence that daughters-in-law rank higher than sons in the hierarchy of obligations to care for an elderly person is a clear example of men's capacity to allocate responsibilities to women. Ungerson's work makes the exercise of patriarchal power visible in a different but interesting way. She has some examples of men acting as the main carers for a disabled wife, as well as women who were caring for husband or parents. In the case of the female carers, she argues, once they had taken on the main responsibility for looking after the infirm person, this was treated by themselves and others as a final settlement, likely to last until that person died. However, in the case of male carers, and especially those who also had a daughter, the settlement was not so final because the possibility of the younger woman's taking over always hovered in the background, and indeed in some cases the daughter already had taken over (Ungerson, 1987, pp. 48–61). Although undoubtedly the daughters in these situations would regard themselves as willing carers, their fathers nonetheless did have the power to call upon their resources for support, whereas women carers have no equivalent power to draw in male relatives.

## Negotiated commitments over time

I have indicated already that I believe that no individual instance of negotiated commitments between relatives can be understood in isolation, simply by looking at the pressure of a particular situation and the processes of negotiation which it engenders. Every negotiation between members of the same family, about whether a particular kind of support is to be provided, draws upon a history of relationships and commitments in that particular family, and anticipates a future. In this section I shall discuss the different elements which need to be considered if we are to understand family obligations as commitments which develop over time – perhaps over the whole lifetime of the individuals involved.

*The history of the relationship*   The first and most obvious element is the history of the relationship between the two individuals involved. There is clear evidence that many instances where, for example, one child takes major responsibility for the care of an elderly parent, are the product of the history of a particular relationship, often the result of decisions taken years earlier, such as the decision to take the parent into your home at a time when they were not infirm, which set the relationship on a particular track (Levin, Sinclair and Gorbach, 1983).

The course of the relationship between a parent and a particular child can be set at a very early stage in the child's life. It may be affected by circumstances such as the timing and spacing of children, so that some are more likely than others to overlap with their parents in adult life (see chapter 3 for further discussion), or by birth order, especially in circumstances where older children are encouraged to move away and younger ones to stay in the parental home for longer. Such factors set the scene for quite different relationships to develop between a parent and their older or younger children (Tilly, 1984). The course of parent–child relationships which people define as bad or unsatisfactory can also be set in childhood. Firth and his colleagues found that where people felt that their relationships with their own parents were poor, childhood events were often offered as an explanation. Common themes were the desertion, divorce and/or remarriage of a parent; although the researchers caution that these events have to be seen as indicative of other tensions, and that whether they actually result in poor relationships in adult life depends upon a range of other circumstances (Firth, Hubert and Forge, 1970, p. 403). If a person has a poor relationship with their children this can be expected to have some effect on the course of negotiations which they conduct about the provision of support in old age, although it is not necessarily an overriding factor, as Qureshi's (1986) data demonstrate (see chapter 1 for further discussion).

Another dimension of the history to a particular relationship, or indeed to a set of relationships, is that there are certain points at which one can anticipate that the relationship will be renegotiated, linked with the normative expectation that there should be what I have called 'patterned change' in family relationships (see chapter 5). Although the character of relationships formed in childhood can have enduring importance, it would be quite wrong to imagine that nothing ever changes. As I have already indicated in chapter 5, there is a clear sense that people expect patterned change in the obligation to give support within families, including a sense that it is quite proper for relationships to be renegotiated at certain points, perhaps most obviously when children first marry. Diana Leonard Barker's (1972) discussion of 'spoiling and keeping close' (which I mentioned in chapter 5) spells out some of the processes through which such renegotiations occur. She shows that parents, especially mothers, spoil their young adult children when they are still living in the parental home by taking little rent from them, buying them gifts and releasing them from the responsibility of helping with domestic tasks (especially if they are boys). As a consequence the ties between parent and child are strengthened and reconstituted on a different basis from childhood and this enables mothers to 'keep them close' when the children establish their own households.

There are also other life events which trigger predictable renegotiations (the renegotiations are predictable even if the events are not). Widowhood is a good example of this, and Marris's study of widows and their families offers a clear account of the new order of social relationships formed following the death of a spouse. Relationships with in-laws become more distant, even if they remain entirely cordial, but at the same time widows can legitimately expect to make larger claims upon their own children (Marris, 1958, pp. 73–8). Divorce and remarriage are also events which one might expect to trigger a renegotiation of relationships with other relatives, although we know very little in detail about how people expect their relationships to change after divorce, either with their own kin, or with former in-laws (see chapter 1 for some discussion of the available literature).

*Developing personal reputations* Focusing on the development of obligations over time highlights another issue to which I have already referred, namely the development of personal reputations and the social identities of individual members of the kin group. The argument here depends partly upon the general insight that people do have a need to maintain a positive social identity in the context of their personal relationships (LaGaipa, 1982) and partly on the specific evidence that families perform the important task of providing a source of positive identity. Writing as an anthropologist who has undertaken a detailed study of eight London households, including their kin relationships, Wallman (1983) argues that families provide certain basic resources for their members, including a sense of identity and belonging. In that sense the family distributes moral as well as economic goods, and these have some impact on the type of support which will be offered and received at any given point in time.

Wallman gives one case example which illustrates this point well; in this instance the personal reputation and social identity which had been built up within the kin group was counter-productive at a point when the woman concerned might have turned to relatives for help. The woman in this case had nine children and was part of a large and close-knit kin network. In that network she had developed the reputation of being a cheerful and easy-going person to whom others could turn for help. At one point she herself suffered a mental breakdown following various problems, including marital violence, and was admitted to a mental hospital for a spell. At the time of this breakdown she felt quite strongly that she could not turn to her relatives for help, because they saw her as someone upon whom other people could always rely (Wallman, 1983, p. 160). In this example, her need for support was out of line with the reputation which she had built up with her kin over time, and her reputation acted therefore as a barrier to her seeking help from them.

Approaching a similar set of issues, but from the quite different standpoint of social philosophers, Leighton, Stalley and Watson emphasize the importance of understanding how a person's history of negotiated commitments goes to make up their own moral and social identity. They base their discussion on material from social workers' case loads. We all live in a social world, they suggest, in which we,

inherit, adopt, negotiate and abandon commitments in a range of social identities such as sons and daughters, mothers and fathers, friends, person helped and person helping, people co-operating. This network of commitments structures our expectations of ourselves and others, gives us purpose and reasons to act. (Leighton, Stalley and Watson, 1982, p. 2)

In this analysis, a person's moral identity can be understood as the sum of these commitments, and their moral integrity is undermined if they fail to honour the commitments which make up that identity. The emphasis of these writers is on moral identity as a personal matter, but one needs only to extend the analysis a little to acknowledge that this also constitutes an individual's reputation, which is the public property of a kin group. It is the social identity which individuals bring to each new stage of negotiations with relatives, and which will influence the course of those negotiations, because each person's reputation carried forward over time embodies a set of expectations about how they will act.

*Cumulative commitments* Finally in relation to this discussion of negotiations over time, I suggest that we can understand the pattern of how these develop by saying that they are cumulative. I am drawing here upon the analysis of commitments developed by Howard Becker (1960) where he spells out how commitments accumulate. This process is not necessarily conscious or deliberate, and it certainly does not mean that people simply gather more and more commitments which they can never shed. Rather Becker's emphasis is upon commitments as part of a pattern of negotiated relationships which themselves change over time, but where the fact that one has developed a particular commitment in the past does have some effect on what is possible in the future. Over a period of time, in Becker's view, a person develops a line of action which has a certain consistency and predictability about it. Social identity and reputation are invested in that consistency, which means that a point is eventually reached where it becomes too 'expensive' to withdraw from the particular course of action, because too much has been invested in it (see Finch, 1987c for further discussion).

Examples of the cumulative nature of commitments can be drawn from the literature on caring for an elderly person, for a parent in particular, where commonly researchers note that far more people seem to 'drift' into caring than ever make a conscious decision to do so. The evidence suggests strongly that a commitment to care develops over a period of time and the idea of drifting comes from the comments which many respondents make, such as 'It just happened' or 'You find it quite impossible to walk away from it' (Lewis and Meredith, 1988, p. 21). I would question, however, whether the concept of drift is appropriate here, implying as it does that the commitment to care derives from a series of events which happen *to* the carer, and in which she is not really a conscious or active participant.

I would argue that the concept of cumulative commitments is an improvement and also that it fits the available evidence. For example, one of Lewis and Meredith's respondents had cared for her own mother before she died, following a history of a relationship where the two had shared a home for many years. The daughter had been married and was widowed in the 1950s. She returned to her mother's home at that point, partly because it was a socially acceptable thing to do and partly because it was cheaper for her. In a sense, from that point onwards she was set on a course which was likely to lead eventually to providing personal care for her mother (p. 22). In a different case an interviewee describes her relationship with her mother in these terms,

My mother and I lived together because we chose to, we liked each other . . . we shared a common home, we could laugh together . . . I was an independent person, so was my mother. We were living together, I wasn't just looking after her. (Lewis and Meredith, 1988, p. 54)

A series of events such as these do not just 'happen to' the participants. Rather people make choices at one particular point in time, for reasons which they are aware of, with benefits accruing to both sides and with consequences of which they are at least partly conscious.

The same could be said of several examples given by Ungerson in her study of carers for elderly people. As I have noted above she shows that, where an elderly man is caring for his infirm wife and they also have a daughter, it is always a possibility that the daughter will take over from him eventually. Again, it seems to me that this represents less of a 'drift' and more of a semi-anticipated series of events, which the daughter nonetheless feels is unavoidable because of the shared understandings developed previously between herself and her parents. Indeed, in one case which Ungerson quoted, the daughter certainly was conscious of what was happening, because her own husband and children were intervening to try to persuade her to take on fewer commitments for her parents. Her GP also had warned her that it might not be a good idea to give up her job to look after her parents, on the grounds that he did not want another depressed and anxious patient on his hands (Ungerson, 1987, pp. 55–6).

I do not wish to imply that commitments which accumulate over time necessarily are experienced as unwelcome (although they may be). But I think that viewing them as cumulative in this way helps to draw together some of the strands of the foregoing discussion – the importance of the time perspective, the significance of personal identity and reputation, the idea of playing to internal and external audiences. The model which is encapsulated by this idea of accumulated commitments helps us to understand, for example, how it is that over a period of time it becomes 'obvious' that one sibling rather than another will take care of elderly parents when that becomes necessary.

### The emotional dimension

This discussion of negotiations would be incomplete without some consideration of the emotional dimension in family relationships, which I have hinted at but not dealt with explicitly. Much of the above discussion in a sense would be peripheral if support between kin were actually offered – or more importantly withheld – because of the quality of the emotional relationships between the two parties which has developed quite separately from any normative structure. In chapter 7 I shall deal with the role which we should accord to emotions in understanding family relationships more generally. At this point I shall confine the discussion to the question of how far negotiations over time about kin support can be said to be shaped by the emotional quality of the relationships involved.

There is no doubt that relationships between close kin can be very painful and hostile, and one would expect the personal commitments developed in such relationships to be governed by those feelings. For example in the study by Lewis and Meredith (1988), of daughters who had cared for their mother before she died, some interviewees made comments which indicated that their relationships had always been poor,

We weren't particularly close, we got on all right and I was the dutiful daughter . . . I mean not grudgingly but I mean we weren't that close really, no.

I think you've got to think a great deal of somebody or have a great sense of duty to be able to do it . . . I think I thought that it was mostly duty . . . there are times when you hate each other when you are in a relationship like that.

(Lewis and Meredith, 1988, pp. 27–8)

In both these cases the daughters had given their mothers significant amounts of personal care despite a rather problematic relationship, which apparently had a long history. That experience could be replicated from a number of other studies and, as I indicated in chapter 1, the available evidence on parent–child relationships in particular suggests that poor relationships generally are not an overriding consideration in whether assistance is given in old age. That may seem curious, but it becomes more understandable if we see emotions themselves, not as free-standing and uncontrollable feelings which are quite separate from the normative structure of duty and obligations, but as linked closely with that structure. In this section I shall expand on that view.

At the most general level, one can argue that emotional relationships in families are shaped by the external contexts which I discussed in chapters 3 and 4. I suggested there, for example, that the rather random factor of birth order can affect profoundly the likelihood that a parent will develop a closer relationship with some children than with others. Another example which I gave concerns the effect of different systems of inheritance. A system such as the traditional English custom of primogeniture, where the oldest son inherits everything, encourages an emotional climate conducive to setting younger children against the oldest son, in a way which is much less likely under an inheritance system which divides property equally. So we can argue that emotional relationships which develop with families cannot be regarded as free-standing and separate from the material circumstances of family life. This point is made very effectively in an article by Medick and Sabean (1984), where they bring together historical and anthropological material to demonstrate that the emotional and material spheres of family life in fact are intimately interwined.

Looking more specifically at the relationships between emotions and the development of family obligations, one needs to take into account that whilst on one level the emotional relationship between the parties may influence their negotiations about providing support, at the same time emotions themselves are subject to normative guidelines.

This is an important point which has been relatively unexplored in writings on family relationships, except in a few very important sources, of which I shall mention particularly Turner (1970) and Hochschild (1975; 1979). It is commonplace in anthropological work to observe that feelings of affection and love are culturally specific, and are taken to be characteristic of family relationships in western societies (Schneider, 1968; Medick and Sabean, 1984). If it is true that people usually do experience these feelings towards their close relatives (and of course it is by no means true universally) – what gives rise to them? Turner's answer is that love has to be seen as a 'social sentiment', and part of a system of organized sentiments which have social meaning in a particular culture. He distinguishes sentiment from emotions, which he sees as rooted in individual psychology and relatively independent of culture. Sentiments, on the other hand, are feelings which are socially defined as appropriate in particular settings. That is not to deny that they have an element of spontaneity, but essentially they have to be learned: we have to learn when a particular sentiment like love is appropriate, how it should be expressed, to whom it should be directed, and so on (Turner, 1970, pp. 216–43).

In her work, Hochschild develops a rather similar analysis, but takes it further through her use of the concept of 'feeling rules'. She argues that these are normative rules which control feelings in a particular social context; 'such rules put a normative floor and ceiling upon feelings by indicating what is appropriate and desirable' (Hochschild, 1975, p. 289). She argues that people do have a clear sense of what they 'should feel' in particular circumstances, which is not necessarily the same thing as what they expect to feel. For the most part, people do experience their actual feelings as being roughly in line with what the normative feeling rules indicate as appropriate, but this does not necessarily arise spontaneously. Hochschild suggests that people monitor and shape their own feelings through emotional work, in which they 'try to feel' those things which they know they 'should feel' (Hochschild, 1979, pp. 564–71).

Both Hochschild's and Turner's work are quite close to the 'social constructionist' perspective in social psychology, where the emotions which people feel depend fundamentally on the language which any culture offers for the expression of emotions, and upon the cultural meaning of such feelings within what Harre calls 'the local moral order' (Harre, 1986). These are issues to which I shall return in chapter 7. I have paused here to explain the basis of these ideas because they are relatively uncommon in discussion of family relationships, yet are of great significance to understanding the relationship between normative guidelines and the negotiation of family obligations.

It must be said that there is very little empirical work on contemporary Britain which would enable us to assess in a systematic way the relevance of these ideas to the negotiation of support within families. However, they do raise important research questions such as: Do people try to align their own feelings about particular relatives with what they believe they 'ought to feel'? Under what circumstances do people try to bring their own feelings into line in this way, and in respect of which relatives? Since we also know that strong feelings of intimacy and loyalty towards members of one's family are more characteristic of women than of men (Stacey and Price, 1981), there are also some important research questions about gender variations. Are women more aware than men of feeling rules? Do women in particular monitor their feelings towards their relatives, to bring them into line with sentiments which are normatively appropriate? Is what counts as 'normatively appropriate' different for women and men?

The questions which I have posed here rather imply that people have negative feelings towards their relatives and then may feel under pressure to give them a more positive cast. But this is not the only way in which emotions can feed into negotiations about support. If we link this with the earlier discussion of creating and sustaining social identities, we can see that the process of negotiating support may be shaped by positive feelings which are linked to an individual's personal reputation and social identity in the kin group, and which get reinforced through the feedback and approval which is part of the negotiating process. The implications of this are spelled out very clearly by Hilary Graham in her discussion of the concept of 'caring' and how it operates in social life. She argues that it is the means by which men's and women's social identities are distinguished,

Caring is 'given' to women: it becomes the defining characteristic of their self-identity and their life's work. At the same time, caring is taken away from men: not-caring becomes a defining characteristic of manhood. Men are marked out as separate and different from women because they are not involved in caring for (and with) others. Their sense of self is achieved by doing things for (and by) themselves. (Graham, 1983, p. 18)

The implication of this is that the process of negotiating kin support is shaped by women's identities as 'people who care', and in turn those identities are reinforced through such negotiations. Again, we lack good data which really could put this to an empirical test in a range of different circumstances, but there is rich potential here for developing further research.

Finally in this consideration of the place of emotions in the negotiation of commitments, there is the possibility that emotions will be 'used' in relationships in a manipulative way. This is referred to in common parlance as emotional blackmail, and is the most dramatic illustration of why it is inappropriate to see emotions as entirely separate from the process of negotiating obligations. A fairly mild example of this (in the sense that it does not appear to involve malicious intent) can be found in Leonard Barker's (1972) account of how parents of young people 'spoil them', so that they can 'keep them close' after they marry, which I mentioned above. Rather less innocuous are examples cited by Firth, Hubert and Forge (1970). Some of their interviewees talked explicitly about parents exercising emotional blackmail over them. In one case, this was to ensure that a woman went on working in the parents' shop, even though she did not want to; in another case a woman said that her parents exploited happy memories of childhood in order to get her to do things which she did not want to do, such as keeping in touch with more distant kin. These examples, by being labelled specifically as emotional blackmail, are being identified by the participants as actions which overstep the mark in terms of normative guidelines – possibly because they disturb the proper balance between dependence and independence in parent–child relationships.

The more recent literature on caring for elderly relatives makes visible the issue of emotional blackmail, and here it is easy to see how it fits into a pattern of negotiations about giving support. Lewis and Meredith give some examples of what they call manipulative behaviour on the part of elderly parents, which evidently contained elements of emotional blackmail, as in the following account,

She was so unpredictable that you couldn't plan anything, you could never say next Saturday we'd just go out, because you could guarantee that Saturday she'd suddenly have one of her bad days; and on her bad days she really did look dreadful. But on the next day she'd be all pinky and perky again. (Lewis and Meredith, 1988, p. 64)

Ungerson discusses explicitly the emotional blackmail which some elderly parents practice on their children, and sees it as highly gendered; that is, women in the younger generation are much more susceptible to being pressured in this way than are men. People who had been at the receiving end spoke of 'feeling guilty if I don't go down to see her' and 'a battle of wills'. One of them spelled out the way in which emotional blackmail worked in these terms,

She considers that daughters *should* be responsible for parents. It's not quite like that any more! She says she won't eat if she goes into Connors House [i.e. short-stay residential care]. She'd make up her mind to die; I'd feel like the executioner! So I think I tend to chicken out. (Ungerson, 1987, p. 96)

In this example, it is clear that emotions are used in the process of negotiating support as a means of bringing about one's own wishes in the face of other people's resistance, and therefore when we are talking about the place of emotions in negotiations we need to link it with the issue of power. In the example above, the mother had the power significantly to influence her daughter's actions, through deploying her own emotions and manipulating her daughter's. If we want to understand how it comes about that one human being has that kind of power to influence the course of a relationship, it is relevant to consider a number of issues which I have raised earlier in this chapter. Certainly the interpersonal history of this particular mother–daughter relationship is likely to be relevant, but we need to look also at the context within which such negotiations take place. How did a shared understanding develop that it is unreasonable for *this* daughter to resist her mother's demands ('I'd feel like the executioner'), despite the fact that she would regard such demands as unreasonable in other circumstances ('It's not quite like that any more')? That understanding certainly did not develop in a social vacuum, but would have been shaped by structural factors including gender, the public morality of family obligations which would endorse the actions of a daughter who made considerable sacrifices for her mother, and the way in which the daughter's personal reputation and social identity had become invested in continuing this commitment to her mother, which on one level she regarded as inappropriate.

### Legitimate excuses

In concluding this discussion of obligations as negotiated commitments, I suggest that much of the material which I have considered can be operationalized empirically by using the concept of 'legitimate excuses'. If we ask the question 'What counts as a legitimate excuse for not offering support in a particular set of circumstances?' we are likely to uncover most of the important facets of negotiating obligations.

First, we will see the boundaries of what counts as acceptable behaviour, and how these relate to normative guidelines about the proper thing to do. The normative guidelines have to be applied in specific cases, but negotiations about how they *can* be applied take place within limits. Those limits are seen by looking at how people try to produce an account of their actions which others will accept as a legitimate application of the guidelines. Second, we highlight the importance of 'accounts' of action, and how the possibilities for successfully establishing a particular account may actually affect what a person does. Third, we see that legitimacy itself is a negotiated issue rather than a fixed criterion. Fourth, we see the importance of placing each decision in the context of others which have gone before, since each negotiation takes place against a history of excuses which have been accepted as legitimate in the past. Fifth, we see the importance of personal reputation and social identity, since the one person may be able to get an excuse accepted as legitimate, whilst another may not. Gender is a very important, although not the only, aspect of this capacity to get a particular excuse accepted as legitimate.

In focusing in this way on legitimate excuses, I do not wish to imply that I see negotiated commitments to support one's relatives in a wholly negative way – that is, as commitments which people always will get out of if they can. I hope it is clear from the foregoing discussion that I see the balance of gains and losses as much more complex than that. Nonetheless I find the concept of legitimate excuses a useful analytical tool, which enables us to get a sharp focus upon the complex and often hidden social processes involved when relatives negotiate their commitments with each other.

# 7

# Are kin relationships 'special'?

## Introduction

In previous chapters I have suggested a number of different ways of looking at support between kin, and at the role played by duty and obligation in its provision. I have ranged from large-scale issues of economic structures and public policies, to questions about the personal relationships which people build with their own relatives, and I have emphasized the inter-connection between the personal and the structural. Each different way of looking at family support and family obligations tends to illuminate some facets, but obscure others. In this chapter I shall draw together the strands of the foregoing discussion by considering several different theoretical models, which have been used to explain kin relationships. Through evaluating these different approaches, I develop a framework for understanding the foundations of support between adult kin in the context of contemporary Britain.

The idea that kin support is founded, in whole or in part, upon duty and obligation, implies that there is 'something special' about social relationships which we have with kin, which makes them distinctively different from all other relationships. Duty, obligation and responsibility are the defining marks of the special character of kinship and are present in these relationships in a way not replicated even with close friends. This idea of the special character of kin relations provides the organizing theme for this chapter. I begin by discussing two theoretical approaches which imply that family relationships are (in this particular sense) 'nothing special', then move to five others which do see kin relationships as special but explain this in rather different ways.

## Support between kin is 'nothing special'

The theoretical positions which I shall consider first are those which suggest that support within kin groups can be explained, in the last resort, without reference to responsibility or duty. I have put in the caveat 'in the last resort', because it is possible to adopt such a theoretical position yet still to recognize that obligation, duty and responsibility are concepts used commonly to describe family life, and therefore have social meaning as ways of presenting our own actions to various audiences. But in the end we have to look elsewhere if we really want to understand the foundations of kin support. In these perspectives, kinship is to be understood as a variation on other types of social relationship, not as special or different in a qualitative sense.

I shall consider two versions of this position. First, there is the view that kin relationships, like the rest of social life, are to be explained by the material conditions under which people live. These are of overriding importance in understanding why individuals act as they do, including occasions on which someone gives support to a relative. Second, there is the argument that all social life, including relationships with kin, is conducted on the basis of self-interest. People give assistance to their relatives because they think they will get something out of it in some way and at some point in the present or the future; although it is acknowledged that such calculations may be difficult for an outsider to uncover.

Although these two positions are distinct analytically, in practice they often are closely intertwined and I shall discuss them together. In a sense they represent two sides of the same coin. Both are concerned to understand family life in material terms, but while the second explanation sees family relationships as instrumental and conducted through individual calculations about self-interest, the first is more concerned with the larger scale level of analysis. Also it leaves space for the connection between economic conditions and family relationships to be traced in different ways, not only through the concept of self-interest.

### *Material conditions: the key to an explanatory framework?*

The first of the two positions which I have outlined implies that examples of support given and received in families are to be understood as transactions, shaped by the economic and material conditions which prevailed at any point in time. It is a version of the argument that all aspects of family relationships are to be explained in the end by economic circumstances. It is economic forces which shape the division of labour in families, who lives with whom, the way children are treated, relationships between spouses, and so on. Equally, beliefs about duty and responsibility towards kin are – like other beliefs about family relationships – ideas shaped in response to a particular set of economic conditions, developed as part of a strategy for coping with those conditions as successfully as possible. But the morality of family support, like other ideas, in the last resort is a dependent variable, as are the actual patterns of assistance developed in any particular kin group. When economic circumstances change we should expect that patterns of support, and also these moral ideas, eventually will change to align with the new conditions.

This line of reasoning has a substantial intellectual pedigree, which it would not be appropriate to discuss in detail here. But it should be noted that versions of this view can be found on both left and right politically. Marxist analyses of family life usually have treated the family as a dependent variable in this sense, beginning with Engels's (1884) classic discussion of the origins of the family, private property and the state. Engels argues that the institution of monogamous marriage and the relationships between women and men associated with it, developed to serve the interests of those who owned property. Once property relations are transformed there will follow a transformation in male–female relationships. The flaws in Engels's argument, as they have been demonstrated by the experience of history, need not be laboured here. From the opposite end of the political spectrum, conservative thought has a long tradition of seeing a particular form of the family (based upon hierarchical and patriarchal authority) as an essential support for an hierarchically organized society. At the same time, the right economic and legal conditions are needed to sustain this particular family form (Nisbet, 1978). Contemporary versions of this can be found in the writings of various commentators who argue, for example, that income support given to families from state resources subverts traditional family relationships, or that more of the cost of supporting young people needs to be shifted back from the state to the family in order to foster a sense of family responsibility (Marsland, 1986; Parker, 1986). In a sense this is remarkably similar to the Marxist position. In both cases, the form that relationships take within families, including the sense of responsibility towards one's relatives, are seen as dependent variables shaped by economic conditions.

Similar ideas have also been influential in academic work. In sociological studies the most obvious example concerns functionalist analyses of the family, especially the cruder versions where the particular form which family relationships take is seen as a consequence of the functions which families perform in the social system as a whole. The family is a dependent variable in the sense that changes in other parts of the social system trigger changes in family relationships. The problems with this type of analysis have been discussed extensively by other writers (see especially Morgan, 1975, ch. 1). I do not propose to rehearse them here, except to point out that one major difficulty of seeing the family as simply a dependent variable in functionalist analysis is that the empirical evidence of how family life operates in practice cannot really be made to fit this analytical scheme.

A more influential source of such ideas in recent years has been the work of social historians in the 'household economics school' to which I referred in chapter 2. In this approach to historical analysis, which has stimulated some very interesting empirical work, individuals who are members of households and families are seen as acting very largely in response to economic pressures and within structural constraints. They respond by developing strategies which will enable them to generate resources and to maximize the benefit which they can get collectively. Exchanges of goods and services in families can be seen as one part of those strategies. As Anderson puts it, 'the norms, meanings and symbols associated with family behaviour are seen, very largely, not as free-floating independent variables but as a corollary of these structural constraints'. (Anderson, 1980, p. 66).

In his discussion of the work generated by this school of thought Anderson points (as those who have criticized functionalist sociology have done) to the problems of relating this analytical scheme to the available empirical data. He argues that it is much easier to give a plausible account of the structural and economic factors to which households are subject, than to document precisely what is the effect of these upon family attitudes and behaviour. He argues also that, whilst the structural accounts may be persuasive of themselves, it is difficult to generate evidence which would demonstrate that they are correct to the exclusion of all other possible explanations, particularly those of writers in the 'sentiments' school, who see change in family life as stimulated by changing ideas about society and individuals. Anderson's own view is that these two types of approach to family history have to be treated as complementary (ibid. pp. 83–4).

Thus in the first instance the argument against this position, which holds that material conditions are the key to an explanatory framework for understanding family life, is that the empirical evidence does not fit the theory. That argument certainly would be supported by much of the evidence which I have reviewed in previous chapters. The reasons why people act as they do towards their relatives, are much more complex than is implied simply by seeing human actions as a response to economic pressures. I have shown, for example, that support between kin is influenced quite fundamentally by the individuals involved, by the personal reputation and social identity established by each person, and by considerations of how one's actions will look to other people.

This is not to suggest that material conditions are of little significance in understanding why people do or do not provide assistance for their relatives. Indeed I have put a good deal of emphasis on their importance, especially in my discussion in chapters 3 and 4. However, I have also argued that the question of *how* material conditions shape actual patterns of family support, and indeed any sense of obligation associated with it, must be more subtle and complex than these particular accounts imply. In that sense they are flawed theoretically as well as empirically. For reasons which I have set out in previous chapters, it makes more sense to look for an explanation which acknowledges that human beings actively construct their own lives out of the materials available to them, including the economic conditions under which they live, rather than seeing external conditions as inevitably and straightforwardly constraining human choices.

### Kin support as instrumental self-interest

The case for rejecting this first position applies in similar ways to the second, that is, the view that support between kin can be explained by instrumental actions arising from self-interest. The argument that support given to kin in reality has a purely instrumental basis in some way is attractive, and one for which there is a good deal of supporting evidence. In this view, there is no reason to suppose that people will continue to assist their relatives if they do not expect that assistance to be returned at some stage. The historical work stimulated by the important contribution of Michael Anderson (1971) offers plenty of evidence that, especially in harsh economic circumstances, people need to know that probably there will be something in it for them before support is offered to adult relatives outside the conjugal household, including parents (see chapter 2).

In this work Anderson used exchange theory as a framework for explaining the dynamics of support between kin, and suggested that exchanges took place in the context of these particular social relationships because kinship provided a structured link between individuals which offered the basis for medium and long-term reciprocal exchange. This kind of argument can be extended to make a much more general case for the instrumental nature of kin support, based on evidence of the widespread and central importance of the principle of reciprocity in kin relationships (see chapters 1 and 5 in particular). One interpretation of that principle is that support is given to a relative only if it can be seen as part of an on-going exchange, in which the giver will benefit eventually. The fact that exchange is not always direct and immediate, and therefore that a particular gift of action does not appear to be instrumental, is not relevant. Provided we understand in a sufficiently subtle way the indirect and long-term nature of many kin exchanges, we will find that in the end it is in the interests of the person who gives a particular item of support to do so. If we pursue this analysis to its conclusion, we have to argue that moral ideas about duty, responsibility and obligation are simply an edifice built upon a set of instrumental relationships.

However, the empirical evidence points to the conclusion that support between kin is not purely an instrumental matter. In particular, the evidence which I considered in chapters 5 and 6 makes it clear that the issue is much more complex than that, involving ideas about the proper thing to do, processes of negotiation in interpersonal relationships and the public presentation of oneself and one's own family. Even if we were to concede that ultimately reciprocity is an instrumental matter, it is not the only principle at work in the negotiation of kin support in practice.

In the end, I think that we cannot sustain the argument that kin relationships are *nothing but* instrumental, especially with close kin. To argue that is to fail to take proper account of all the research evidence which demonstrates that the principle of duty or obligation looms much larger than self-interest in most people's understanding of relationships, with close kin especially (Firth, Hubert and Forge, 1970, especially ch. 4), or evidence of the type which I discussed in chapter 5 which clearly suggests that self-interest is not the only possible basis for offering support to relatives. Again, especially in respect of genealogically close kin, the research evidence suggests that women who provide practical support and personal care for relatives sometimes are doing this despite their own self-interest, and despite a distant or even hostile relationship with the person for whom they are caring (see, for example, Cornwell, 1984; Qureshi, 1986).

We need to take seriously the possibility that self-interest is one element in kin support in many instances, but not to accord it overriding theoretical significance. In empirical examples of kin support it is important to look for self-interest, which may well be built into exchanges in a concealed way. Also the evidence which I reviewed in chapter 1 suggests that there are certain relationships where we might expect to find it quite prominently, and others where it will be more muted. In particular any structures of support built with more distant kin, and even with siblings, seem typically to be founded on mutual self-interest and require that the rewards to keep flowing in both directions for the relationship to be sustained. However, relationships with closer kin, especially with parents or children, often are of a different order and are sustained even when it does not appear to be in the interests of one of the parties to do so.

Finally, there is a fundamental problem with both the explanations which I have considered here, namely that they do not help us to answer the question 'Why kin?'. Both explanations require us to conclude that they can be explained in the same terms as any other social relationships. In that sense they do not need to address the question 'Why kin?'. However, that still leaves the problem of trying to understand why in practice most people do develop, with at least some of their kin, relationships which are characterized by the giving and receiving of support and which they understand to be qualitatively different from other relationships. The explanations to which I now turn have the common theme that they do treat kin relationships as 'something special'.

## Kin relations are 'something special'

The ideas which I shall examine in this section have the common feature that they start from the premise that relationships between relatives do have a distinctive dimension, which is not accounted for simply by economic or instrumental considerations. However, they vary quite markedly in explaining why this special relationship exists. I shall consider five different approaches to that issue (none of which I regard as wholly satisfactory), as a way of assessing how we can best understand the distinctive character of kin relationships, and how we might account for its basis.

## Nature and biology

The first set of ideas concerns the belief that family ties are a natural part of human existence, ultimately to be explained by biology. That rather broad statement covers a range of different intellectual positions, from the implicit and unconsidered to the rather more carefully thought out. In political terms it is closely associated with right-wing thought, and links perhaps in a slightly curious way with the idea that the correct economic conditions have to prevail for appropriate family relationships to flourish. Commentators who adopt this position are inclined to invoke the idea of the 'natural' or the 'normal' to describe the kind of family life which they wish to promote, whilst at the same time arguing that state activity in providing various types of welfare services can dangerously undermine this natural unit (see for example, Anderson and Dawson, 1986).

*Socio-biology*  The work of socio-biologists, and certain philosophers who have been influenced by them, represents the clearest attempt to spell out in a more rigorous way the idea that nature or biology is at the centre of mutual support in families. A central tenet of the socio-biologists' explanation of social behaviour is that people 'favour their own' because of the biological relationship between them – quite literally because they share the same genes. Thus the basis of the special relationship between kin, and the motivation for support given to kin over and above that which would be given to other people, is the survival of one's own genes. This is not to argue that people will never act altruistically towards others outside their own kin group. But the socio-biologists' position would be that such behaviour occurs only when people expect some benefit to accrue to themselves or to their own family. Only within the kin group do we find what Wilson (1978) calls 'hard core altruism', that is, behaviour which is not influenced by expectations of reward or indeed punishment.

The theory which underscores these ideas is traced to Darwin's theory of evolution, specifically, to the point where he argues that the principle of natural selection operates at the level of the organism. Socio-biologists have developed these ideas as the basis of their theory of altruism between kin (Dawkins, 1976; Wilson, 1975; 1978). The argument is that people act in such a way as to enhance the survival chances of their own genetic material, which is shared with blood relatives in different proportions: 50 per cent with children, 50 per cent with siblings, 25 per cent with nieces or nephews and so on. This explains why people sometimes do give support to a relative, even when apparently this is against their own self interest. At the same time, the fact that the tendency to look after one's own gets weaker with genealogically more distant relatives is a result of sharing a decreasing proportion of genetic material with more distant kin. Another concept linked with this by some writers is the idea of 'inclusive fitness', which builds on Darwin's notion of the survival of the fittest. The argument is that, if I act altruistically towards my sister I am thereby lowering my own 'fitness' but increasing hers; however, since I have a genetic stake in her fitness, the net effect of my action may be to improve the 'average inclusive fitness' of all the people in my own kin network. The prospects for this can be calculated mathematically (Wilson, 1975, pp. 117–20).

These ideas have been taken and developed by some philosophers such as Singer, who argues that various social reformers have tried to weaken the tendency for people to look after 'their own', yet there is always a preference for this: 'A bias towards the interests of our own family, rather than those of the community in general, is a persistent tendency in human behaviour for good biological reasons' (Singer, 1981 p. 36). Singer's argument in fact ends up as more complex than this, since he also wants to build in rationality as a component in morality, but the basic premise upon which his theory rests is clearly the biological one.

There is another twist to theories of socio-biology which it is also important to mention in this context and which concerns relationships between women and men. The fundamental idea here is that men and women have different genes and that men's genes direct them to perform gender-specific actions which include men's domination of women, whose genes in turn direct them to be nurturing and submissive. This would imply that women's greater involvement in giving support to their relatives, especially personal care, has a genetic basis. These ideas have been exposed to substantial critical analysis by feminist writers (see, for example, Sayers, 1982; Birke, 1986).

Although there may be a relatively small number of writers who would acknowledge that they have been influenced directly by socio-biology, ideas of this kind do have widespread currency nonetheless, because they are common (possibly in a more muted form) in other intellectual traditions. Within academic anthropology, for example, there are scholars who would argue that women are programmed genetically to act differently from men, especially in relation to parenthood activities, and that this is an important reason why different social roles are assigned to them (Barnes, 1973). Not surprisingly there are other anthropologists who would dispute the view that women are subject to the dictates of nature and biology more than, or in a different way from, men (MacCormack and Strathern, 1980). Other writers, especially feminist writers, have echoed this theme, arguing their case on empirical grounds, namely that socio-biologists cannot provide evidence which would support their theory adequately, because they cannot spell out the biological mechanisms which allegedly direct women and men to act differently (Chodorow, 1978; MacCormack and Strathern, 1980). Others make their argument on political grounds emphasizing that all conservative thinkers, including socio-biologists, use the concept of 'nature' to legitimate the dominance of men over women (Levitas, 1986).

*The blood tie*  Despite their empirical and theoretical flaws, these ideas about nature or biology as the basis of the special relationship do have a certain appeal, because of the commonsense understanding that kinship represents a 'blood tie' which, along with the contractual arrangement of marriage, is the mechanism by which kin are acquired. Indeed there is empirical evidence that 'blood' relations, by and large, are seen as having a stronger claim than relations acquired by marriage (Firth, Hubert and Forge, 1970, pp. 89–94; see also chapter 1 for a review of relevant evidence). But in the end the blood tie cannot explain completely why people act as they do towards their kin.

The reasons for this have been explored by a number of writers, and I shall refer to them only briefly here. One line of argument draws on the substantial evidence generated by anthropologists, which shows that the social meaning of blood ties varies in different societies, therefore has very different implications for kin relationships. For example, traditional kinship systems in Jamaica are based on the belief that 'mother-blood is stronger than father-blood', as the basis for a domestic and family organization which accords women a much more central role than kinship systems in western Europe (Smith, 1973). Even if we were to concede that part of the socio-biologists' argument which accords a role to genetic ties as the basis of kin relationships, at the very least we must conclude that the effect of biological relationship is mediated and modified through the social meaning of kinship.

If we accept that the blood tie cannot be said to account for the character of kin relationships in any straightforward sense, we can then begin to look at how different societies define who counts as kin for particular purposes, and the role which blood ties play in that. In my view this is a more fruitful line of analysis than the rather sterile debates about whether kin relationships are 'really' explained by biology or not. This perspective leads us to look at the distinctions between biological and social definitions of kinship, and the circumstances in which they are applied.

That distinction can be shown up most effectively in the critical case of parenthood, by looking at how different societies define who 'counts' as the parent of a particular child. Whilst in some societies, the overwhelming criterion is biological, the physiological mother and father being counted as the child's parents for all practical purposes, this is not so everywhere. The work of anthropologists shows clearly that 'social' parenthood, especially social fatherhood, is of considerable importance in many societies, so that a man other than the biological father has responsibility for raising the child and may also have legal rights and responsibilities associated with being 'counted' as the child's father. The person may be another blood relative, for example, the mother's brother. In these examples we see that the allocation of responsibilities and duties between kin may be linked more importantly with social kinship than with biological kinship. This does not mean necessarily that biological relationships are irrelevant, simply that they are accorded less significance in some societies than in others. In her review and analysis of this issue, Esther Goody argues that we have to recognize 'that there are different "kinds" of parenthood – physiological, jural, educational – which are differently weighted in different societies. This weighting is not arbitrary but a response to a balance of cultural and institutional features in any given social system' (Goody, 1982, p. 19).

One example of these factors being given different 'weighting', even within a single society, concerns the practice of adoption in Britain, and of course elsewhere. Adoption entails people who are not genetic parents of a child becoming its social parents for all purposes. In official terms it is a practice of relatively recent origin, having been made legal under English law only in 1926 (Hoggett and Pearl, 1987). Although for the most part British kinship places more weight than do some other societies on the biological dimension of parenthood, in the case of people who have been adopted the significance of that element is greatly diminished. It is interesting that, over the past 60 years, there has been considerable debate about whether to sever all links with the biological parent after a child is adopted. Contemporary practice tends to favour the opportunity to retain some links, after a period in which considerable attempts were made to conceal many adopted children's biological origins. As one commentator on this issue has put it, this change represents a shift from a situation where biological ties and social ties were seen as crudely opposed alternatives, to one which acknowledges that both might have some significance for the adopted person (Richards, 1987).

I have explored the issue of the social dimensions of kinship through discussing parenthood because this is the key case, where the biological links are most evident. If the social dimensions are prominent here, then they will be also with other kin relationships. It is clear that if we wish to understand the basis of support between kin, and the extent to which it is founded upon a 'special relationship' characterized by duty and obligation, we cannot allow our explanation to rest on arguments about nature and biology.

At the same time it seems important to give due weight to nature and biology in a different sense: not as 'causes' of kin support but as representing beliefs which are used at commonsense level to talk about kinship, most obviously represented by phrases such as 'blood is thicker than water', or 'my own flesh and blood'. Wherever we find widespread adherence to the *belief* that blood ties should be treated as special, that is bound to have some bearing upon the way people conduct their own relationships. One of the most important discussions of these issues is contained in the work of Schneider (1968), writing of

American society, who argues that the idea that kinship is founded on nature and biology is itself an important element in the system of cultural beliefs and symbolic meanings which defines American kinship. The *idea* that certain actions are determined or required by nature is important because of the symbolic meaning this gives to kinship, not because it is literally true.

## The economics of family altruism

The idea that altruistic behaviour is specially characteristic of families in a sense is re-stating the problem which I am discussing, rather than offering an explanation. However, it deserves to be identified as a perspective in its own right, partly because the idea that families are altruistic units is pervasive, especially in certain social policy literature which treats altruism as a natural attribute of family life (Pinker, 1971, ch. 1). However, other writers define family altruism in a somewhat different way, and it is these upon whom I concentrate here.

Certain economists have developed the concept of family altruism as a way of dealing with a problem in classical economic theory, namely that it does not really leave space for explaining why people do not always and invariably act to maximize their own economic interests (Phelps, 1975). A leading proponent of the theory of family altruism as a way of resolving this problem is Gary Becker (1981a, 1981b). Becker argues that although the principle of selfishness (that is, self-interest) is characteristic of people's behaviour in the market-place, a quite different principle applies in the family, namely altruism. This view has some affinities with work by those sociologists and historians who see the family as a 'haven in a heartless world' (see especially Lasch, 1977). Becker sets out to build a whole separate economic theory of family life, based upon this distinctive principle. Although his work is concerned with decisions about consumption and production within the household, rather than with the sharing of practical assistance across households, his ideas can be applied by extension to situations concerned with support and obligations between kin. His fundamental thesis is that in family life people act in the interests of other people, not just of themselves, as a matter of routine.

It is apparent that this analysis of family altruism is, like socio-biology, a way of explaining why people 'favour their own'. The idea of 'inclusive fitness' as used in socio-biology draws on a similar logic about maximizing the opportunities of the kin group as a whole. However, the theory of the economics of family altruism differs from socio-biology, in that it does not presume that nature or biology is the basis of family support, but rather the rational choices made by so-called 'economic man'. This leaves open the possibility that some people do not act rationally, which in this context means selfishly rather than altruistically.

Becker develops this argument in respect of parent–child relationships, where he suggests that 'altruistic' families invest more in their children than 'selfish' families, but in the end this investment usually pays off because their children are more successful than the children of parents who have invested less in this kind of human capital. By the same reasoning, he says that one can explain why parents give more to children than children to parents: children are intrinsically more worth investing in, because they have more of their lives remaining. Even if you assume that all parties are equally altruistic, parents could be expected to give more (Becker, 1981b, pp. 194-7). Where people's natural impulses are not altruistic, they can nonetheless be induced to act altruistically by appeals to self-interest – they will then act 'as if' they cared for the other people more than they actually do.

This definition of altruism as a rather curious blend of genuine regard for others and totally calculating self-interest does have the merit of demystifying the concept of altruism, which otherwise can be used merely as a way of referring to behaviour whose nature we do not really understand, but of which we vaguely approve. Another important source of demystification is the work of feminist writers, who have seen very clearly that altruistic qualities, especially in family relationships, are more frequently associated with women than men, and that therefore altruism is a concept which legitimizes the many self-sacrifices women make for other members of their family (Blum, et al., 1976; Ve, 1984; Land and Rose, 1985).

The economic theory of family altruism certainly has some attractions as a way of making sense of the data presented in earlier chapters, especially the evidence about generational flows of support which demonstrate that, in practice, older generations give support to younger and that younger generations normally continue as net beneficiaries throughout their lifetimes (see chapter 1 for discussion of relevant evidence). The theory of family altruism would predict this pattern of investment in the younger generation. One also could argue that these patterns are supported at the normative level by the strong pressures for old people to remain independent of their children, since dependence of the older generation upon the younger always represents a reversal of the logic of family altruism.

However, there are a number of problems with this theory as an explanation of assistance within families, and the extent to which this is underpinned by a sense of obligation. First, its explanatory power essentially is restricted to generational relationships and it is much less obviously applicable to examples of assistance between other kin, for example between siblings. Second, it is an explanation which claims to be universally applicable, in the sense that it is not tied to any particular cultural and social arrangements. This means that it cannot deal adequately with evidence that in practice there is a great deal of diversity even in the way in which parents and children support each other. The simple distinction between altruistic and non-altruistic families does not begin to capture the complexity observed in the data on parent–child relationships in different societies, or even among different cultural groups in British society where, for example, the expectations about dependence between different generations vary for people of white, Asian and Caribbean origin (see chapters 1 and 5). Third, a case can be made against this perspective on the grounds that I discussed in relation to all explanations which presume that family life can be explained in economic terms – namely, that the data do not fit this type of explanation. People's relationships with their relatives, and the commitments which develop between them to give assistance of various types, can be shown to stem from the past history of the relationship, the construction of an individual's social identity, and a number of other factors which are connected with economic circumstances only in a complex and indirect way.

In my view this theory is of limited value to understanding family support, although it does serve to alert us to look for circumstances in which people's assistance to their relatives is blended with self-interest in an apparently rational way. However, such circumstances almost certainly will require a more subtle analytical approach than that implied by the concept of family altruism.

## Emotional ties

The third set of ideas which I shall consider in this section are different again from the first two, although they still locate the explanation of family obligations in the individual personality, and in relationships as they have developed between close kin in the private sphere of family life, rather than explaining them with reference to social or economic forces. These ideas can be summarized as: when adults have special or distinctive relationships with their kin, this is a consequence of emotional bonds and patterns of relationship which were formed in their early lives. The relationship with parents, therefore, is likely to be particularly significant because of the central part which they play in childhood experience.

The most obvious, certainly the most influential, source of such ideas is the work of Freud and other psychoanalysts who place a premium on early experiences in understanding adult personalities and relationships. There is considerable variation between different schools of psychoanalytical theory about the meaning of these experiences and how irrevocable they are in their effects upon adult lives. But all versions agree on the supreme significance of childhood, whether at a conscious or an unconscious level, in understanding adults (Corey, 1986). This emphasis is also to be found quite widely in the discipline of psychology, among writers who would not necessarily locate themselves within psycho-analysis. In reviewing psychological evidence about this, Rutter (1986, ch. 9) points out that the research is rather inconclusive. His own evaluation is that one cannot write off early experiences as having *no* importance, but that they almost certainly are less significant than many psychologists have presumed.

The view that family life is to be explained by the quality of emotional ties built up between individuals has practical significance in the context of family therapy. Mainstream family therapy has tended to operate with a concept of each family as a 'system', in which the behaviour of each affects the other, in a complex sequence built up over the lifetime of each member (for an extended discussion of family systems theorizing see Morgan, 1985, pp. 132–58). In family therapy considerable importance is placed upon childhood experiences, but it is also acknowledged that people are not necessarily bound by their past. The whole point of therapy is that it presumes that it is possible for relationships to change in adult life.

What is the relevance of any of these ideas to understanding the nature of the special relationship between adult kin? In principle we might expect them to be rather fruitful. As I have noted in previous chapters (see especially chapter 6), the evidence of existing research is that adults are highly selective about which kin they identify as people with whom they have close and confiding relationships, for example choosing one child but not another (Hoyt and Babchuk, 1983; O'Connor and Brown, 1984). Since at the same time there seems to be relatively little correlation between closeness in this sense and frequency of contact, the history of that particular relationship is an obvious possible explanation. We know that such relationships often do have very long histories. In her study of elderly people living in rural Wales, Wenger found that most did name someone who was a close confidant, and in three-quarters of cases, the person named was someone whom the respondent had known for 30 years or more; in more than two-thirds of her cases, the relationship had lasted for over 50 years (Wenger, 1984, pp. 98–9). A long-standing pattern of relationships between people does not always constitute positive support of course. I have used previously a case example taken from Wallman's (1983) work, concerning a woman who was part of a large, close kin network, but felt unable to turn to any of her relatives when she suffered a breakdown, precisely because she herself had always been the person who supported others in that network; the form of relationships which she had developed with her kin made it impossible for her to seek their help when she needed it.

This kind of evidence suggests that the interpersonal and emotional history of relationships with kin might provide a very fruitful line of explanation of the special nature of kin relations. It is an explanation which would seem to fit with the analysis I developed in chapter 6, concerning the cumulative nature of negotiated commitments to kin. However, neither systems theorizing nor the various therapeutic theories have really concerned themselves to any great extent with relationships in the adult kin group (Richards, 1987). Indeed the meaning of the term 'family' in family systems theory, for example, remains curiously hazy. It seems often to imply the household or the conjugal family, but the question of whether other kin are inside or outside the 'family system' is often unclear (Morgan, 1985, pp. 151–6).

There are some exceptions to this, notably a school of thought in therapy and casework which argues that a broad spectrum of family relationships (not only those between parents and children) can be understood with reference to experiences in early life, and that therapists working with adult clients should consider these possibilities in their attempt to uncover a person's problem. An early and interesting example of this is work by Leichter and Mitchell (1967), based upon a study of American Jewish families. They argue that because the culture which they were studying accords relationships with kin a 'morally binding quality', individuals can get locked into a set of relationships which have to be understood as part of the kin group network. Commenting on more recent work, Lieberman (1981) identifies an 'extended family school' of family therapy, which likewise focuses upon relationships in the kin group in adult life and beyond the conjugal family. He suggests that the experiences of some adults can be understood only with reference to long-standing patterns of relationship with their kin. There can be, for example, the transmission of certain beliefs and behaviours across generations so that children, as it were, inherit and are moulded by specific ways of relating to members of their family. These patterns are carried over into adult life, in ways that the person concerned simply may not be aware of.

In Britain an influential source of such ideas has been the work of Lily Pincus, through her writing and through her involvement in the Tavistock Institute for Marital Studies. Especially in her work on family 'secrets' (Pincus and Dare, 1978), she has developed a theory of how patterns of behaviour are transmitted across generations of adults within the same kin group, especially between parents and children. This is based on the idea that an adult may have developed unconscious – but very strong – feelings about family relationships, and will pass on these 'secrets' to their own children, leading them to repeat the pattern in their own adult lives. Such secrets can be transmitted across several generations in the form of family mythology, with each generation repeating and reinforcing the pattern which has its origins well in the past. For example, in one case cited by Pincus and Dare, three generations of women in the same family repeated a pattern in which they relied almost exclusively on each other for their emotional support and support with child rearing, to the effective exclusion of the men with whom they were associated. The authors acknowledge that in many respects this was a very satisfactory arrangement between three generations of strong, warm and emotionally close women. They use this case to pursue their analysis that the foundation of this pattern repeated over three generations lay in the early married life of the grandmother, who had interpreted her experiences as meaning that men cannot really be relied upon and that it is 'best to live and have children without the support of men' (p. 11). Since this apparently had proved a rather satisfactory basis for her own life, she had transmitted the 'secret' to her own daughters who then did the same. Of course the whole point of this analysis is to argue that such secrets are capable of challenge, and that therapy is one means whereby people can be helped to break the pattern. One does not have to accept the particular judgement made about *which* patterns need to be broken to appreciate the force of the underlying analysis.

This account has some affinities with the work of Chodorow (1978) on the reproduction of mothering, although the two writers are located in very different intellectual and ideological positions. Chodorow, like Pincus, is concerned with understanding how patterns of relationships are reproduced from one generation to the next; in her case the focus is upon the reproduction of mothering, as a means to understanding the sexual division of labour between women and men. The nub of her argument is,

Because women are themselves mothered by women, they grow up with relational capacities and needs, and a psychological definition of self-in-relationship, which commits them to mothering. Men, because they are mothered by women do not. Women mother daughters who, when they become women, mother. (Chodorow, 1978, p. 209).

The intellectual position which she adopts is based in psychoanalysis, and draws specifically upon object-relations theory, modified by feminism. It must be said that the case which she makes has received substantial criticism, some of it from other feminists (Sayers, 1982). The details of these debates are not directly relevant to my present argument. What I want to take from Chodorow's work in this context is that it represents an attempt to understand how the family relationships of adult women and men are shaped by their early upbringing, which in turn is 'socially patterned' by elements of social structure (p. 50). To take an example which is relevant to the giving and receiving of support between kin, she argues that men and women receive different early experiences, because both are mothered by women, and these produce differing capacities for close relationships in adult life. Women have a greater capacity for a rich emotional life than do men, and when their male sexual partners are unable to gratify this they turn naturally to other women. Chodorow argues that this is most apparent in those societies where women and men are socially segregated and women spend most of their time with other women, but it also can be seen in evidence from western societies about the importance of women's relationships with each other (pp. 199–200). If we were to apply this to evidence reviewed in earlier chapters about support in kin groups, we could argue that it is to be expected that women are more involved in this than men, especially in giving and receiving emotional support.

These various perspectives at least hint at the potential for further developments in both theory and empirical research, centring on the significance of the emotional history of relationships for understanding kin support in adult life. In trying to construct a rounded explanation of the distinctive nature of kin ties, I would argue that potentially this provides us with an important element, but only one. As Morgan (1988) has argued in his discussion of family therapy, the boundaries between emotion and sentiment on the one hand, and rationality and economic calculation on the other, are considerably more permeable than much academic work implies. Any account of the emotional history of a relationship needs to be integrated with other elements, which are important to understanding the foundations of family support and family obligations, two in particular.

First, the emotional history of a relationship needs to be set in its social context. At the most fundamental level, this means questioning what emotions actually 'are' and where they come from. Both the sociological accounts of emotions which I discussed in chapter 6, and the 'social constructionist' school of thought in social psychology, reject the idea that emotions can be seen as uncontrollable feelings which well up from inside human beings without any reference to social relationships or circumstances. As Harre puts it, 'Emotions do not just happen. They are part of the unfolding of quite standard dramatic scenarios' (Harre, 1986, p. 13).

The 'standard dramatic scenarios' to which Harre refers would include all situations in which, in a given culture, it is regarded as appropriate to express a particular emotion: grief after death, apprehension before childbirth, anger after a trust has been betrayed, and so on. As I indicated in chapter 6, there is evidence in studies of family life that people try to bring their emotions in line with what they 'ought to feel' in a given set of circumstances. These circumstances of course are specific to a given society: an emotion which is regarded as appropriate in one culture could well be disapproved of in another, as the contributors to Harre's (1986) volume demonstrate. Many examples could be cited which are relevant to family obligations. To take just one which I used in chapter 4, men living in Britain who are of Asian descent are reported to experience strong feelings of anxiety and shame if they are unable to provide financially for their parents. While British men – and women for that matter – appear to be free from these strong emotions. The fact that emotions are culturally specific in this way, further strengthens the argument that they can only be understood within their specific social context.

Second, our understanding of the significance of the emotional history of any relationship needs to give due weight to the possibilities for changing the character of relationships, through events which occur in adult life. Concentrating upon childhood experiences and the overriding importance of the mother–child bond is unconvincing as the foundation of an explanation for support between relatives in adult life. A similar argument has been made by Richards (1987) about the rather different issue of understanding the long-term impact of divorce and remarriage. This perspective does not fit with the evidence (see especially chapter 6) that obligations to give support within families have the character of negotiated commitments over time. This requires a view of social life which, as I have previously spelled out, sees the meaning of actions and relationships as developed and renegotiated, not fixed for ever at one point in time.

Essentially the problem with explaining adult relationships by events which happened much earlier in life is that this kind of explanation leaves insufficient space for people to change. As Gerth and Wright Mills (1954) put it in their classic discussion of individual character and social structure, the uniqueness of an individual is in one sense made up from accumulated past experience, but it is not *only* that. Individual characteristics (and by extension, one can argue, a particular pattern of family relationships), have to be understood at any particular point in time in relation to the present circumstances of that person's life, as well as their accumulated past experiences. The future is also important, since individuals anticipate a certain type of future for themselves and to an extent act in such a way as to bring it about. Thus a decision, for example, to bring a parent into one's own home with a view to looking after them when they are frail, may have something to do with a close tie formed in childhood, but it may have a great deal more to do with a history of reciprocal support in adult life, the need for the parent's company or support in the present, and an anticipated future in which you think it would be easier to move geographically if you can take your responsibilities with you in your own household, rather than be faced with a more difficult decision about leaving the parent behind.

### Universalistic vs particularistic social relationships

The final two explanations which I shall consider place much more emphasis on 'the social' than those which I have so far considered. By this I mean that they look for explanations of the distinctive character of kinship in the social organization of particular societies, rather than as something which is inherent in human nature.

I shall consider first the work of Talcott Parsons (1964) on the idea that relationships within families are 'particularistic', in the sense that people are defined as distinctive individuals who can and should be given special treatment. In most other social relationships in industrialized societies (especially in the sphere of work), it is a requirement that one does not show favouritism, treats everyone in an equivalent position alike, and does not take into account their particular individual characteristics – that is, other relationships are conducted on a 'universalistic' basis. Parsons believes that one can delineate these common features of kin relationships in all societies, although he allows for some variations according to the particular conditions which prevail.

The moral aspects of kinship, which Parsons sees as common to all societies, can be expressed more generally in terms of his 'pattern variables'. They are characterized by the variable particularistic/neutrality/diffuseness, or particularistic/neutrality/affectivity (ibid. pp. 185–6). My understanding of what Parsons means by these terms can be expressed as follows. Kin relationships are always characterized by obligations which are all-embracing rather than specific; these should override personal interest and inclination; actions towards kin should express solidarity and loyalty; in honouring obligations to kin one should not necessarily expect any reward.

One problem with Parsons's work is that although he is explicitly constructing a general theory of society, it is sometimes difficult to decide whether he is simply describing what does actually happen (as he sees it), or providing an explanation of why social relationships are organized in these particular ways. In general Parsons is arguing that the form which all social relationships take can be understood by considering the functions they perform for the society as a whole. In this case, the characteristic form of family relationships derives from a human need to have some people to whom one relates on a personal basis and to whom one is known as an individual, especially in a society where for the most part people are known by the positions which they occupy (in work and as citizens), rather than for their own distinctive characteristics. The real difficulty of evaluating that view, as Morgan (1975) has pointed out, is that Parsons provides little empirical evidence to support his claims that people do have, or need to have, distinctively different relationships with their families. A further problem is that Parsons's discussion of relationships with kin outside the conjugal family is somewhat ambiguous. Although he did suggest that obligations to other kin are weaker than those to a spouse and immature children, he did not specify the nature of those obligations, or why they might vary (Allan, 1985, p. 13). Finally there is the general problem of analysing societies in functionalist terms, to which I have already referred (and see Morgan, 1975).

Although there would be considerable difficulty in relying upon Parsons's scheme as a total explanation of the distinctive character of kin relationships, it has certain merits in highlighting features which would need to be built into such an explanation. Simply on a descriptive level, the particularistic/universalistic distinction can be a useful way of referring to the distinctive shape of family relationships, provided that we understand that this may apply appropriately to family relationships in a particular time and place (as for Parsons, in middle-class America), but may be an entirely inappropriate description of kin relationships in a different social and cultural context. Using Parsons's work more analytically, it is useful to be reminded that we may need to understand the special character of relationships with relatives as one in contrast with other social relationships, as relationships which have their distinctive character precisely because of the need for such contrasts. I shall return to this point when I have considered the fifth and final body of ideas which we might use to think about these issues.

### The moral character of kinship

The final explanation which I shall consider of the special character of kin relations is drawn from the work of anthropologists and was developed initially in the context of their studies of pre-industrial societies. This is the idea that the fundamental distinguishing mark of kin relations is that they have a 'moral' character which marks them off from other kinds of social relations, the morality of 'prescriptive altruism'. This morality is defined – to use the phrase of Meyer Fortes with whom these ideas are centrally associated – as 'sharing without reckoning', that is an impulse to give support which is not conditional upon instrumental considerations, including the capacity of other people to reciprocate. The idea of the moral character of kinship is in a sense the polar opposite of the ideas which I considered at the beginning of this chapter, which suggest that in the last resort kin support is an instrumental matter. This concept of kinship as defined by its moral character suggests that in the last resort kinship is the one type of social relationship which is *not* instrumental, and that it is marked off from all other social relationships by its moral dimension. These ideas have been linked also with the concept of social solidarity which has its origins in the work of Durkheim. This suggests that moral rules play a key role in binding a society together, and that therefore they need to be upheld, even when it is not in the material interests of individuals to obey them. This theoretical position has been very influential in anthropology – and indeed in sociology – although, as one commentator has put it, not all anthropologists have invariably been 'dazzled by the Durkheimian view of social solidarity' (Firth, 1975).

These ideas have generated substantial debate in anthropology, which can be pursued through a number of sources (Worsley, 1956; Leach, 1961; Fortes, 1969; Bloch, 1973). The debate centres upon questioning whether morality as such has any real explanatory power in social life. Critics take the view that moral (and indeed legal) rules and sanctions, which operate in a given society, cannot be understood separately from the material circumstances in which people have to exist, and the economic interests which are embodied in those rules. These debates formed part of broader changes in the discipline of anthropology, stimulated by an interest in the ideas of Marx, about the place to be accorded to economic interests in explanations of social life. Fortes' reply to his critics is scathing about their attempts to find 'the hidden hand of economic compulsion everywhere'. He makes a forceful case that many of the moral rules and sanctions associated with kinship, such as the incest taboo, simply cannot be explained by economic self-interest. He argues that all kinship institutions are associated with moral rules of conduct, which are based on prescriptive altruism as the central value premise; 'What I wish to stress is the basic premise: kinship is binding; it creates inescapable moral claims and obligations' (Fortes, 1969, p. 242).

Thus far, Fortes' work might be taken as providing a descriptive generalization of what happens in practice, but without necessarily suggesting why this occurs. His explanation centres upon the idea that the principle of prescriptive altruism divides an individual's social world into two categories: those to whom this principle applies and those to whom it does not. It means that the people in my own social world consist of a small number to whom I have clear social and moral obligations, and a much larger number to whom I do not. Those obligations hold, whatever my circumstances, if someone who I recognize as kin asks me to lend them money, or to give them a home on a temporary basis, or to do anything else which would count as the kind of thing which you can expect a relative to do for you. If anyone else makes such claims there is not the same specifically moral duty laid upon me to assist them, although of course I may decide to do so. If we see kinship in this light, its effect is to give the social world of each individual shape and structure and to root each person as a member of a group to which she or he distinctively 'belongs'. This analysis is an example of what I referred to earlier as an explanation which focuses on 'the social'; that is, kin relationships are seen as part of the organization of society as a whole, not based upon features inherent in human nature.

One can see how such explanations developed in the discipline of anthropology, given that anthropologists traditionally have studied societies in which kin groups have formed an important element in social and economic organization. Such explanations have considerable force in understanding the basis of kin support in societies which still have that type of social organization, for example in the Mediterranean and Islamic societies discussed in earlier chapters (see especially chapters 1 and 6). In the British context, does it make sense to say that kinship has this distinctive moral character, which divides the social world into people to whom we have obligations and the rest, and gives each of us a social place? I believe that it does.

When we apply these ideas to the material which I have reviewed on kinship in British society, it seems to me that they do have some force, provided that we take seriously the point made by critics of this position, and acknowledge that material self-interest is a powerful force in kin relations which works alongside – and may possibly conflict with – the more imperative built into the character of kinship. I shall expand that argument in the next section, linking it with ideas drawn from the other perspectives which I have considered.

### Evaluation: the special relationship of kinship

I have reviewed five possible and rather different explanations of the special nature of kinship, and have pointed out some of the strengths and weaknesses of each. I shall now use them as the basis for suggesting what a more adequate account of the 'special relationship' of kinship should consist of. There are obvious dangers in drawing eclectically and selectively from a number of different intellectual positions, but it seems to me that whilst none of those on offer is adequate of itself, several provide insights which should be included in a more rounded conceptual framework.

What should be the main features of that framework? Certainly it should be firmly rooted in the social world, as opposed to an explanation concerned with inherent features of human nature. Other than that, I would take from the work of Parsons and Fortes an idea common to them both, that of contrasts. Both argue, from rather different positions, that the special relationships which people have with their kin are to be understood by comparison with other social relationships. This idea of contrasts seems to me to accord clearly with the evidence which we have about how people conceptualize kin relationships. It accords, for example, with the distinction between kinship and friendship which Allan (1979) has demonstrated. Quite simply relatives are people whom you treat differently.

Taking this as the starting-point I want to make three qualifications immediately. First, 'treating differently' should not be taken to imply active contact. We know that many people do not keep in regular and active contact with many of their kin, and yet they still feel that the relationship does constitute 'something special'. The important point is that kin are people whom you *can* treat differently, and they can make assumptions about how you will treat them. You may not have seen your cousin for a long time because she lives at the other end of the country, but if you are visiting that area and need accommodation for a few days, you know that you can ask and can expect to be welcomed. This interpretation is in line with much of the material which I reviewed in chapter 1 which implies, as I noted there, that the real importance of kin support in practice seems to be its reliability: not that it is being used constantly, but you know that you always *can* fall back on it.

My second qualification is that the principle that relatives are to be treated differently still leaves open the question of precisely which individuals count as relatives for this purpose. In the context of the majority experience in Britain these rules of kinship are rather unclear. I suggested in chapter 1 that the outermost circle of kin (those whose existence is acknowledged, but with whom no contact is maintained) are not relevant, from the point of view of assessing what support passes between relatives. But the very fact that these people's existence is acknowledged and that they are recognized *as kin* means that potentially they could be drawn into structures of kin support. Decisions about who counts as effective kin are not necessarily made once and fixed forever: as I have indicated, people who have not been part of a particular support structure can get defined into it as circumstances change; equally people who have been inside can get defined out. Cutting someone out of your will represents the most dramatic gesture of the latter, in popular imagery of family life.

Third, we need to recognize that distinctions are made *within* the kin network about different forms of 'treating differently'. I used the example above of asking for a few days accommodation from a cousin whom you have not seen for a long time. That example was chosen deliberately to represent the kind of request which probably would be regarded as appropriate by most people in those circumstances. But, as my review in chapter 1 makes clear, there are certain types of support which it would be quite inappropriate to ask for: free accommodation for a year rather than a couple of days, a loan of money, a commitment to providing regular child care. These are examples of support which, when they occur at all, are characteristic of relationships between closer kin: the 'inner' rather than the 'outer' circle. Of course that inner/outer division itself is not fixed: certainly one can find examples where cousins have been defined into the inner circle, but that does not apply in my example. Gender also represents a principle through which different treatment is filtered: you treat male and female relatives differently, in many cases, even when they fall in the inner circle. Important distinctions are made, even within the group of people whom you treat differently, about what type of different treatment is appropriate. Nonetheless the distinctive contrast in social relationships is between kin and non-kin.

To push this line of explanation further, why should human life be organized in this way around the principle of contrasting social relations? Again, I would look for reasons in the realm of the social rather than to some notion of an inherent human need for different types of relationship. As Fortes' work suggests in particular, the special set of relationships based upon kinship has the effect of placing people in the social order, in relation to those outside the kin group as well as those within it. These relationships give me a place which both I and others can understand, in relation to social structure as a whole and which give me a basis of getting on with the practical business of living (Harris, 1983, pp. 14–15). In the context of a society like Britain, of course, kinship does not 'fix' the social position of an individual irrevocably in the same way in which it does in some of the societies studied by anthropologists. Nonetheless people who have to find their place in the world in the context of a fluid social structure and an impersonal urban environment, if anything, may be in particular need of an identifiable social place to which they clearly 'belong' (Morgan, 1975, pp. 65–6). Kinship does create such a place, although it is obvious that it may not do so exclusively.

Why should kin relationships in particular be the ones with which this sense of social place is associated? Membership of a kin network has one feature not shared by other groups to which people belong. Except in the case of people who have been adopted, you do not have to 'become' a member of your family of origin. You are a member and remain so whatever else happens in your life – in all other social groups, membership can be revoked or withdrawn, either by your own action or those of others. Irrevocable membership helps to explain why the sense of obligation to in-laws is frequently reported as being more ambiguous than that to blood relatives, and why the position of step-relatives commonly is experienced as problematic. Membership of the in-laws' family could always be revoked, especially since we know that death as well as separation or divorce is seen as an occurrence which ought to lead to change in these particular relationships (Marris, 1958, ch. VI; Schneider, 1968, pp. 77–89).

Irrevocable membership of a family of origin places each person in a series of two-way relationships with a number of individuals: with a mother, a father, a sister, an aunt, a cousin, and so on. However, these are not conducted in isolation, but develop as part of a set of relationships within the kin network as a whole. Relationships between two individuals are visible to other people, who themselves may have some interest in their development. Hence, as I have noted in chapter 6 and elsewhere, the character of a person's relationship with a brother or an uncle may be shaped in part by their relationships to closer kin: cordial contacts are maintained, and perhaps assistance of various kinds offered, 'for the sake of' the mother or father who stands between the two in genealogical terms. Whilst irrevocable membership of the kin group, in my view, is an important element in understanding the special responsibilities which people feel towards kin, its consequences are many and various. It is at this point that I would also want to highlight the importance of emotional ties and the history of relationships in which they are embedded. I argued earlier that these are not of themselves a sufficient explanation of the special basis of kinship, but the fact that your family of origin (although not of course the family into which you may marry) are people with whom you have interacted over your whole lifetime builds into these relationships a dynamic which can significantly reinforce the social definition of kin as people whom you treat differently. In a sense, that applies even when the history of the relationship has been stormy – it remains a relationship with a long history and has distinctively strong emotions associated with it. Taking account of the emotional history of a particular relationship clearly can be very important in understanding the circumstances of individuals. As the basis of a more general explanation of the character of kin relationships, I find it useful as one element in a theoretical scheme, provided that one recognizes that relationships are not fixed in childhood, never to be altered, but do have an on-going history in which the past is modified, even if it can never be abandoned completely.

This brings me to another key element which I believe needs to be built into a rounded explanation of the special nature of kin relationships, that is the negotiated element. I set out the case for seeing the central significance of this in chapter 6 and I will not repeat it here. The importance of negotiation in family relationships fits well with the emphasis which I have now given to the idea that kin relationships 'place' a person in the social order because, as the social order itself changes, individuals need to recreate and adjust their own sense of place within it. Many negotiations about support between kin could be seen as attempts to make individual adjustments of this kind, whilst at the same time retaining in general terms a sense of the distinctiveness of kin relationships as a necessary mechanism for continually recreating and sustaining a sense of social identity. In this context we can understand why people need to reassert the values associated with close personal relationships, at the very point when they are in the process of breaking such a relationship (LaGaipa, 1982; see chapter 6 for further discussion), and equally the evidence that people retain a strong sense of the 'ideal norm' of kinship obligations, even when they acknowledge that there is often a gap between this and their own actions in practice (Firth, Hubert and Forge, 1970, pp. 102–5).

It seems to me that the distinctive feature of kin relationships properly can be described as an issue of morality, which puts relationships with kin on a different basis from those with other people. Kin relationships are conceptualized and explained in practice as having 'a peculiar, inescapable moral quality of obligation attached to them' (Firth, Hubert and Forge, 1970, p. 114). However, this can only be understood with reference to the sense which it enables people to make of their own position in the social world, rather than as a fixed set of prescriptive rules which people follow (see chapter 5). When it stops giving meaning and shape to the social world, the power of the moral imperative is reduced considerably, as it is when it conflicts with material self-interest. Neither circumstance, however, means necessarily that the principle will be abandoned, because all such relationships have a long history, which incorporates people other than those directly concerned. As I argued in chapter 6, at a time when a person begins to realize that they might prefer a different pattern of relationships with their kin, their past actions may have committed them to a particular course from which it is too expensive to withdraw.

I would argue that these are the key features which enable us to understand the distinctive features of kin relationships, and in particular the 'sense of obligation' to give support. A distinctive morality does mark the boundaries between kin and other relationships, but it is a morality rooted in real ties between one person and another and the social meaning which these give to individuals' lives. It needs to be built up over time, reaffirmed and reinforced if it is to be sustained, and the ways in which it gets translated into actions and commitments will be affected profoundly by the material conditions under which the participants live. Demographic structures, the economic climate, the law and public policy all shape the need for kin support and the capacity to provide it. They create the conditions under which people 'make their own lives', but the shape which kin relationships take for any single individual is a product of that person's own actions, especially the way in which they have developed relationships over time: sometimes acting consciously and sometimes not; sometimes feeling constrained by circumstances and other times more in control of the situation; sometimes feeling obliged to reciprocate support given in the past without really wanting to, and other times wanting to find a way of paying back without being able to; sometimes finding that their words and deeds have committed them to a course of actions which they had not anticipated.

# Conclusion

The family is the place where we care for each other, where we practise consideration for each other. Caring families are the basis of a society that cares.

This much-quoted statement about the nature of family life comes from a speech made by James Callaghan when he was Labour Prime Minister in 1978 (*Guardian* 23.5.78.; Finch and Groves, 1980; Morgan, 1985). It has been quoted extensively because it represents a succinct statement of the politics of the family in recent years. But what does it mean? Is it description or prescription? Was the Prime Minister congratulating the British population on its virtue or exhorting it to do better?

Taken out of context the meaning is ambiguous. In context it is quite plain. He was doing as politicians of various persuasions have done for many years: justifying government policies which were restricting access to state provision of services, by extolling the superior virtues of family support. The use of the word 'caring' gives the hint that women are seen as the most suitable providers of such assistance. It is *pre*scription presented as *de*scription. There is a long history in Britain of politicians describing family life as they would like it to be, but presenting that description as if it were a simple account of how most people live in reality. The implication is clear of course: if we don't live like this, then we ought to.

The evidence which I have reviewed in previous chapters, and the analysis which I have developed, offer the basis for evaluating this kind of statement both as description and as prescription. Does the concept of 'caring families', of the idea that 'caring' is distinctively associated with family life, make any sense as a description of how most people in Britain live in the later part of the twentieth century? Does it represent a model of family life which most people would regard as right and proper, an ideal to which they ought to aspire? When governments try to encourage this model, are they simply supporting what the majority of people do in any case? In posing such questions in this concluding chapter I am returning to debates about the politics of family support and family obligations which I opened up in the introduction, and which give the issues I have addressed in this book an importance well beyond specialist academic concerns.

I do not propose to summarize the arguments of the preceding chapters in a straightforward way here, but to draw on them to construct an account of assistance within kin groups which addresses the issues as they are formulated within the contemporary politics of the family. The arguments which follow all grow out of earlier chapters, but I shall not repeat the detail here. I believe that my arguments can be supported by the evidence I have reviewed, although – as I have noted throughout – the whole analysis must be taken as provisional, because we lack systematic and up-to-date data which could settle these questions more authoritatively.

## Support in practice

Throughout this discussion I have emphasized the importance of keeping separate the question of what assistance people actually give to their relatives, from the reasons why they give it, especially the part played by duty, obligation or responsibility. I shall begin therefore with the question of what happens in practice. Are families characterized uniquely by the giving and receiving of support of various kinds? How important is assistance from relatives to most adults in contemporary Britain?

The evidence which I have reviewed in this book suggests that assistance from relatives still is of considerable importance to many people – in some respects more so than is often imagined, for example the use of kin networks to help in finding jobs. The lives of some people (most of them women) are dominated by the assistance which they give to a relative, especially people who are the main carer for someone who is handicapped and infirm. Yet at the same time kin support in many ways is unpredictable. By this, I mean that we cannot predict simply from knowing that someone has a sister, or a father, or five grand-children, what assistance if any is passing between them now, or has ever done. Nor is it easy to predict what will happen when a particular set of circumstances arises where a person needs some help – financial difficulties caused by unemployment, a car accident in which they sustained broken bones, the grief of a bereavement, or whatever. They may well get assistance from relatives, but we cannot be sure precisely what they can expect, or from whom. It all depends on their particular circumstances.

The 'all depends on circumstances' argument can be a rather lame one, an excuse for not considering the evidence sufficiently rigorously. That is not my intention here. I believe that the evidence about how family support works in practice points to considerable room for variation between one family and the next, even between two families who are in similar circumstances, and indeed that there is a sense in which people feel it is proper that there *should* be room for manoeuvre. I wish therefore to use the 'all depends on circumstances' line of argument in a strong sense: the substantial space for variation tells us something important about how family support operates. It tells us that for the most part people do not regard a loan of money, or the offer of temporary accommodation, or anything else, as given automatically by reflex action on the part of relatives. Rather, the appropriateness of offering a particular type of assistance is something to be weighed up and judged in particular circumstances, and to be negotiated between the parties concerned.

I have stressed the unpredictable character of kin support, but I do not mean to imply that it is completely random. We can detect some patterns in who gives what to whom, but often those patterns are not visible unless we know a good deal about the individuals concerned. The most visible elements concern gender, ethnicity, generation and economic position. The details are contained in earlier chapters and I do not propose to repeat them here, but we can predict, for example, that older generations give support to younger more than the other way round; that people of Asian descent living in Britain are more likely than white British people to be giving help to their in-laws; that giving financial assistance is more common in better-off families than in poorer ones; that most women are involved more extensively than most men in exchanges of assistance between relatives. I am not suggesting that any of these patterns is a fixed and immutable part of family life: we can see how they derive at least in part from social and economic circumstances. Women are more involved than men because they need to be: the division of labour in our society accords them a range of domestic and caring responsibilities for which they need the support of others. Given the circumstances of Britain in the late twentieth century, these are common patterns, which leave nonetheless plenty of scope for individual variations.

There are also relatively predictable variations within the kin network itself: assistance, especially significant assistance, is more likely to pass between certain kin than others. I have spoken of inner and outer circles, and corresponding variations in support. That metaphor holds good provided we recognize that the boundaries between circles are not fixed. The most we can say is that, for the white majority, one's own parents and children normally fall in the inner circle, and that people as distant as aunts or cousins normally do not, but there are considerable variations between kin groups in precisely who gets defined in, and this itself can change over time. Further, many individuals will be members of more than one 'inner circle'. This overlapping membership, within a kin network which itself is rather fluid, creates both room for manoeuvre and some constraints. I cannot afford to do too much decorating for my husband's sister, because my own sister will notice and feel hurt unless I do the same for her; on the other hand, having to be fair to both is rather a good excuse when my sister-in-law asks me once too often. In this hypothetical example, I am using my membership of overlapping inner circles (one comprising my own siblings and parents; the other made up of my husband's siblings and parents) to create a pattern of kin support with which I feel comfortable.

The least visible source of variation in family assistance is the principle of reciprocity, which in many ways is the key to under-standing how patterns of support build up over time. An expectation that assistance should flow in two directions, and that no one should end up in a position where they are receiving more than they are giving, is at the heart of many of the negotiations which take place about support in families. This does not necessarily mean direct and immediate 'paying back': the reciprocal gift may come much later, and perhaps be given to another person. The important thing is that each person's balance sheets should be kept even. The only partial exception to this is parents' gifts (of various kinds) to their children, where it seems quite common for parents to continue to be net givers of gifts throughout their lifetimes without any real pressure on children to pay back an equivalent amount. Even here there is a reciprocal element if the children have children themselves, whom they will treat in the same way. The reciprocal element plays a large part in the unpredictability of family support, since over a period of time it creates a pattern of commitments which are not necessarily anticipated by the participants themselves, let alone accessible to an outsider.

Support between kin *is* important to many people in contemporary Britain, but it does not operate to the kind of fixed rules implied by the idea that caring is 'naturally' part of family relationships. In particular the idea, promoted by various governments, that the family should be the first port of call for people who need some assistance, does not align with what happens in practice. Indeed I have made the case in earlier chapters that most people see their kin as a 'last resort' rather than a first. Kin support is reliable in this sense only: you know that you can fall back on your relatives – especially your close kin – if all else fails. Even then you cannot assume that assistance will be given automatically, as I have already indicated. For most people the desirable situation is never to have to use that safety-net except for relatively minor assistance which can be repaid easily.

## The sense of obligation

The other dimension to family support is what I have called throughout the 'sense of obligation'. This is the 'ought' dimension, reflected in political debate by the belief that people *should* be prepared to assist their relatives, even if this does not always happen in practice. For many people this sense of obligation is the key defining characteristic of family ties, especially between close kin. You feel 'duty bound' to help your family, and this gives kin support an inescapable quality. As I argued in the introduction to this book, the Victorian connotations of these ideas should not blind us to their contemporary significance, at least in political terms. The assumption that it is natural to feel a sense of obligation to one's kin informs much contemporary social policy.

Do people assist their kin because they have this sense of obligation or duty? Are kin relationships a special category of relationship because of this? How does the sense of obligation get mobilized? I have argued in this book that kin relationships *are* marked out distinctively by this sense of obligation, which in the end is a matter of morality rather than individual feelings or emotions. However, that morality does not operate on the basis of fixed rules, of the kind that would tell me I should be prepared to look after my father when he is ill, but that I need not make the same offer for my uncle, or that I could ask my brother for a loan of £200 but not £2,000.

The distinctive morality which marks out kin relationships operates more subtly than that, and on the basis of normative guidelines or principles which are more concerned with how to work out what to do, than with specifying precisely what you should do in particular circumstances. The principle of reciprocity is one of these. Another is ensuring that each adult keeps an appropriate amount of independence from the rest. Yet another is a sense that there is a 'right time' in people's lives when they can ask for or give assistance, but at other times this would not be appropriate. Expectations about gender differences permeate all of these.

These principles come into play when people negotiate their relationships with one another and work out what to do in particular circumstances. Such negotiations are conducted between real people, not simply between human beings who occupy the social positions 'daughter' 'grandfather' 'brother' and so on. Those real people have a history of interpersonal relationships stretching over many years in most cases, and their relationships have an anticipated future. That is why the commitments which I develop towards my mother will have their own distinctive character: she is *my* mother, not simply *a* mother.

Why should these commitments develop with kin rather than other people? Of course they are not necessarily confined exclusively to kin: some people do develop very strong and long-lasting commitments to friends. I have argued in earlier chapters that having a set of relationships which is marked distinctively by commitments and obligations gives shape and meaning to the social world for each individual. Kin relationships are especially suited to this (although not exclusively so), because membership of the kin group into which you were born is automatic and irrevocable: you do not join and there is a sense in which you cannot leave. The lifelong nature of relationships with one's family of origin mark them as distinctive and different from all others. This makes them especially suited to developing relationships, in which people become committed to assist each other. I would place considerable emphasis upon the 'become'. Commitments to assist one's kin are not automatically 'there', ready-made for the fully-fledged adult to take on board. They develop and change over time; they get reaffirmed through reciprocal assistance; they help to establish an individual's personal reputation and social identity, which then in turn influences the course of future negotiations.

In reality, the 'sense of obligation' which marks the distinctive character of kin relationships is nothing like its image in political debate, where it appears as a set of ready-made moral rules which all right-thinking people accept and put into practice. It is actually much less reliable than that. It is nurtured and grows over time between some individuals more strongly than between others, and its practical consequences are highly variable. It does have a binding quality, but that derives from commitments built up between real people over many years, not from an abstract set of moral values.

## Family obligations in the public domain

I have placed the emphasis so far on the personal and negotiated elements in both family support and the morality of obligation which underscores it. But it is plain that such negotiations do not take place in a social vacuum. Indeed, governments' attempts to encourage people do develop a sense of responsibility towards their relatives place these arrangements firmly in the public domain, and imply that apparently private arrangements are open to pressure – even manipulation – from outside.

I have emphasized in earlier chapters that social and economic circumstances in general do have an important bearing upon the structures of support which are developed in families. The economic climate, as it affects individuals and their relatives, creates the conditions under which some people have need for support and others have the capacity to provide it. The demographic structure of the population at any given point in time affects the shape of individual kin groups, and therefore the range of options for giving, receiving and sharing assistance. Most dramatically at the present time, demographic change has created much larger numbers of very elderly people than ever had to be supported by previous generations, at a time when the numbers of people born in succeeding generations has shrunk.

If we take a fairly long historical perspective, we can see that people in the present are not necessarily any more or less willing to support their relatives than in the past; but the circumstances under which they have to work out these commitments themselves have changed and created new problems to be solved. External conditions of this kind do not straightforwardly determine what any of us does for our relatives, but they do form part of the materials out of which we have to create our own commitments. They affect the nature of the choices which present themselves. For example (to stay with the question of the care of elderly people), a decision about whether you should take an elderly father to live with you looks very different if you are an only child, than it would have done under the demographic conditions of earlier generations, when you could expect to have several siblings. It looks different again if economic circumstances have worked in your favour, so that you can afford to pay a professional nurse to look after him, by comparison with someone for whom the choice about co-residence also entails using their own labour to provide nursing care.

Into this complex equation we also have to insert the action of governments who, through the law and through their policies, modify the external circumstances under which commitments to relatives are negotiated. How important a factor is this? Can governments make us do more for our kin, or even alter the morality of family obligations, to fit their own policy preferences? If government keeps up the pressure, will we find in the future that the family becomes the first, rather than the last, port of call when any of us needs assistance?

We move into the realms of speculation here, but that speculation can be informed by looking at what has happened in similar circumstances in the past. There have been several times during the last two centuries when governments have tightened the screws, to try to ensure that people relied on their families rather than on the state for financial assistance: the creation of the New Poor Law in 1834; the tightening of Poor Law regulations in the late nineteenth century; the creation of the household means test for unemployed people in the 1930s. The historical evidence suggests that on each occasion the measures were less successful than their hard-line advocates would have wished. On each occasion when government was attempting to impose a version of family responsibilities which people regarded as unreasonable, many responded by developing avoidance strategies: moving to another household, losing touch with their relatives, cheating the system. If anything it has been the state's assuming some responsibility for individuals – such as the granting of old age pensions – which has freed people to develop closer and more supportive relationships with their kin. It seems that it is not in the power of governments straight-forwardly to manipulate what we do for our relatives, let alone what we believe to be proper.

Of course we cannot tell precisely what governments will try to do in the future, nor what the consequences will be. But the lesson of our past is that governments are quite capable of promoting a view of family obligations which is out of step with what most people regard as proper or reasonable, and with the commitments people have arrived at themselves, through the delicate processes of negotiation described above. Undoubtedly that situation creates great difficulties for some people, who feel that they are under sustained and unreasonable pressure, and eventually some will give in. But on the evidence of the past, many will not. Governments in this situation may try to ensure that their own views prevail, but their chances of success are probably partial at best. Happily, I should like to add.

# References

Abrams, P. (1982). *Historical Sociology*, London: Open Books.

Allan, G. (1979). *A Sociology of Friendship and Kinship*. London: Allen and Unwin.

Allan, G. (1982). Property and Family Solidarity. In P. G. Hollowell (ed.) *Property and Social Relations*. London: Heinemann.

Allan, G. (1983). Informal networks of care: issues raised by Barclay. *British Journal of Social Work*, 13, 417–433.

Allan, G. (1985). *Family Life*. Oxford: Basil Blackwell.

Allatt, P. and Yeandle, S. (1986). It's not fair, is it? Young unemployment, family relations and the social contract. In S. Allen, A. Watson, K. Purcell and S. Wood (eds) *The Experience of Unemployment*. London: Macmillan.

Ambrose, P., Harper, J. and Pemberton, R. (1983). *Surviving Divorce: Men Beyond Marriage*. Brighton: Wheatsheaf.

Anderson, D. and Dawson, G. (eds) (1986) *Family Portraits*. London: Social Affairs Unit.

Anderson, D., Lait, J. and Marsland, D. (1981). *Breaking the Spell of the Welfare State*. London: Social Affairs Unit.

Anderson, M. (1971). *Family Structure in Nineteenth Century Lancashire*. Cambridge: Cambridge University Press.

Anderson, M. (1972). Household structure and the industrial revolution: mid-nineteenth century Preston in perspective. In P. Laslett and R. Wall (eds) *Household and Family in Past Time*. Cambridge: Cambridge University Press.

Anderson, M. (1977). The impact on the family relationships of the elderly of changes since Victorian times in governmental income-maintenance provision. In E. Shanas and M. B. Sussman (eds) *Family Bureaucracy and the Elderly*. Durham, N.C.: Duke University Press.

Anderson, M. (1980). *Approaches to the History of the Western Family 1500–1914*. London: Macmillan.

Anderson, M. (1985). The emergence of the modern life cycle in Britain. *Social History*, 10, 1, 69–87.

Anthias, F. and Yuval-Davis, N. (1983). Contextualising feminism: gender, ethnic and class division. *Feminist Review*, 15, 62–75.

Anwar, M. (1985). *Pakistanis in Britain*. London: New Century Publishers.

Arensberg, C. M. and Kimball, S. T. (1968). *Family and Community in Ireland.* Cambridge, Mass.: Harvard University Press.

Argyle, M. and Henderson, M. (1984). The rules of friendship. *Journal of Personal and Social Relationships*, 1, 211–37.

Argyle, M. and Henderson, M. (1985). *The Anatomy of Relationships.* Harmondsworth: Penguin.

Aries, P. (1972). *Centuries of Childhood,* London: Peregrine.

Arrow, K. J. (1975). Gifts and Exchanges. In E. S. Phelps (ed.) *Altruism, Morality and Economic Theory.* New York: Russell Sage Foundation.

Askham, J. (1984). *Identity and Stability in Marriage.* Cambridge: Cambridge University Press.

Atkins, A. and Hoggett, B. (1984). *Women and the Law.* Oxford: Basil Blackwell.

Audit Commission for Local Authorities in England and Wales (1985). *Managing Social Services for the Elderly More Effectively.* London: Her Majesty's Stationery Office.

Baier, K. (1970). The moral point of view. In G. Wallace and A. D. M. Walker (eds) *The Definition of Morality.* London: Methuen.

Bakke, E. W. (1933). *The Unemployed Man: A Social Study.* London: Nisbet and Co. Ltd.

Ballard, C. (1979). Conflict, Continuity and Change: Second-generation South Asians. In V. Saifullah Khan (ed.) *Minority Families in Britain.* London: Macmillan.

Baldwin, S. (1985). *The Costs of Caring: Families with Disabled Children.* London: Routledge and Kegan Paul.

Banks, J. A. (1954). *Prosperity and Parenthood; A Study of Family Planning among the Victorian Middle Class.* London: Routledge and Kegan Paul.

Barker, D. L. (1972). Young people and their homes: spoiling and 'keeping close' in a South Wales town. *Sociological Review*, 20, 4, 569–90.

Barker, J. (1984). *Black and Asian Old People in Britain.* Mitcham, Surrey: Age Concern Research Unit.

Barnes, J. A. (1973). Genetrix: genitor-nature: culture? In J. Goody (ed.) *The Character of Kinship.* Cambridge: Cambridge University Press.

Bayley, M. (1973). *Mental Handicap and Community Care.* London: Routledge and Kegan Paul.

Bebbington, A. and Davies, B. (1983). Equity and efficiency in the personal social services. *Journal of Social Policy*, 12, 3, 309–30.

Becker, G. (1981a). Altruism in the family and selfishness in the market place. *Economics*, 48, 1–15.

Becker, G. S. (1981b). *A Treatise on the Family.* Cambridge, Mass: Harvard University Press.

Becker, H. S. (1960). Notes on the concept of commitment. *American Journal of Sociology*, 66, 32–40. Reprinted in H. S. Becker, (1970) *Sociological Work: Method and Substance.* Chicago: Aldine.

Bell, C. (1968). *Middle Class Families.* London: Routledge and Kegan Paul.

Bell, C., McKee, L. and Priestley, K. (1983). *Fathers, Childbirth and Work.* Manchester: Equal Opportunities Commission.

Benedict, P. (1976). Aspects of the domestic cycle in a Turkish provincial town. In J. G. Peristiany (ed.) *Mediterranean Family Structures.* Cambridge: Cambridge University Press.

Berger, P. and Kellner, H. (1964). Marriage and the construction of reality. *Diogenes*, 46, 1–24.

Bergmann, K., Foster, E. M., Justice, A. W. and Matthews, V. (1978).

Management of the demented elderly patient in the community. *British Journal of Psychiatry*, 132, 441–49.

Berkner, L. K. (1975). The use and misuse of census data for the historical analysis of family structure. *The Journal of Interdisciplinary History*, 4, 1, 721–38.

Bernardes, J. (1985). Do we really know what 'The Family' is? In P. Close and R. Collins (eds) *Family and Economy*. London: Macmillan.

Bernardes, J. (1986). Multidimensional developmental pathways: a proposal to facilitate the conceptualisation of 'Family Diversity'. *Sociological Review*, 34, 3, 590–610.

Bernardes, J. (1988). Founding the New 'Family Studies'. *Sociological Review*, 36, 1, 57–86.

Birke, L. (1986). *Women, Feminism and Biology*. Brighton: Wheatsheaf.

Blaxter, M. and Paterson, E. (1982). *Mothers and Daughters: A Three Generation Study of Health Attitudes and Behaviour*. London: Heinemann.

Blenkner, M. (1965). Social work and family relationships in later life: some thoughts on filial maturity. In E. Shanas and G. F. Streib (eds) *Social Structure and the Family: Generational Relations*. Englewood Cliffs: Prentice-Hall.

Bloch, M. (1973). The long term and the short term: the economics and political significance of the morality of kinship. In J. Goody (ed.) *The Character of Kinship*. Cambridge: Cambridge University Press.

Blum, L., Homiak, M., Housman J., and Scheman, N. (1976). Altruism and women's oppression. In C. Gould and M. Wartofsky (eds) *Women and Philosophy*. New York: G. P. Putman's Sons.

Booth, C. (1892a) *Pauperism and The Endowment of Old Age*. London: Macmillan.

Booth, C. (1892b). *The Life and Labour of the People of London*. London: Macmillan.

Bosanquet, H. (1906). *The Family*. London: Macmillan.

Bott, E. (1957). *The Family and Social Network*. London: Tavistock.

Brah, A. (1986). Unemployment and racism: Asian youth on the dole. In S. Allen, A. Watson, K. Purcell and S. Wood (eds) *The Experience of Unemployment*. London: Macmillan.

Brannen, J. and Collard, J. (1982). *Marriages in Trouble: the Process of Seeking Help*, London: Tavistock.

Brittan, A. and Maynard, M. (1984) *Sexism, Racism and Oppression*. Oxford: Basil Blackwell.

Britton, M. and Edison, N. (1986). The changing balance of the sexes in England and Wales 1851–2001. *Population Trends*, 46, 22–5.

Brody, E. (1981). Women in the middle and family help to older people. *The Gerontologist*, 21, 471–80.

Brown, C. (1984). *Black and White Britain*. London: Policy Studies Institute.

Brown, G. and Harris, T. (1978). *The Social Origins of Depression*. London: Tavistock.

Bulmer, M. (1985). The rejuvenation of community studies: neighbours, networks and policy. *Sociological Review*, 33, 3, 430–48.

Bulmer, M. (1986). *Neighbours: The Work of Philip Abrams*. Cambridge: Cambridge University Press.

Bulmer, M. (1987). *The Social Basis of Community Care*. London: Allen and Unwin.

Burgoyne, J. and Clark, D. (1984). *Making A Go Of It: A Study of Step Families in Sheffield*. London: Routledge and Kegan Paul.

Butler, S. (1903). *The Way of All Flesh*, London: G. Richards.

Butler, S. (1919). *The Note Books of Samuel Butler, 1835–1902.* ed. by H. Festing Jones. London: Firfield.

Charles, N. and Kerr, M. (1988). *Women, Food and Families.* Manchester: Manchester University Press.

Charlesworth, A., Wilkin, D. and Durie, A. (1984). *Carers and Services: A Comparison of Men and Women Caring For Dependent Relatives.* Manchester: Equal Opportunities Commission.

Chaytor, M. (1980). Household and kinship: Ryton in the late sixteenth and early seventeenth centuries. *History Workshop Journal*, 10, 25–60.

Cheal, D. J. (1983). Intergenerational family transfers. *Journal of Marriage and the Family*, 45, 805–13.

Chodorow, N. (1978). *The Reproduction of Mothering.* Berkeley: University of California Press.

Cicourel, A. V. (1973). Interpretive procedures and normative rules in the negotiation of status and role. In A. Cicourel, *Cognitive Sociology.* Harmondsworth: Penguin.

Clark, E. (1982). Some aspects of social security in medieval England. *Journal of Family History*, 7, 4, 307–20.

Cole, G. D. H. and Cole, M. I. (1937). *The Condition of Britain.* London: Victor Gollancz.

Cooke, K. (1987). The withdrawal from paid work of the wives of unemployed men: a review of research. *Journal of Social Policy*, 16, 3.

Corey, G. (1986). *Theory and Practice of Counselling and Psychotherapy.* 3rd edn. Monterey, Cal.: Brooks/Cole Publishing Co. Ltd.

Cornwell, J. (1984). *Hard Earned Lives: Accounts of Health and Illness from East London.* London: Tavistock.

Craig, J. (1983). The growth of the elderly population. *Population Trends*, 32, 28–33.

Cretney, S. (1984). *Principles of Family Law.* 2nd Edn. London: Sweet and Maxwell.

Croll, E. (1978). Rural China: segregation to solidarity. In P. Caplan and J. Bujra (eds) *Women United, Women Divided.* London: Tavistock.

Cromwell, R. and Olson, D. H. (eds) (1975). *Power in Families.* Beverly Hills: Sage.

Crowther, M. A. (1982). Family responsibility and state responsibility in Britain before the Welfare State. *Historical Journal*, 25, 1, 131–45.

Cuisenier, J. (1976). The domestic cycle in the traditional family organisation in Tunisia. In J. G. Peristiany (ed.) *Mediterranean Family Structures.* Cambridge: Cambridge University Press.

Cunningham-Burley, S. (1985). Constructing grandparenthood: anticipating appropriate action. *Sociology*, 19, 3, 421–36.

Cusack, S. and Roll, J. (1984). *Families Rent Apart: A Study of Young People's Contribution to their Parents' Housing Costs.* London: CPAG.

Daatland, S. O. (1983). Care Systems. *Ageing and Society*, 3, 1, 1–21.

Dale, J. and Foster, P. (1986). *Feminists and State Welfare.* London: Routledge and Kegan Paul.

Davidoff, L. (1979). The separation of home and work? Landladies and lodgers in nineteenth- and twentieth-century England. In S. Burman (ed.) *Fit Work For Women.* London: Croom Helm.

Davidoff, L. and Hall, C. (1987). *Family Fortunes: Men and Women of the English Middle Class 1780–1850.* London: Hutchinson.

Dawkins, R. (1976). *The Selfish Gene.* Oxford: Oxford University Press.

Deacon, A. and Bradshaw, J. (1983). *Reserved for the Poor: the Means Test in British Social Policy*. Oxford: Basil Blackwell.

Douglas, J. (1971). *American Social Order*. New York: Free Press.

Engels, F. (1884). *The Origins of the Family, Private Property and the State*, Republished in 1985. Harmondsworth: Penguin.

Equal Opportunities Commission (1982). *Caring for the Elderly and Handicapped: Community Care Policies and Women's Lives*. Manchester: EOC.

Family Policy Studies Centre (1984). *The Forgotten Army: Family Care and Elderly People*. London: FPSC.

Finch, J. (1984). Community Care: developing non-sexist alternatives. *Critical Social Policy*, 9, 6–18.

Finch, J. (1986a). Age. In R. Burgess (ed.) *Key Variables in Social Investigation*. London: Routledge and Kegan Paul.

Finch, J. (1986b). Community care and the invisible welfare state. *Radical Community Medicine*, Summer, 15–22.

Finch, J. (1987a). The vignette technique in survey research. *Sociology*, Vol. 21, 1, pp. 105–14.

Finch, J. (1987b). Whose responsibility? Women and the future of family care. In I. Allen, M. Wicks, J. Finch and D. Leat, *Informal Care Tomorrow*. London: Policy Studies Institute.

Finch, J. (1987c). Family obligations and the life course. In A. Bryman, B. Bytheway, P. Allatt and T. Keil (eds) *Rethinking the Life Cycle*. London: Macmillan.

Finch, J. and Groves, D. (1980). Community care and the family: a case for equal opportunities? *Journal of Social Policy*, 9, 4, pp. 487–514.

Finch, J. and Mason, J. (forthcoming). Decision taking in the fieldwork process: theoretical sampling and collaborative working. In R. G. Burgess (ed.) *Studies in Qualitative Methods*. London: JAI Press.

Firth, R. (1975). The sceptical anthropologist? Social anthropology and Marxist views of society. In Bloch M. (ed.) *Marxist Analyses and Social Anthropology*. London: Malaby.

Firth, R., Hubert, J. and Forge, A. (1970). *Families and their Relatives*. London: Routledge and Kegan Paul.

Fishman, P. M. (1978). Interaction: the work women do. *Social Problems*, 25, 4, pp. 397–406.

Flandrin, J. L. (1979). *Families in Former Time*. Cambridge: Cambridge University Press.

Fortes, M. (1969). *Kinship and the Social Order*. Chicago: Aldine.

Foster, P. (1983). *Access to Welfare: an Introduction to Welfare Rationing*. London: Macmillan.

Freedman, J., Hammond, E., Masson, J. and Morris, N. (1988). *Property and Marriage: An Integrated Approach*. Report series no. 29. London: Institute for Fiscal Studies.

Gerth, H. and Wright Mills, C. (1954). *Character and Social Structure*. London: Routledge and Kegan Paul.

Giddens, A. (1979). *Central Problems in Social Theory*. London: Macmillan.

Gilhooly, M. (1982). Social aspects of senile dementia. In R. Taylor and A. Gilmore (eds) *Current Trends in Gerontology*. Aldershot: Gower.

Gilligan, C. (1982). *In A Different Voice: Psychological Theory and Women's Development*. Cambridge, Mass: Harvard University Press.

Gittins, D. (1985). *The Family in Question*. London: Macmillan.

Gittins, D. (1986). Marital Status, Work and Kinship, 1850–1930. In J. Lewis (ed.)

*Labour and Love: Women's Experience of Home and Family 1850–1940*. Oxford: Basil Blackwell.

Glendinning, F. (ed.) (1983). *The Elders in Ethnic Minorities*. Keele: Beth Johnson Foundation.

Gluckman, M. (1963). Gossip and Scandal. *Current Anthropology*, 4, 307–16.

Goddard, V. (1987). Honour and Shame: the control of women's sexuality and group identity in Naples. In P. Caplan (ed.) *The Cultural Construction of Sexuality*. London: Tavistock.

Goldthorpe, J., Llewellyn, C. and Payne, C. (1980). *Social Class in Modern Britain*. Oxford: Clarendon.

Goody, E. (1982). *Parenthood and Social Reproduction*. Cambridge: Cambridge University Press.

Gouldner, A. W. (1973). *For Sociology: Renewal and Critique in Sociology Today*. London: Allen Lane.

Graham, H. (1983). Caring: a Labour of Love. In J. Finch and D. Groves (eds) *A Labour of Love: Women, Work and Caring*. London: Routledge and Kegan Paul.

Graham, H. (1984). *Women, Health and the Family*. Brighton: Wheatsheaf.

Graham, H. (1985). Providers, negotiators and mediators: women as the hidden carers. In E. Lewin and V. Olesen (eds) *Women, Health and Healing: Toward a New Perspective*. London: Tavistock.

Green, K. (1988). The English woman's castle – inheritance and private property today. *Modern Law Review*, 51, 187–209.

Grieco, M. (1987). *Keeping It In The Family: Social Networks and Employment Change*. London: Tavistock.

Griffiths, Sir R. (1988). *Community Care: Agenda for Action*. A Report to the Secretary of State for Social Services. London: Her Majesty's Stationery Office.

Grimshaw, J. (1986). *Feminist Philosophers: Women's Perspectives on Philosophical Traditions*. Brighton: Harvester.

Groves, D. (1987). Occupational pensions and women's poverty in old age. C. Glendinning and J. Millar (eds) *Women and Poverty in Britain*. Brighton: Wheatsheaf.

Groves, D. and Finch J. (1983). Natural selection: perspectives on entitlement to the Invalid Care Allowance. In J. Finch and D. Groves (eds) *A Labour of Love: Women, Work and Caring*. London: Routledge and Kegan Paul.

Guillemaud, A. (1983). Introduction. In A. Guillemaud (ed.) *Old Age and the Welfare State*. London: Sage.

Halsey, A. H. (1985). On methods and morals. In M. Abrams, D. Gerrard and N. Timms (eds) *Values and Social Change in Britain*. London: Macmillan.

Hannington, W. (1937). *The Problem of the Distressed Areas*. London: Victor Gollancz.

Hareven, T. (1978). Family time and historical time. In A. Ross, J. Kagan and T. Hareven (eds) *The Family*. New York: Norton.

Harre, R. (1977). Rules in the explanation of social behaviour. In P. Collett (ed.) *Social Rules and Social Behaviour*. Rowman, N. J.: Rowman and Littlefield.

Harre, R. (1986). An outline of the social constructionist viewpoint. In R. Harre (ed.) *The Social Construction of Emotions*. Oxford: Basil Blackwell.

Harris, C. (1983). *The Family and Industrial Society*. London: Allen and Unwin.

Haskey, J. (1983). Social class patterns of marriage. *Population Trends*, 34, 12–19.

Haskey, J. (1986). One-parent families in Great Britain. *Population Trends*, 45, 5–14.

Haskey, J. (1987a) Trends in marriage and divorce in England and Wales 1837–1987. *Population Trends*, 48, 11–19.

Haskey, J. (1987b). Social class differentials in remarriage after divorce. *Population Trends*, 47, 34–42.

Haskey, J. (1988). Regional patterns of divorce in England and Wales. *Population Trends*, 52, 5–14.

Henwood, M. and Wicks, M. (1985). Community care, family trends and social change. *Quarterly Journal of Social Affairs*, 1, 4, 357–71.

Hill, R. (1970). *Family Development in Three Generations*. Cambridge, Mass: Schenkman.

Hochschild, A. (1975). The sociology of feeling and emotion: selected possibilities. In M. Millman and R. Kanter (eds) *Another Voice: Feminist Perspectives on Social Life and Social Science*. New York: Anehar.

Hochschild, A. R. (1979). Emotion work, feeling rules and social structure. *American Journal of Sociology*, no. 85, 551–75.

Hoggett, B. and Pearl, D. (1987). *The Family, Law and Society: Cases and Materials*. 2nd edn. London: Butterworth.

Holmans, A. (1981). Housing careers of recently married couples. *Population Trends*, 24, 10–14.

Hoyt, D. R. and Babchuk, N. (1983). Adult kinship networks: the selective formaton of intimate ties with kin. *Social Forces*, 62, 1, 84–101.

Humphries, J. (1977). Class struggle and the persistence of the working class family. *Cambridge Journal of Economics*, 1, 241–58.

Hunt, A. (1978). *The Elderly At Home*. London: Her Majesty's Stationery Office.

Hurstfield, J. (1986). Women's unemployment in the 1930s: some comparison with the 1980s. In S. Allen, A. Watson, K. Purcell and S. Wood (eds) *The Experience of Unemployment*. London: Macmillan.

Hurt, J. S. (1979). *Elementary Schooling and the Working Classes 1860–1918*. London: Routledge and Kegan Paul.

Hutson, J. (1987). Fathers and sons: family farms, family businesses and the farming industry. *Sociology*, 21, 2, 215–29.

Jamieson, L. (1986). Limited resources limiting conventions: working-class mothers and daughters in urban Scotland c. 1890–1925. In J. Lewis (ed.) *Labour and Love: Women's Experience of Home and Family 1850–1940*. Oxford: Basil Blackwell.

Jerrome, D. (1981). The significance of friendship for women in later life. *Ageing and Society*, 1, 2, 175–77.

Johansson, S. R. (1977). Sex and death in Victorian England: an examination of age- and sex-specific death rates 1840–1910. In M. Vicinus (ed.) *A Widening Sphere: Changing Roles of Victorian Women*. London: Methuen.

Jones, G. (1987). Leaving the parental home: an analysis of early housing careers. *Journal of Social Policy*, 16, 1, 49–74.

Kiernan, K. and Eldridge, S. (1987). Age at marriage: inter and intra cohort variation. *British Journal of Sociology*, XXXVIII, 1, 44–65.

Kreps, J. (1977). Intergenerational transfers and the bureaucracy. In E. Shanas and M. B. Sussman (eds) *Family, Bureaucracy and the Elderly*. Durham, N. C.: Duke University Press.

La Fontaine, J. S. (1985). Anthropological perspectives on the family and social change. *Quarterly Journal of Social Affairs*, 1, 1, 29–60.

LaGaipa, J. L. (1982). Rules and rituals in disengaging from relationships. In S. Duck (ed.) *Personal Relationships 4: Dissolving Personal Relationships*. London: Academic Press.

Lakhani, B. (1988). *National Welfare Benefits Handbook*. London Child Poverty Action Group.

Land, H. (1978). Who cares for the family? *Journal of Social Policy*, 7, 3, 257–84.

Land, H. (1983). Who still cares for the family? Recent developments in income maintenance, taxation and family law. In J. Lewis (ed.) *Women's Welfare, Women's Rights*. London: Croom Helm.

Land, H. and Parker, R. (1979). Family policy in Britain. In S. Kamerman and A. Kahn (eds) *Family Policy in Fourteen Countries*. Columbia: Columbia University Press.

Land, H. and Rose H. (1985). Compulsory altruism for some or an altruistic society for all? In P. Bean, J. Ferris and D. Wynes (eds) *In Defence of Welfare*. London: Tavistock.

Lasch, C. (1977). *Haven in a Heartless World*. New York: Basic Books.

Laslett, P. (1972a). Introduction: the history of family. In P. Laslett and R. Wall (eds). *Household and Family in the Past Time*. Cambridge: Cambridge University Press.

Laslett, P. (1972b). Mean household size in England since the sixteenth century. In P. Laslett and R. Wall (eds) *Household and Family in Past Time*. Cambridge: Cambridge University Press.

Leach, E. R. (1961). *Pul Eliya: A Village in Ceylon*. Cambridge: Cambridge University Press.

Leichter H. J. and Mitchell, W. E. (1967). *Kinship and Casework*. New York: Russell Sage Foundation.

Leighton, N., Stalley, R. and Watson, D. (1982). *Rights and Responsibilities*. London: Heinemann.

Leira, A. (1983). Women's work strategies: an analysis of the organisation of everyday life in an urban neighbourhood. In A. Leira (ed.) *Work and Womanhood: Norwegian Studies*. Oslo, Norway: Institute For Social Research.

Leonard, D. (1980). *Sex and Generation: a Study of Courtship and Weddings*. London: Tavistock.

Levin, E., Sinclair, I. and Gorbach, P. (1983). *The Supporters of Confused Elderly Persons at Home*. London: National Institute for Social Work.

Levi-Strauss, C. (1969). *The Elementary Structure of Kinship*. Boston: Beacon Press.

Levitas, R. (1986). Competition and compliance. In R. Levitas (ed.) *The Ideology of the New Right*. Cambridge: Polity Press.

Lewis, J. (1984). *Women in England 1870–1950: Sexual Divisions and Social Change*. Brighton: Wheatsheaf.

Lewis, J. and Meredith, B. (1988). *Daughters Who Care*. London: Routledge.

Lieberman, S. (1981). The 'extended family' school of family therapy. In S. Walrond-Skinner (ed.) *Developments in Family Therapy*. London: Routledge and Kegan Paul.

Litwak, E. (1965). Extended kin relations in a democratic industrial society. In E. Shanas and G. Streib (eds) *Social Structure and the Family: Generational Relations*. New York: Prentice Hall.

Lynes, T. (1985). *Penguin Supplementary Benefits Handbook*. 5th edn. Harmondsworth: Penguin.

MacCormack, J. and Strathern, M. (1980). *Nature, Culture and Gender*. Cambridge: Cambridge University Press.

MacFarlane, A. (1978). *The Origins of English Individualism*. Oxford: Basil Blackwell.

McGregor, O. R. (1973). *Family Breakdown and Social Policy*. Proceedings of the British Academy, vol. LIX. London: Oxford University Press.

McKee, L. (1987). Households during unemployment: the resourcefulness of the unemployed. In J. Brannen and G Wilson (eds) *Give and Take in Families*. London: Allen and Unwin.

McKee, L. and Bell, C. (1985). Marital and family relations in times of male unemployment. In B. Roberts, R. Finnegan and D. Gallie (eds) *New Approaches to Economic Life*. Manchester: Manchester University Press.

McKee, L. and Bell, C. (1986). His unemployment, her problem: the domestic and marital consequences of male unemployment. In S. Allen, A. Watson, K. Purcell and S. Wood (eds) *The Experience of Unemployment*. London: Macmillan.

Madge, J. and Brown, C. (1981). *First Homes: A Survey of the Housing Circumstances of Young Married Couples*. London: Policy Studies Institute.

Manners, J. and Rauta, I. (1979). *Family Property in Scotland*. London: Her Majesty's Stationery Office.

Mansfield, P. and Collard, J. (1988). *The Beginning of the Rest of Your Life? A Portrait of Newly-Wed Marriage*. London: Macmillan.

Marris, P. (1958). *Widows and their Families*. London: Routledge and Kegan Paul.

Marsden, T. (1984). Capitalist farming and the farm family. *Sociology*, 18, 2, 205–24.

Marsland, D. (1986). Young People, the family and the state. In D. Anderson and G. Dawson (eds) *Family Portraits*. London: Social Affairs Unit.

Martin, J. and Roberts, C. (1984). *Women and Employment: a Lifetime Perspective*. London: Her Majesty's Stationery Office.

Mason, J. (1987). *Gender Inequalities in Long-Term Marriage*. Ph.D. Thesis. University of Kent.

Matthewman, J. and Calvert, H. (1987). *Tolley's Guide to the Social Security Act 1986*. Croydon: Tolley Publishing Company.

Mays, N. (1983). Elderly South Asians in Britain: a survey of relevant literature and themes for future research. *Ageing and Society*, 3, 1, 71–97.

Means, R. (1987). Older people in housing studies: rediscovery and emerging issues for research. *Housing Studies*, 2, 2, 82–98.

Means, R. and Smith, R. (1985). *The Development of Welfare Services for Elderly People*. London: Croom Helm.

Medick, H. and Sabean, D. W. (1984). Interest and emotion in family and kinship studies: a critique of social history and anthropology. In H. Medick and D. W. Sabean (eds) *Interest and Emotion: Essays on the Study of Family and Kinship*. Cambridge: Cambridge University Press.

Morgan, D. H. J. (1975). *Social Theory and the Family*. London: Routledge and Kegan Paul.

Morgan, D. H. J. (1985). *The Family, Politics and Social Theory*. London: Routledge and Kegan Paul.

Morgan, D. H. J. (1988). Two faces of the family: the possible contribution of sociology to family therapy. *Journal of Family Therapy*, 10, 233–53.

Morris, L. (1983). Redundancy and patterns of household finance. *Sociological Review*, 32, 3, 492–523.

Morris, L. (1985). Renegotiation of the domestic division of labour in the context of male redundancy. In B. Roberts, R. Finnegan and D. Gallie (eds) *New Approaches to Economic Life*. Manchester: Manchester University Press.

Mount, F. (1982). *The Subversive Family: an Alternative History of Love and Marriage*. London: Jonathan Cape.

Moylan, S., Davies, B. and Millar, J. (1984). *For Richer For Poorer? Cohort Study of Men Entering Unemployment*. London: DHSS.

Murie, A. and Forrest, R. (1980). Wealth, inheritance and housing policy. *Policy and Politics*, 8, 1, 1–19.

Murphy, M. and Sullivan, O. (1986). Unemployment, housing and household structure among young adults. *Journal of Social Policy*, 15, 2, 205–22.

National Institute for Social Work (1982). *Social Workers: Their Roles and Tasks*. The Barclay Report. London: Bedford Square Press.

Nisbet, R. A. (1978). Conservatism. In R. Nisbet and T. Bottomore (eds) *A History of Sociological Analysis*. London: Heinemann.

Nissel, M. and Bonnerjea, L. (1982). *Family Care of the Handicapped Elderly: Who Pays?* London: Policy Studies Institute.

Noddings, N. (1984). *Caring: A Feminine Approach to Ethics and Moral Education*. Berkeley: University of California Press.

Oakley, R. (1979). Family, kinship and patronage: the Cypriot migration to Britain. In V. Saifullah Khan (ed.) *Minority Families in Britain*. London: Macmillan.

O'Connor, P. and Brown, G. W. (1984). Supportive relationships: fact or fancy? *Journal of Social and Personal Relationships*, 1, 159–75.

Oppenheim, C. (1987). *A Tax on All the People: The Poll Tax*. London: Child Poverty Action Group.

Oren, L. (1973). The welfare of women in labouring families: England 1860–1950. *Feminist Studies*, I. Winter–Spring, 107–25.

Osterud, N. G. (1986). Gender Divisions and the organisation of work in the Leicester hosiery industry. In A. John (ed.) *Unequal Opportunities: Women's Employment in England 1800–1918*. Oxford: Basil Blackwell.

Pahl, J. (1983). The allocation of money and the structuring of inequality within marriage. *Sociological Review*, 31, 2, 237–62.

Pahl, J. (1984). The allocation of money within the household. In M. Freeman (ed.) *The State, the Law and the Family*. London: Tavistock.

Pahl, R. E. (1984). *Divisions of Labour*. Oxford: Basil Blackwell.

Palmer, R. (1977). The Italians: patterns of migration to London. In J. L. Watson (ed.) *Between Two Cultures*. Oxford: Basil Blackwell.

Parker, G. (1985). *With Due Care and Attention*. London: Family Policy Studies Centre.

Parker, H. (1986). Family income support: government subversion of the traditional family. In D. Anderson and G. Dawson (eds) *Family Portraits*. London: Social Affairs Unit.

Parsons, T. (1964). *The Social System*. London: Routledge and Kegan Paul.

Parsons, T. and Fox, R. (1968). Illness, therapy and the modern urban American family. In N. W. Bell and E. F. Vogel (eds) *A Modern Introduction to the Family*. New York: Free Press.

Pascall, G. (1986). *Social Policy: A Feminist Analysis*. London: Tavistock.

Patterson, S. (1977). The Poles: an exile community in Britain. In J. L. Watson (ed.) *Between Two Cultures*. Oxford: Basil Blackwell.

Peristiany, J. G. (ed.) (1968). *Honour and Shame: The Values of Mediterranean Society*. London: Weidenfeld and Nicholson.

Peristiany, J. G. (ed.) (1976). *Mediterranean Family Structures*. Cambridge: Cambridge University Press.

Phelps, E. S. (ed.) (1975). *Altruism, Morality and Economic Theory*. New York: Russel Sage Foundation.

Philpott, S. B. (1977). The Monserratians: migration dependency and the maintenance of Island ties in England. In J. L. Watson (ed.) *Between Two Cultures*. Oxford: Basil Blackwell.

Pilgrim Trust (1938). *Men Without Work*. Cambridge: Cambridge University Press.

Pinchbeck, I. and Hewitt, M. (1973). *Children in English Society*. Vol. 2, London: Routledge and Kegan Paul.

Pincus, L. and Dare, C. (1978). *Secrets in the Family*. London: Faber and Faber.

Pinker, R. (1971). *Social Theory and Social Policy*. London: Heinemann.

Pinker, R. (1979). *The Idea of Welfare*. London: Heinemann.

Plant, R., Lesser, H. and Taylor-Gooby, P. (1980). *Political Philosophy and Social Welfare: Essays on the Normative Basis of Welfare Provisions*. London: Routledge and Kegan Paul.

Powis, J. (1984). *Aristocracy*. Oxford: Basil Blackwell.

Quadagno, J. (1982). *Aging in Early Industrial Society: Work, Family and Social Policy in Nineteenth Century England*. London: Academic Press.

Qureshi, H. (1986). Responses to dependency: reciprocity, affect and power in family relationships. In C. Phillipson, M. Bernard and P. Strang (eds) *Dependency and Interdependency in Old Age*. London: Croom Helm.

Qureshi, H. and Simons, K. (1987). Resources within families: caring for elderly people. In J. Brannen and G. Wilson (eds) *Give and Take in Families*. London: Allen and Unwin.

Rathbone, E. (1924). *The Disinherited Family*. Republished 1986. Bristol: Falling Wall Press.

Rawls, J. (1967). Two concepts of rules. In P. Foot (ed.) *Theories of Ethics*. Oxford: Oxford University Press.

Reiss, D. (1981). *The Family's Construction Reality*. Cambridge, Mass: Harvard University Press.

Richards, M. (1987). Children, parents and families: developmental psychology and the re-ordering of relationships after divorce. *International Journal of Law and the Family*, 1, 295–317.

Rimmer, L. and Wicks, M. (1983). The challenge of change: demographic trends, the family and social policy. In H. Glennerster (ed.) *The Future of the Welfare State*. London: Heinemann.

Roberts, E. (1984). *A Woman's Place: an Oral History of Working Class Women 1890–1940*. Oxford: Basil Blackwell.

Roberts, R. (1971). *The Classic Slum: Salford Life in the First Quarter of the Century*. Manchester: Manchester University Press.

Roebuck, J. and Slaughter, J. (1979). Ladies and pensioners: stereotypes and public policy affecting old women in England 1880–1940. *Journal of Social History*, 13, 1, 105–14.

Roll, J. (1988). *Young People at the Crossroads*. London: Family Policy Studies Centre.

Rose, H. (1981). Re-reading Titmuss: the sexual division of welfare. *Journal of Social Policy*, 10, 4, 521–38.

Rosenmayr, L. and Kockeis, E. (1963). Propositions for a sociological theory of aging and the family. *International Social Science Journal*, 15, 410–26.

Rosnow, R. L. and Fine, G. A. (1976). *Rumor and Gossip: The Social Psychology of Hearsay*. New York: Elsevier.

Ross, E. (1983). Survival networks: women's neighbourhood sharing in London before World War I. *History Workshop*, 15, 4–27.

Rubin, J. and Brown, B. R. (1975). *The Social Psychology of Bargaining and Negotiaton*. New York: Academic Press.

Rutter, M. (1986). *Maternal Deprivation Reassessed*. Harmondsworth: Penguin.

Sahlins, M. (1965). On the sociology of primitive exchange. In M. Branton (ed.) *The Relevance of Models in Social Anthropology*. London: Tavistock.

Saifullah Khan, V. (1976). *Purdah* in the British situation. In D. Leonard Barker and S. Allen (eds) *Dependence and Exploitation in Work and Marriage*. London: Longmans.

Saifullah Khan, V. (1977). The Pakistanis: Mirpur villagers at home and in Bradford. In J. L. Watson (ed.) *Between Two Cultures*. Oxford: Basil Blackwell.

Salvage, A. V. (1985). *Domiciliary Care Schemes for the Elderly*. London: Research Team for the Care of the Elderly.

Sayers, J. (1982). *Biological Politics*. London: Tavistock.

Scanzoni, J. (1979). Social processes and power in families in W. Burr, R. Hill, I. Nye and I. Reiss (eds) *Contemporary Theories about the Family*. Glencoe: Free Press.

Schneider, D. M. (1968). *American Kinship: A Cultural Account*. Englewood Cliffs: Prentice-Hall.

Scott, J. (1982). *The Upper Classes: Property and Privilege in Britain*. London: Macmillan.

Scott, J. (1986). *Capitalist Property and Financial Power*. Brighton: Wheatsheaf.

Segalen, M. (1984). 'Avoir sa part': sibling relations in partible inheritance in Brittany. In H. Medick and D. W. Sabean (eds) *Interest and Emotion: Essays on the Study of Family and Kinship*. Cambridge: Cambridge University Press.

Shanas, E. (1979). The family as support system in old age. *The Gerontologist*, 19, 169–74.

Shorter, E. (1975). *The Making of the Modern Family*. London: Fontana/Collins.

Singer, P. (1981). *The Expanding Circle: Ethics and Sociobiology*. Oxford: Clarendon.

Sixsmith, A. J. (1980). Independence and home in later life. In C. Phillipson, M. Bernard and P. Strang (eds) *Dependency and Interdependency in Old Age*. London: Croom Helm.

Smart, C. (1984). *The Ties That Bind: Law, Marriage and the Reproduction of Patriarchal Relations*. London: Routledge and Kegan Paul.

Smith, R. I. (1973). The matrifocal family. In J. Goody (ed.) *The Character of Kinship*. Cambridge: Cambridge University Press.

Smith, R. M. (1984). The structured dependence of the elderly: some sceptical historical thoughts. *Ageing and Society*, 4, 4, 408–29.

Smyer, M. (1984). Aging and social policy: contrasting Western Europe and the United States. *Journal of Social Issues*, 5, 2, 239–53.

Social Services Inspectorate Development Group (1985). *Assessment Procedures for Elderly People Referred Local Authority Residential Care*. London: Department of Health and Social Security.

Sprigge, T. L. S. (1970). Definition of moral judgement. In G. Wallace and A. D. M. Walker (eds) *The Definition of Morality*. London: Methuen.

Stacey, M. (1981). The division of labour revisited or overcoming the Two Adams. In P. Abrams, R. Deem, J. Finch and P. Rock (eds) *Practice and Progress: British Sociology 1950–1980*. London: Allen and Unwin.

Stacey, M. and Price M. (1981). *Women, Power and Politics*. London: Tavistock.

Stack, C. B. (1975). *All Our Kin: Strategies For Survival in a Black Community*. New York: Harper and Row.

Stirling, P. (1965). *Turkish Village*. London: Weidenfeld and Nicholson.

Stivens, M. (1981). Women, kinship and capitalist development. In K. Young, C. Wokowitcz and R. McCullagh (eds) *Of Marriage and the Market*. London: Routledge and Kegan Paul.

Stone, L. (1977). *The Family, Sex and Marriage in England 1500–1800*. London: Weidenfeld and Nicholson.

Strauss, A. (1978). *Negotiations*. San Francisco: Jossey Bass.

Study Commission on the Family (1982). *Values and the Changing Family.* London: Study Commission.

Spurling, H. (1974). *Ivy When Young: The Early Life of I. Compton-Burnett 1884–1919.* London: Gollancz.

Sullivan, O. (1986). Housing movements of the divorced and separated. *Housing Studies*, 1, 1, 35–48.

Summerfield, P. (1984). *Women Workers in the Second World War.* London: Croom Helm.

Summerfield, P. (1986). Review of Elizabeth Roberts *A Woman's Place, Social History*, 11, 3, 409–13.

Sussman, M. (1965). Relationships of adult children and their parents in the United States. In E. Shanas and G. Streib (eds) *Social Structure and the Family.* Englewood Cliffs: Prentice-Hall.

Thane, P. (1982). *Foundations of the Welfare State.* London: Longmans.

Thompson C. and West P. (1984). The public appeal of sheltered housing. *Ageing and Society*, 4, 3, 305–26.

Thorogood, N. (1987). Race, class and gender: the politics of housework. In J. Brannen and G. Wilson (eds) *Give and Take in Families.* London: Unwin Hyman.

Tillion, J. G. (1983). *The Republic of Cousins: Women's Oppression in Mediterranean Society.* First published 1966. London: Alsaqi Books.

Tilly, L. (1984). Linen was their life: family survival strategies and parent–child relations in nineteenth century France. In H. Medick and D. W. Sabean (eds) *Interest and Emotion: Essays on the Study of Family and Kinship.* Cambridge: Cambridge University Press.

Titmuss, R. (1958). The position of women. In R. Titmuss. *Essays on the Welfare State.* 2nd edn, 1963. London: Allen and Unwin.

Titmuss R. (1970). *The Gift Relationship.* London: Allen and Unwin.

Todd, J. and Jones, L. (1972). *Matrimonial Property.* London. Her Majesty's Stationery Office.

Townsend, P. (1957). *The Family Life of Old People.* London: Routledge and Kegan Paul.

Townsend, P. (1965). The effects of family structure on the likelihood of admission to an institution in old age: an application of general theory. In E. Shanas and G. F. Streib (eds) *Social Structure and the Family: Generational Relations.* Englewood Cliffs, N.J.: Prentice-Hall.

Townsend, P. (1979). *Poverty in the United Kingdom.* Harmondsworth: Penguin.

Turner, R. H. (1970). *Family Interactions.* New York: John Wiley.

Ungerson, C. (1983). Why do women care? In J. Finch and D. Groves (eds) *A Labour of Love: Women, Work and Caring.* London: Routledge and Kegan Paul.

Ungerson, C. (1987). *Policy is Personal: Sex, Gender and Informal Care.* London: Tavistock.

Ve H. (1984). Women's mutual alliances: altruism as a premise for interaction. In H. Holter (ed.) *Patriarchy in a Welfare Society.* Oslo, Norway: Universitetsforlagets.

Voysey M. (1975). *A Constant Burden: The Reconstitution of Family Life.* London: Routledge and Kegan Paul.

Walker, A. (ed.) (1982). *Community Care: the Family, the State and Social Policy.* Oxford: Martin Robertson/Basil Blackwell.

Walker, A. (1987). The poor relation: poverty among old women. In C. Glendinning and J. Millar (eds) *Women and Poverty in Britain.* Brighton: Wheatsheaf.

Wall, R. (1972). Mean household size in England from printed sources. In P. Laslett and R. Wall (eds) *Household and Family Past Time*. Cambridge: Cambridge University Press.

Wall, R. (1977). The responsibilities of kin. *Local Population Studies*, 19, 58–60.

Wall, R. (1984). Residential isolation of the elderly: a comparison over time. *Ageing and Society*, 4, 4, 483–503.

Wall, R. (1986). Work, welfare and family. In L. Bonfield, R. Smith and K. Wrightson (eds) *The World We have Gained: Histories of Population and Social Structure*. Oxford: Basil Blackwell.

Wallace, G. and Walker, A. D. M. (1970). Introduction. In G. Wallace and A. D. M. Walker, *The Definition of Morality*. London: Methuen.

Wallman, S. (1983). *Eight London Households*. London: Tavistock.

Warnock, G. J. (1971). *The Object of Morality*. London: Methuen.

Watson, J. L. (1977). The Chinese: Hong Kong Villagers in the British catering trade. In J. L. Watson (ed.) *Between Two Cultures*. Oxford: Basil Blackwell.

Wenger, G. C. (1984). *The Supportive Network*. London: Allen and Unwin.

Wenger, G. C. (1986). What do dependency measures measure? In C. Phillipson, M. Bernard and P. Strang (eds) *Dependency and Interdependency in Old Age*. London: Croom Helm.

West, P. (1984). The family, the welfare state and community care: political rhetoric and public attitudes. *Journal of Social Policy*, 13, 4, 417–46.

West, P., Illsley, R. and Kelman, H. (1984). Public preferences for the care of dependency groups. *Social Science and Medicine*, 18, 4, 287–95.

Wilkin D. (1979). *Caring for the Mentally Handicapped Child*. London: Croom Helm.

Williams, R. (1973). *The Country and the City*. London: Chatto.

Willmott, P. and Young M. (1960). *Family and Class in a London Suburb*. London: Routledge and Kegan Paul.

Wilson, A. (1978). *Finding a Voice: Asian Women in Britain*. London: Virago.

Wilson, E. O. (1975). *Sociobiology: The Newsynthesis*. Cambridge, Mass: Harvard University Press.

Wilson, E. O. (1978). *On Human Nature*. Harvard, Mass: Cambridge University Press.

Wilson, G. (1987). Women's Work: the role of grandparents in inter-generational transfers. *Sociological Review*, 35, 4, 703–20.

Wilson, P. and Pahl, R. (1988). The changing sociological construct of the family. *Sociological Review*, 36, 2, 233–72.

Wolf, M. (1985). *Revolution Postponed: Women in Contemporary China*. Stanford: Stanford University Press.

Wolfram, S. (1987). *In-Laws and Out-Laws: Kinship and Marriage in England*. London: Croom Helm.

Worsley, P. (1956). The kinship system of the Tallensi: a re-evaluation. *Journal of the Royal Anthropological Institute*.

Wright Mills, C. (1940). Situated actions and vocabularies of motive. *American Sociological Review*, October.

Yeandle, S. (1984). *Women's Working Lives: Patterns and Strategies*. London: Tavistock.

Young, M. and Willmott, P. (1957). *Family and Kinship in East London*. London: Routledge and Kegan Paul.

# Index

*Index by Barbara Hird*